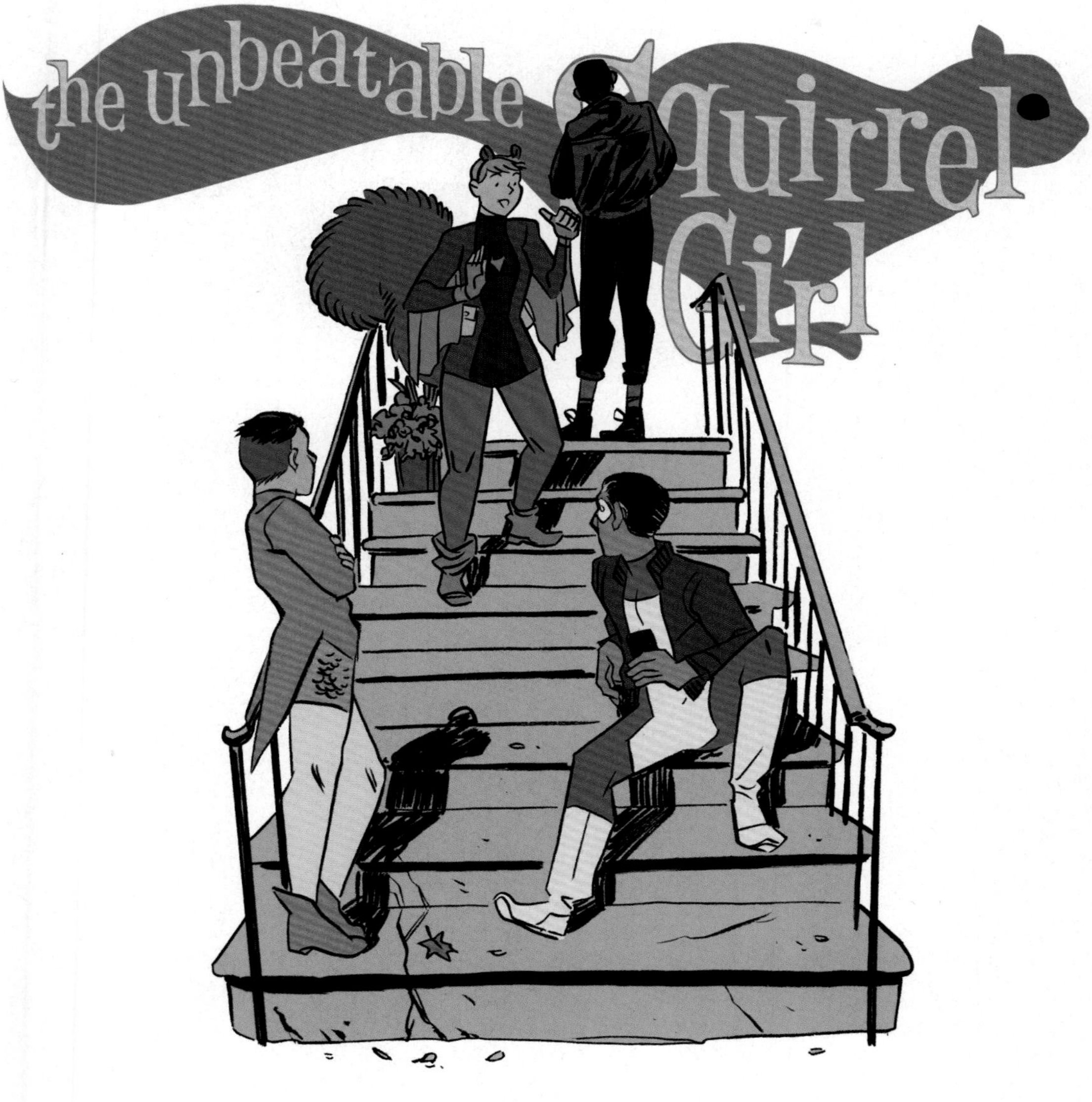
the unbeatable Squirrel Girl

Who Run the World? Squirrels

the unbeatab

COLLECTION EDITOR: **JENNIFER GRÜNWALD**
ASSISTANT EDITOR: **CAITLIN O'CONNELL**
ASSOCIATE MANAGING EDITOR: **KATERI WOODY**
EDITOR, SPECIAL PROJECTS: **MARK D. BEAZLEY**
VP PRODUCTION & SPECIAL PROJECTS: **JEFF YOUNGQUIST**
SVP PRINT, SALES & MARKETING: **DAVID GABRIEL**
BOOK DESIGNER: **JAY BOWEN**

EDITOR IN CHIEF: **AXEL ALONSO**
CHIEF CREATIVE OFFICER: **JOE QUESADA**
PRESIDENT: **DAN BUCKLEY**
EXECUTIVE PRODUCER: **ALAN FINE**

THE UNBEATABLE SQUIRREL GIRL VOL. 6: WHO RUN THE WORLD? SQUIRRELS. Contains material originally published in magazine form as THE UNBEATABLE SQUIRREL GIRL #17-21. First printing 2017. ISBN# 978-1-302-90664-1. Published by MARVEL WORLDWIDE, INC., a subsidiary of MARVEL ENTERTAINMENT, LLC. OFFICE OF PUBLICATION: 135 West 50th Street, New York, NY 10020. Copyright © 2017 MARVEL No similarity between any of the names, characters, persons, and/or institutions in this magazine with those of any living or dead person or institution is intended, and any such similarity which may exist is purely coincidental. **Printed in Canada.** DAN BUCKLEY, President, Marvel Entertainment; JOE QUESADA, Chief Creative Officer; TOM BREVOORT, SVP of Publishing; DAVID BOGART, SVP of Business Affairs & Operations, Publishing & Partnership; C.B. CEBULSKI, VP of Brand Management & Development, Asia; DAVID GABRIEL, SVP of Sales & Marketing, Publishing; JEFF YOUNGQUIST, VP of Production & Special Projects; DAN CARR, Executive Director of Publishing Technology; ALEX MORALES, Director of Publishing Operations; SUSAN CRESPI, Production Manager; STAN LEE, Chairman Emeritus. For information regarding advertising in Marvel Comics or on Marvel.com, please contact Vit DeBellis, Integrated Sales Manager, at vdebellis@marvel.com. For Marvel subscription inquiries, please call 888-511-5480. **Manufactured between 8/4/2017 and 9/5/2017 by SOLISCO PRINTERS, SCOTT, QC, CANADA.**

10 9 8 7 6 5 4 3 2 1

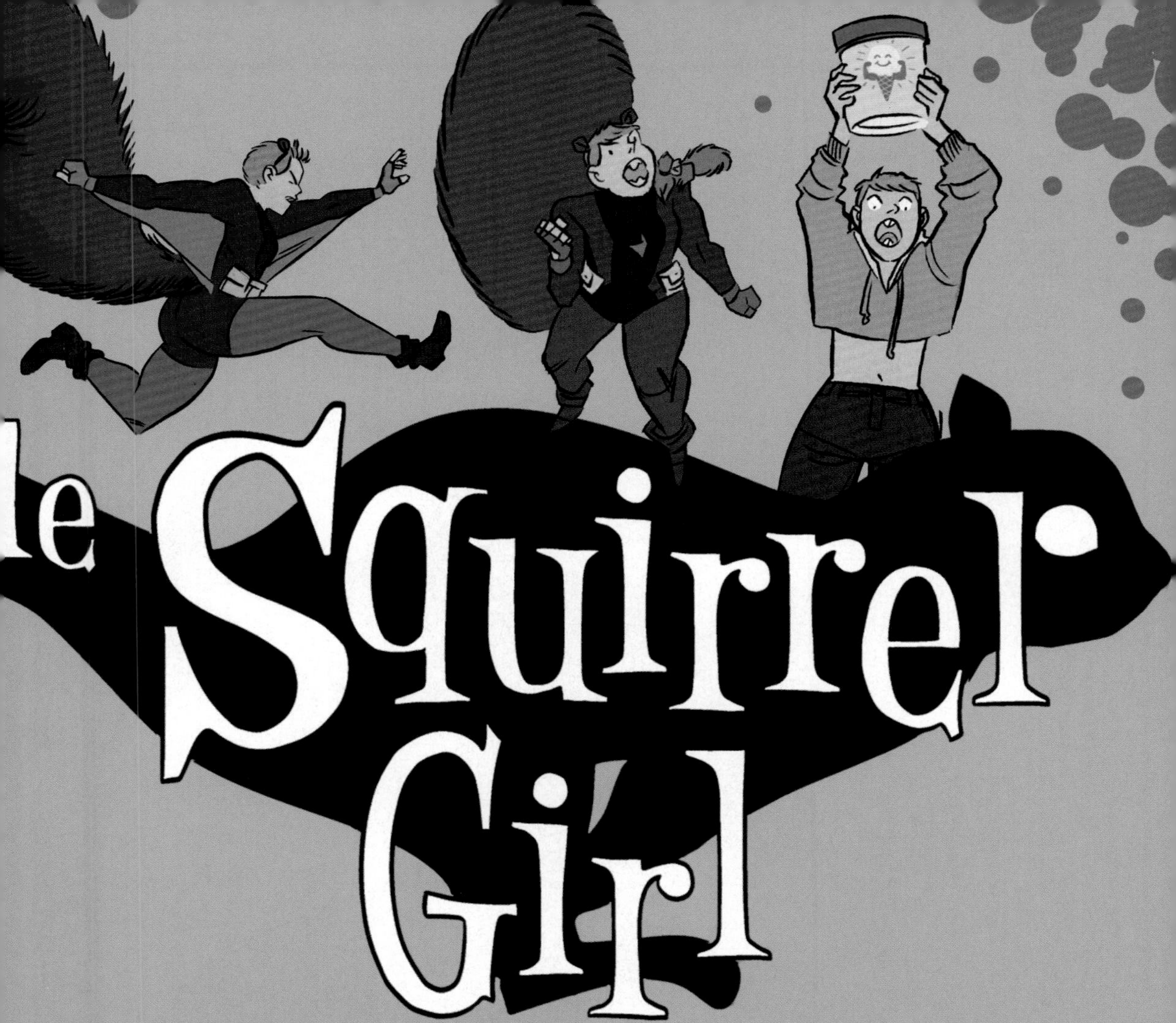
le Squirrel
Girl

Ryan North
WRITER

Erica Henderson
ARTIST

Chris Schweizer
VULTURE & SANDMAN PANELS, #17

Rico Renzi
COLOR ARTIST

VC's Travis Lanham
LETTERER

Erica Henderson
COVER ART

Charles Beacham
ASSISTANT EDITOR

Sarah Brunstad
ASSOCIATE EDITOR

Wil Moss
EDITOR

LOGO DESIGN BY **MICHAEL ALLRED**

SPECIAL THANKS TO **CK RUSSELL**

SQUIRREL GIRL CREATED BY **WILL MURRAY** & **STEVE DITKO**

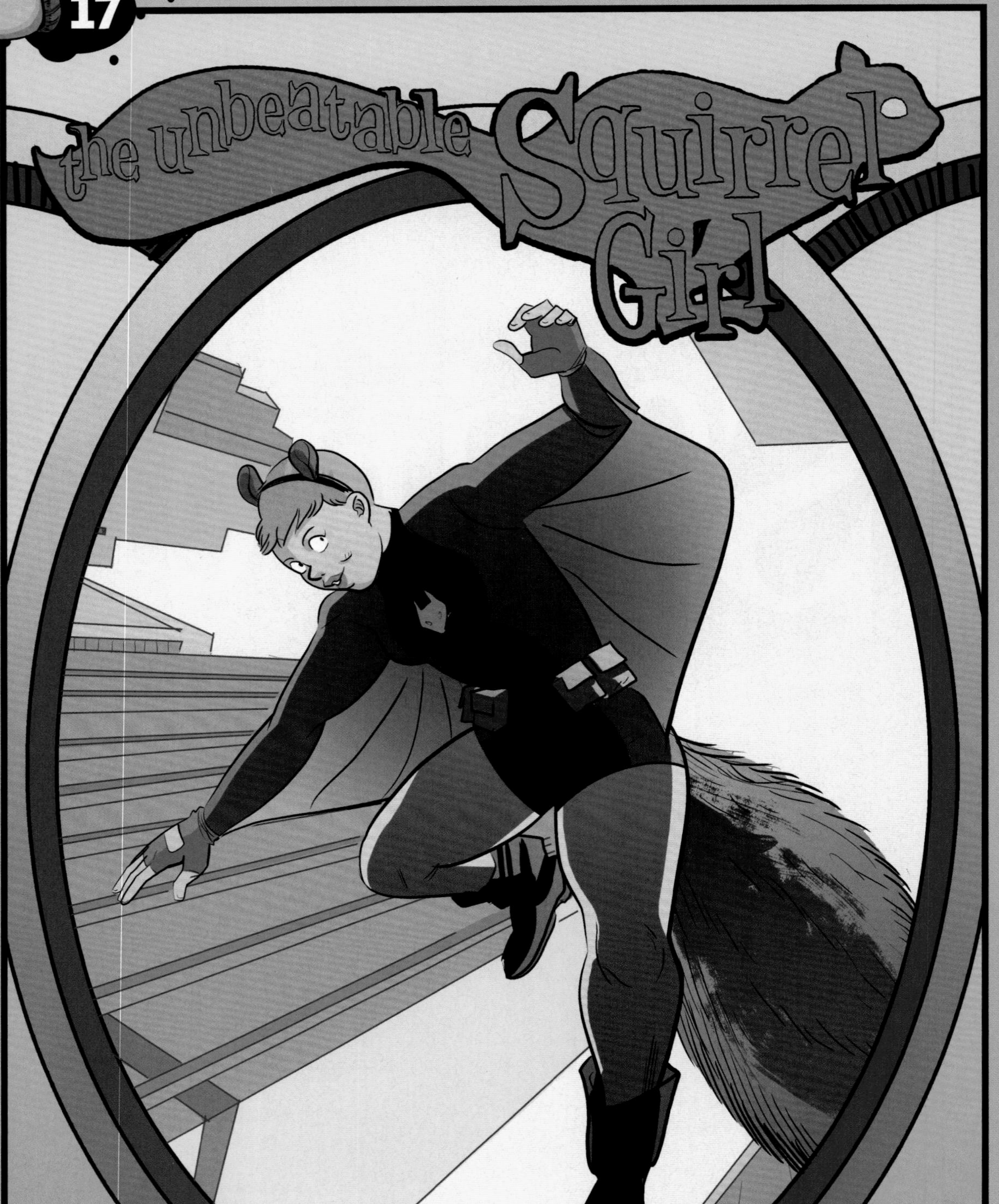
the unbeatable Squirrel Girl

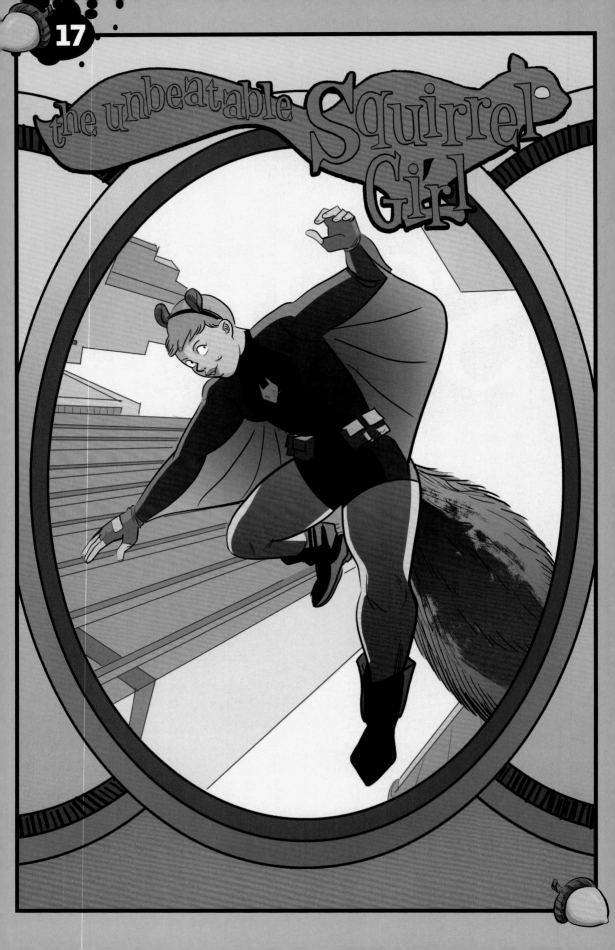

Doreen Green isn't just a second-year computer science student: she secretly also has all the powers of both squirrel and girl! She uses her amazing abilities to fight crime **and** *be as awesome as possible. You know her as...* ***The Unbeatable Squirrel Girl!***
Find out what she's been up to, with...

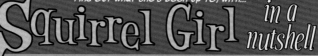

Squirrel Girl *in a nutshell*

Squirrel Girl @unbeatablesg
Roses are red / Violets are dull / Guess who just had her birthday party crashed by THE FRIGGIN' RED SKULL

Squirrel Girl @unbeatablesg
Answer: me.

Squirrel Girl @unbeatablesg
Well haha not JUST me since it was a party filled with pals like KOI BOI, CHIPMUNK HUNK, SPIDER-MAN, BLACK WIDOW, IRON MAN, and MORE??

Squirrel Girl @unbeatablesg
Anyway, I punched the Red Skull right through the roof and he's in jail now. PRESUMABLY FOREVER?? THAT SEEMS LIKELY, YES?

Squirrel Girl @unbeatablesg
Which MAYBE just goes to show you the dangers of crashing someone's party when she's friends with LITERAL SUPER HEROES? hmm hard to say

Egg @imduderadtude
@unbeatablesg can u get a mesasge to spider man for me

Squirrel Girl @unbeatablesg
@imduderadtude no

Egg @imduderadtude
@unbeatablesg please he has me blocked and i just want to ask him Y he has me blokced

Squirrel Girl @unbeatablesg
@imduderadtude Dude, real talk, you don't want to be following him anyway, he posts the worst stuff

Squirrel Girl @unbeatablesg
@imduderadtude like he's a good guy for fighting crime but not necessarily the best at providing entertaining #content in 140 characters

Spider-Man @aspidercan
if someone is a jerk on here i reply with "wow looks like u got bitten by a radioactive JERK," so yeah feel free to use that if you want

Spider-Man @aspidercan
hi everyone i'm having a lot of fun here on the world......................................wide............ ....WEB

Spider-Man @aspidercan
If you're wondering who I've got blocked, it's @wealth and @fame

Spider-Man @aspidercan
....because wealth and fame i've ignored

Spider-Man @aspidercan
#actionismyreward

Squirrel Girl @unbeatablesg
@imduderadtude I rest my case

xKravenTheHunterx @unshavenkraven
@unbeatablesg Happy belated birthday, girl of squirrels.

Squirrel Girl @unbeatablesg
@unshavenkraven Thanks, Kraven!

xKravenTheHunterx @unshavenkraven
@unbeatablesg I'm sorry I could not attend your party.

Squirrel Girl @unbeatablesg
@unshavenkraven It's okay! We'll hang out sometime soon. We'll have to catch up later, I've got to get to a thing for class!

Squirrel Girl @unbeatablesg
@unshavenkraven I mean my friend has got to get to a thing for class.

Squirrel Girl @unbeatablesg
@unshavenkraven I mean, my friend has to get to a thing for class and I'm helping her...go there?

Squirrel Girl @unbeatablesg
@unshavenkraven She goes to a different school

Squirrel Girl @unbeatablesg
@unshavenkraven in Canada

xKravenTheHunterx @unshavenkraven
@unbeatablesg You can just delete these posts.

Squirrel Girl @unbeatablesg
@unshavenkraven YEP, ALREADY ON IT

search!

#computerengineering
#regularengineering
#catthor
#doghulk
#alfredo4life

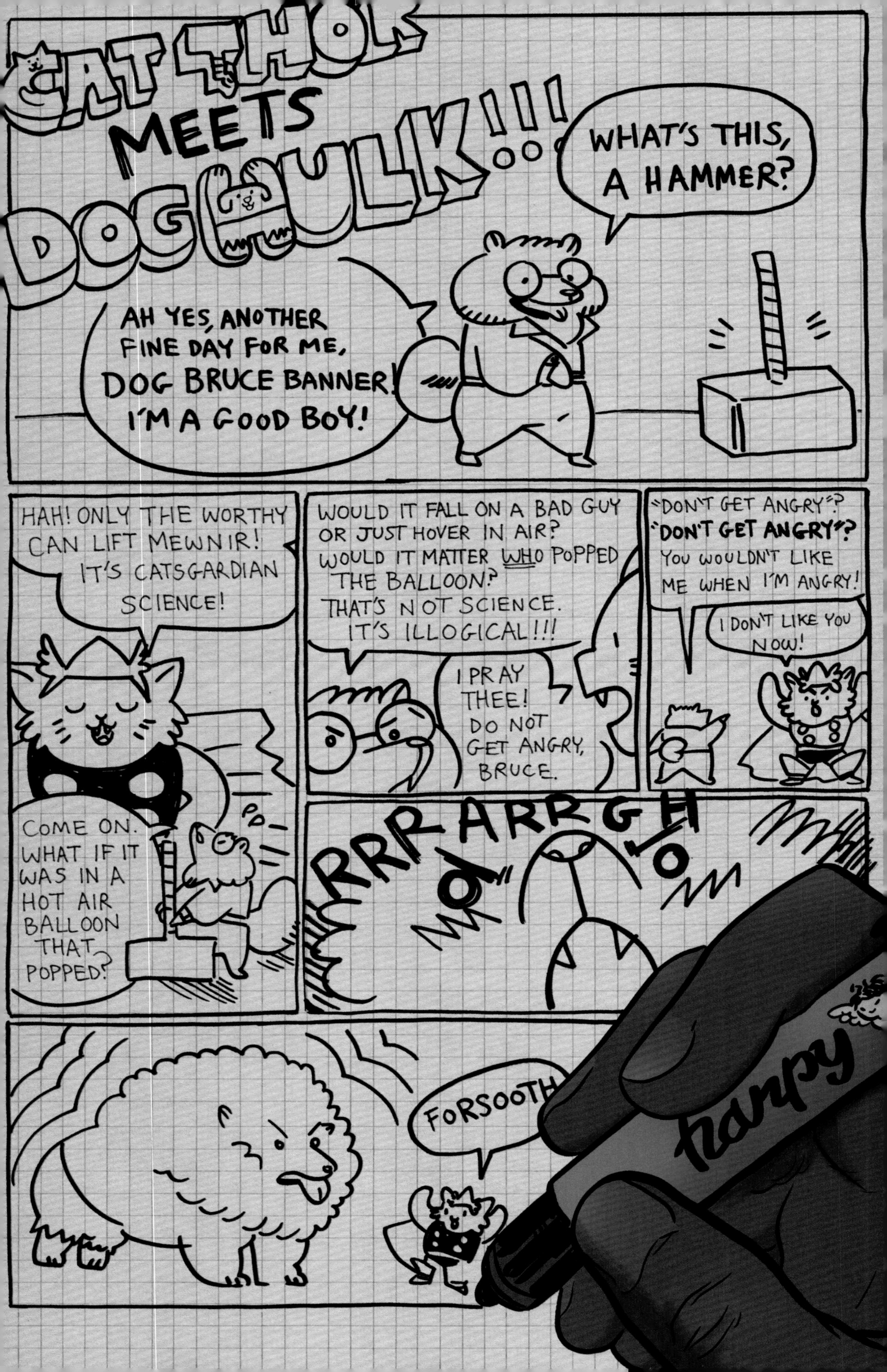

CAT THOR MEETS DOG HULK!!!
WHAT'S THIS, A HAMMER?
AH YES, ANOTHER FINE DAY FOR ME, DOG BRUCE BANNER! I'M A GOOD BOY!
HAH! ONLY THE WORTHY CAN LIFT MEWNIR! IT'S CATSGARDIAN SCIENCE!
COME ON. WHAT IF IT WAS IN A HOT AIR BALLOON THAT POPPED?
WOULD IT FALL ON A BAD GUY OR JUST HOVER IN AIR? WOULD IT MATTER WHO POPPED THE BALLOON? THAT'S NOT SCIENCE. IT'S ILLOGICAL!!!
I PRAY THEE! DO NOT GET ANGRY, BRUCE.
"DON'T GET ANGRY"? "DON'T GET ANGRY"? YOU WOULDN'T LIKE ME WHEN I'M ANGRY!
I DON'T LIKE YOU NOW!
RRRARRRGH
FORSOOTH

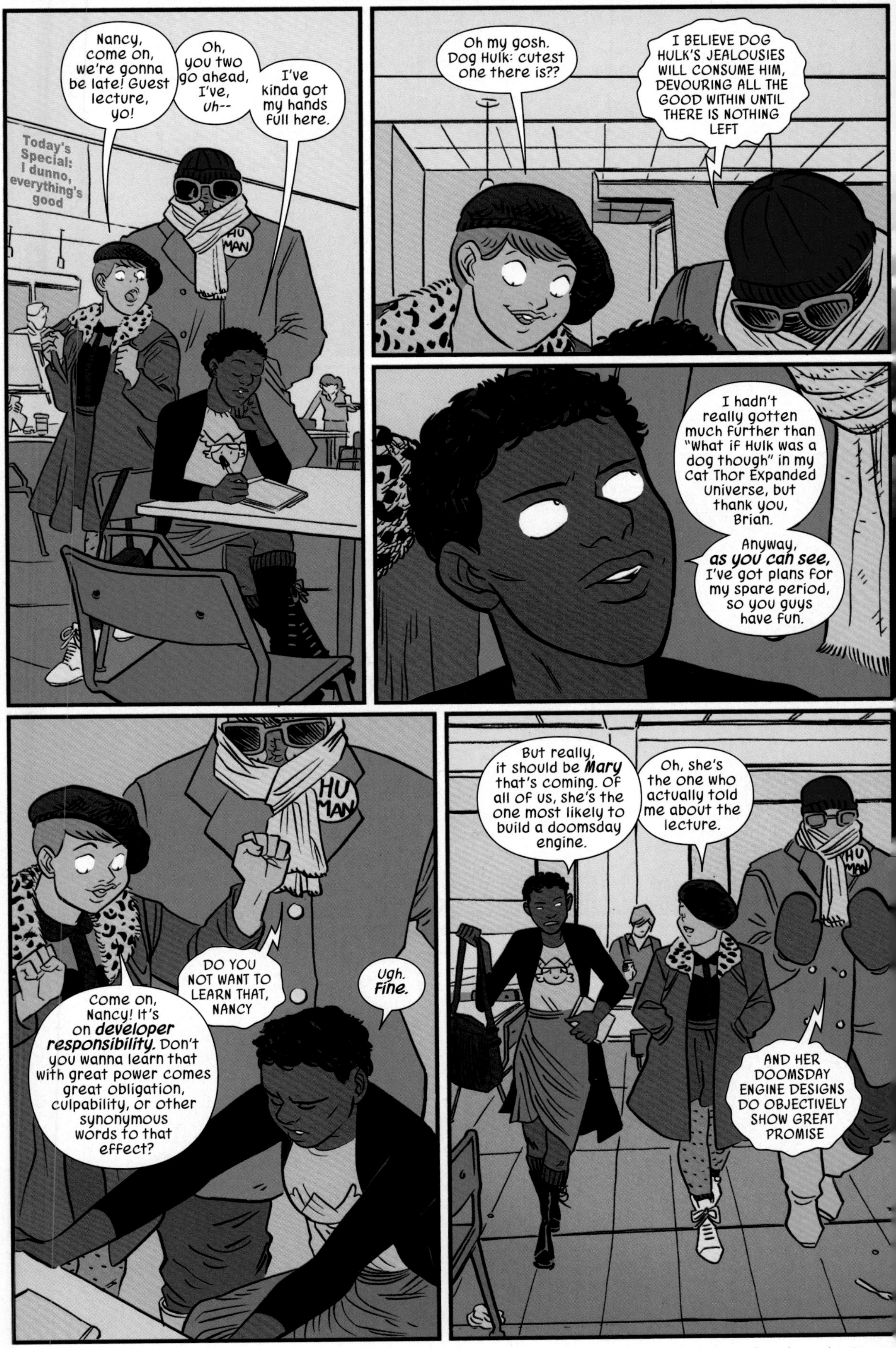
Nancy, come on, we're gonna be late! Guest lecture, yo!
Oh, you two go ahead, I've, uh--
I've kinda got my hands full here.
Today's Special: I dunno, everything's good
HU MAN
Oh my gosh. Dog Hulk: cutest one there is??
I BELIEVE DOG HULK'S JEALOUSIES WILL CONSUME HIM, DEVOURING ALL THE GOOD WITHIN UNTIL THERE IS NOTHING LEFT
I hadn't really gotten much further than "What if Hulk was a dog though" in my Cat Thor Expanded Universe, but thank you, Brian.
Anyway, *as you can see,* I've got plans for my spare period, so you guys have fun.
Come on, Nancy! It's on ***developer responsibility.*** Don't you wanna learn that with great power comes great obligation, culpability, or other synonymous words to that effect?
DO YOU NOT WANT TO LEARN THAT, NANCY
Ugh. ***Fine.***
But really, it should be ***Mary*** that's coming. Of all of us, she's the one most likely to build a doomsday engine.
Oh, she's the one who actually told me about the lecture.
AND HER DOOMSDAY ENGINE DESIGNS DO OBJECTIVELY SHOW GREAT PROMISE

ESU student, definitely not a robot, will evaluate your doomsday engines and provide constructive feedback. Looking to trade for lessons in passing as a human, not because I need them, ***obviously,*** I just want to see if ***you*** know.

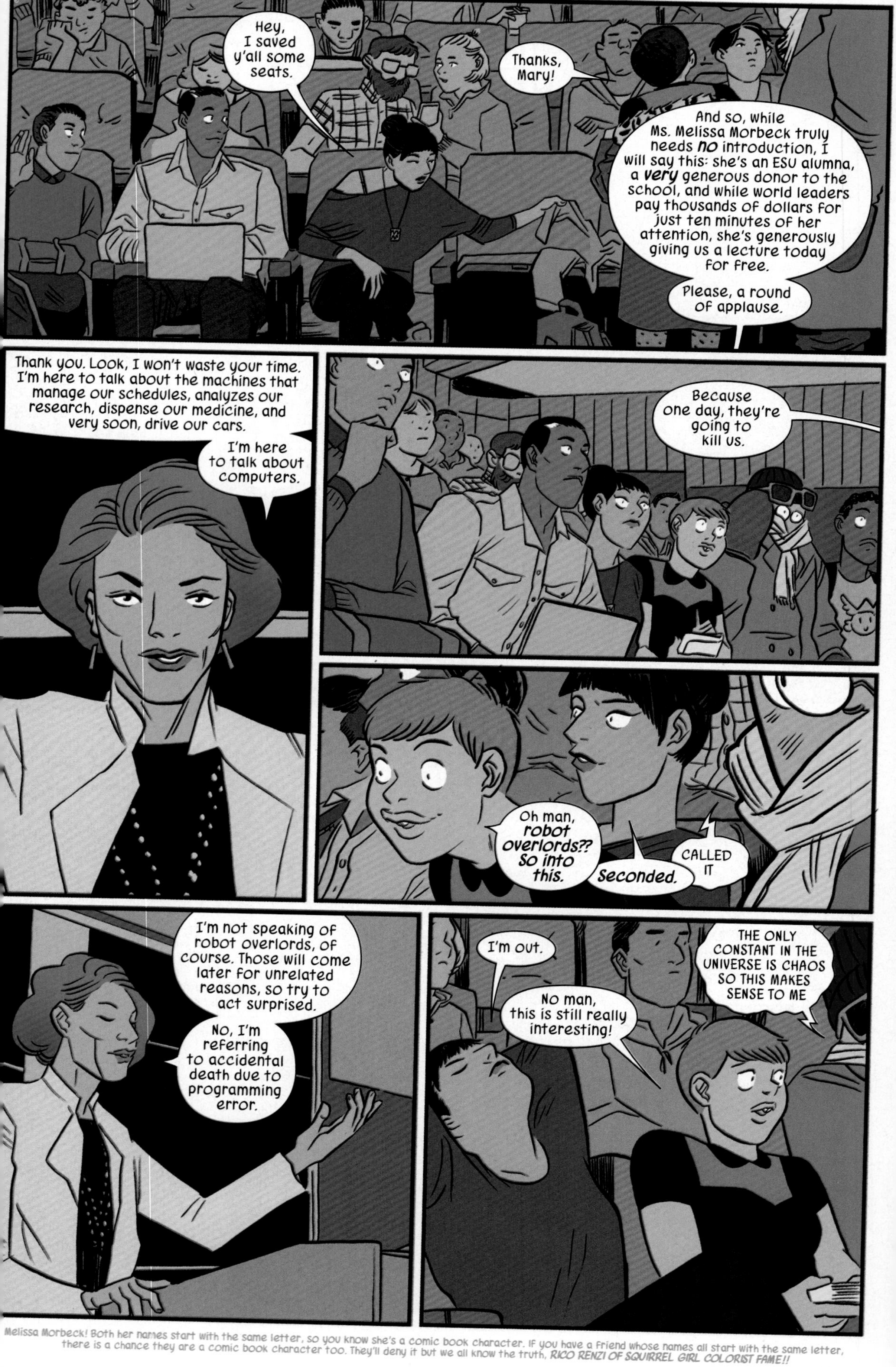
Hey, I saved y'all some seats.
Thanks, Mary!
And so, while Ms. Melissa Morbeck truly needs *no* introduction, I will say this: she's an ESU alumna, a *very* generous donor to the school, and while world leaders pay thousands of dollars for just ten minutes of her attention, she's generously giving us a lecture today for free.
Please, a round of applause.
Thank you. Look, I won't waste your time. I'm here to talk about the machines that manage our schedules, analyzes our research, dispense our medicine, and very soon, drive our cars.
I'm here to talk about computers.
Because one day, they're going to kill us.
Oh man, *robot overlords?? So into this.*
Seconded.
CALLED IT
I'm not speaking of robot overlords, of course. Those will come later for unrelated reasons, so try to act surprised.
No, I'm referring to accidental death due to programming error.
I'm out.
No man, this is still really interesting!
THE ONLY CONSTANT IN THE UNIVERSE IS CHAOS SO THIS MAKES SENSE TO ME

Melissa Morbeck! Both her names start with the same letter, so you know she's a comic book character. If you have a friend whose names all start with the same letter, there is a chance they are a comic book character too. They'll deny it but we all know the truth, *RICO RENZI OF SQUIRREL GIRL COLORIST FAME!!*

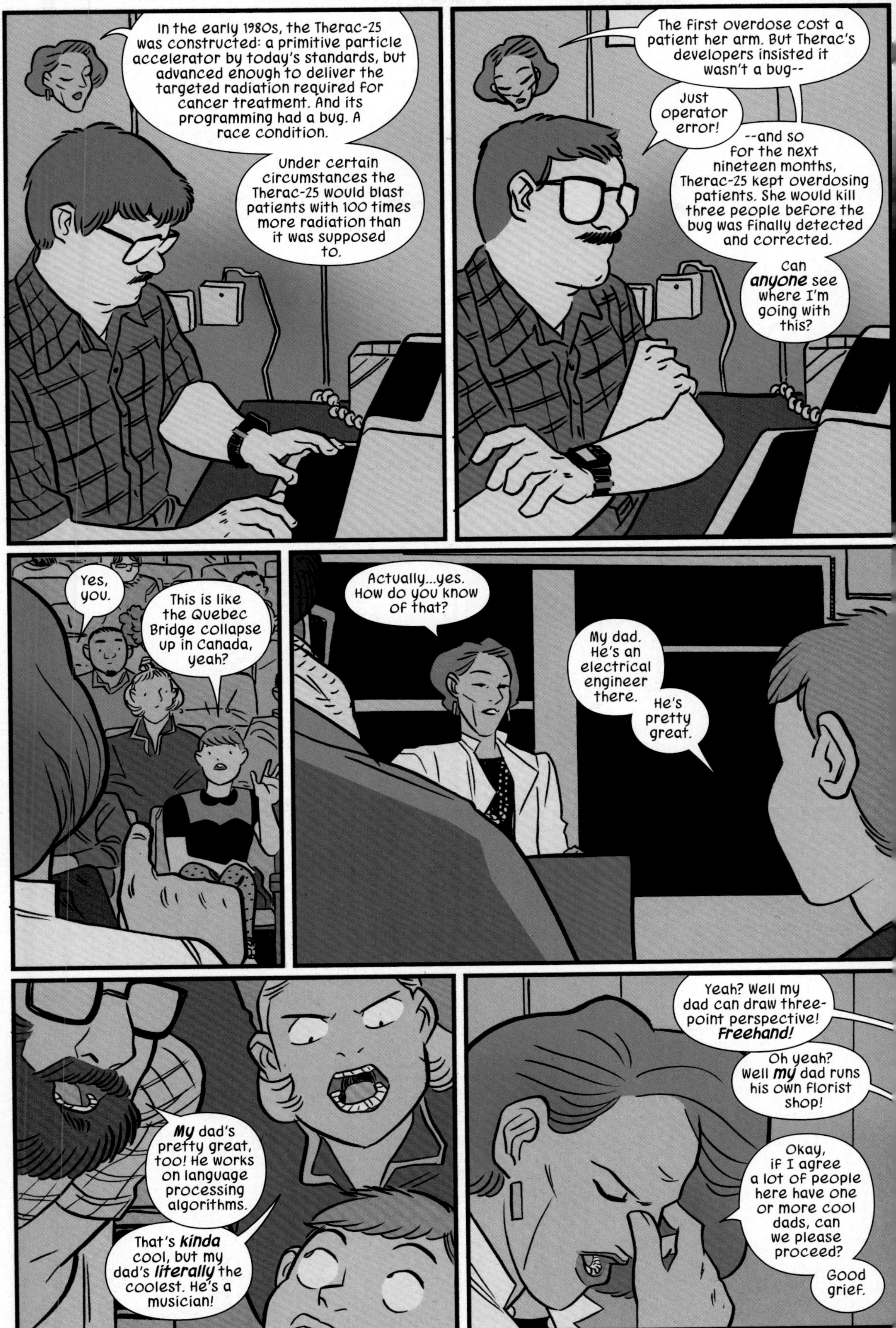
In the early 1980s, the Therac-25 was constructed: a primitive particle accelerator by today's standards, but advanced enough to deliver the targeted radiation required for cancer treatment. And its programming had a bug. A race condition.
Under certain circumstances the Therac-25 would blast patients with 100 times more radiation than it was supposed to.
The first overdose cost a patient her arm. But Therac's developers insisted it wasn't a bug--
Just operator error!
--and so for the next nineteen months, Therac-25 kept overdosing patients. She would kill three people before the bug was finally detected and corrected.
Can *anyone* see where I'm going with this?
Yes, you.
This is like the Quebec Bridge collapse up in Canada, yeah?
Actually...yes. How do you know of that?
My dad. He's an electrical engineer there.
He's pretty great.
My dad's pretty great, too! He works on language processing algorithms.
That's *kinda* cool, but my dad's *literally* the coolest. He's a musician!
Yeah? Well my dad can draw three-point perspective! *Freehand!*
Oh yeah? Well *my* dad runs his own florist shop!
Okay, if I agree a lot of people here have one or more cool dads, can we please proceed?
Good grief.

Other cool dads not mentioned here include the dad who knows how to ramp his skateboard off a pipe, the dad who trains falcons, and the dad who makes his own ice cream but still shares it with people even if they didn't help make it. All solid, 100% cool dads.

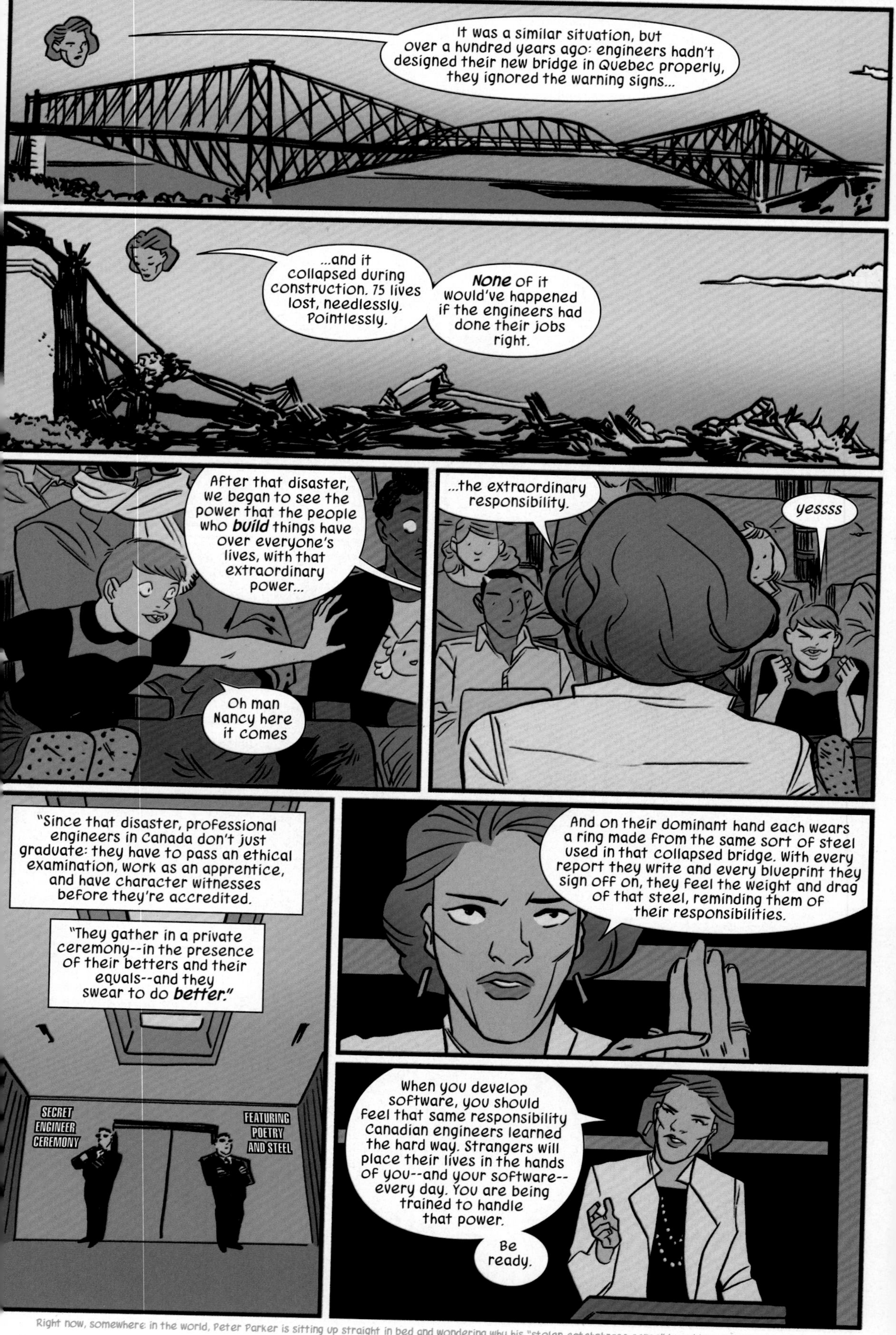
It was a similar situation, but over a hundred years ago: engineers hadn't designed their new bridge in Quebec properly, they ignored the warning signs...
...and it collapsed during construction. 75 lives lost, needlessly. Pointlessly.
None of it would've happened if the engineers had done their jobs right.
After that disaster, we began to see the power that the people who ***build*** things have over everyone's lives, with that extraordinary power...
Oh man Nancy here it comes
...the extraordinary responsibility.
yessss
"Since that disaster, professional engineers in Canada don't just graduate: they have to pass an ethical examination, work as an apprentice, and have character witnesses before they're accredited.
"They gather in a private ceremony--in the presence of their betters and their equals--and they swear to do ***better.***"
SECRET ENGINEER CEREMONY
FEATURING POETRY AND STEEL
And on their dominant hand each wears a ring made from the same sort of steel used in that collapsed bridge. With every report they write and every blueprint they sign off on, they feel the weight and drag of that steel, reminding them of their responsibilities.
When you develop software, you should feel that same responsibility Canadian engineers learned the hard way. Strangers will place their lives in the hands of you--and your software--every day. You are being trained to handle that power.
Be ready.

Right now, somewhere in the world, Peter Parker is sitting up straight in bed and wondering why his "stolen catchphrase-sense" is suddenly tingling *so much.*

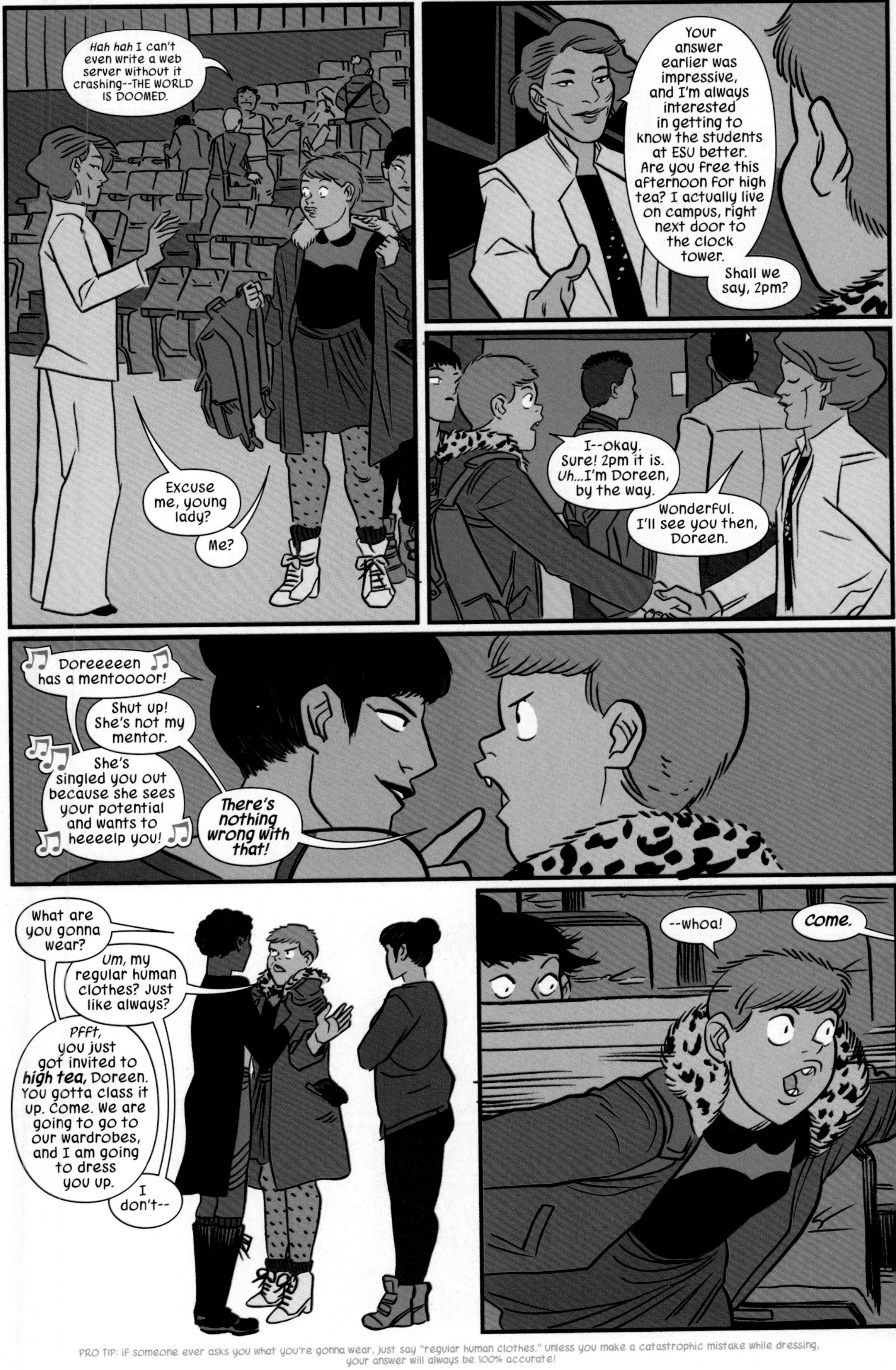
Hah hah I can't even write a web server without it crashing--THE WORLD IS DOOMED.
Excuse me, young lady?
Me?
Your answer earlier was impressive, and I'm always interested in getting to know the students at ESU better. Are you free this afternoon for high tea? I actually live on campus, right next door to the clock tower.
Shall we say, 2pm?
I--okay. Sure! 2pm it is. Uh...I'm Doreen, by the way.
Wonderful. I'll see you then, Doreen.
Doreeeeen has a mentoooor!
Shut up! She's not my mentor.
She's singled you out because she sees your potential and wants to heeeelp you!
There's nothing wrong with that!
What are you gonna wear?
Um, my regular human clothes? Just like always?
Pfft, you just got invited to high tea, Doreen. You gotta class it up. Come. We are going to go to our wardrobes, and I am going to dress you up.
I don't--
--Whoa!
Come.

PRO TIP: If someone ever asks you what you're gonna wear, just say "regular human clothes." Unless you make a catastrophic mistake while dressing, your answer will always be 100% accurate!

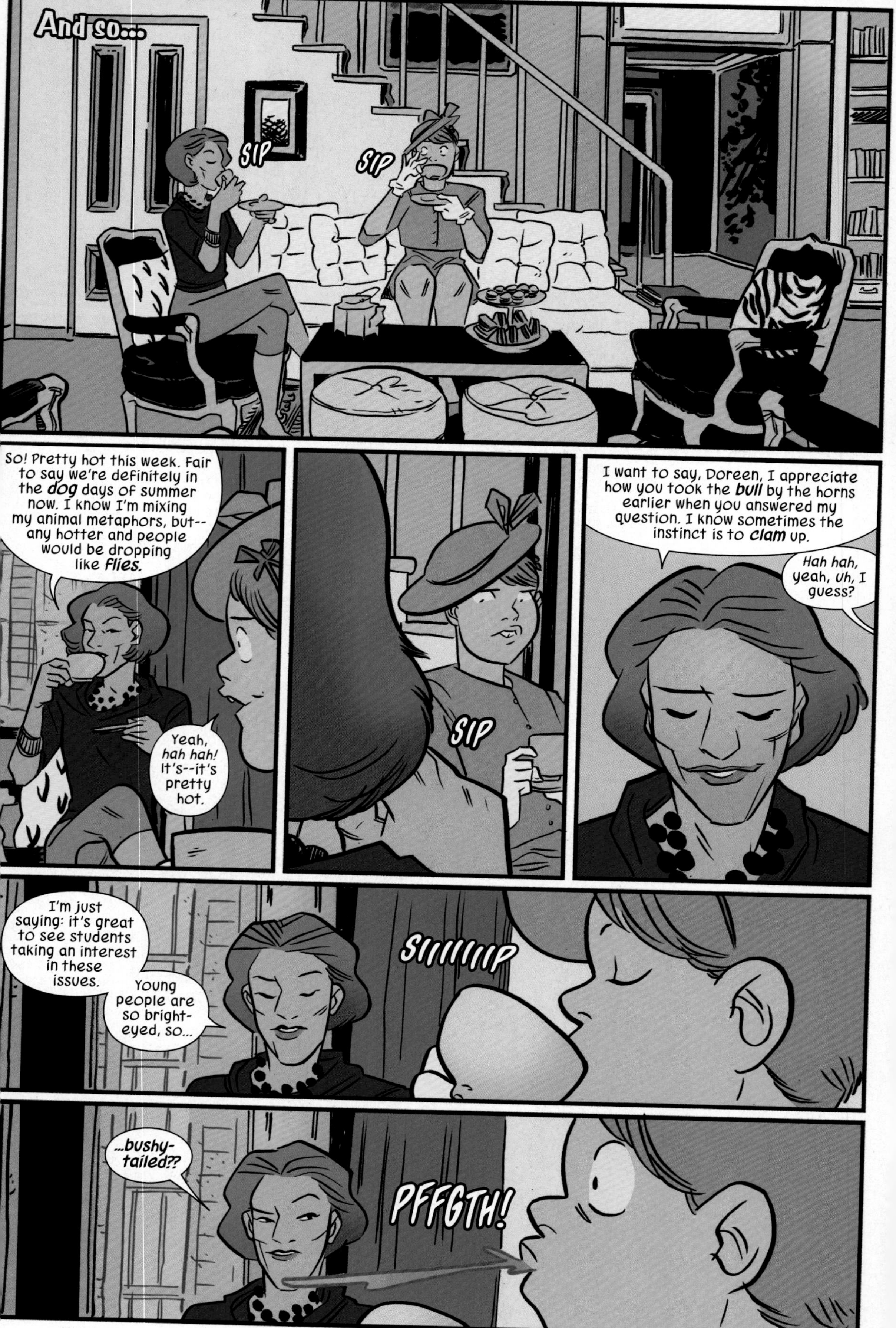
And so...
SIP
SIP
So! Pretty hot this week. Fair to say we're definitely in the *dog* days of summer now. I know I'm mixing my animal metaphors, but-- any hotter and people would be dropping like *flies.*
Yeah, hah hah! It's--it's pretty hot.
SIP
I want to say, Doreen, I appreciate how you took the *bull* by the horns earlier when you answered my question. I know sometimes the instinct is to *clam* up.
Hah hah, yeah, uh, I guess?
I'm just saying: it's great to see students taking an interest in these issues.
Young people are so bright-eyed, so...
SIIIIIIP
...bushy-tailed??
PFFGTH!

After many experiments I can finally confirm that, yes, "pffgth" is the sound I make when spitting out tea. Anyway, thanks for having me over, I gotta go, good luck with all your moistened walls!!

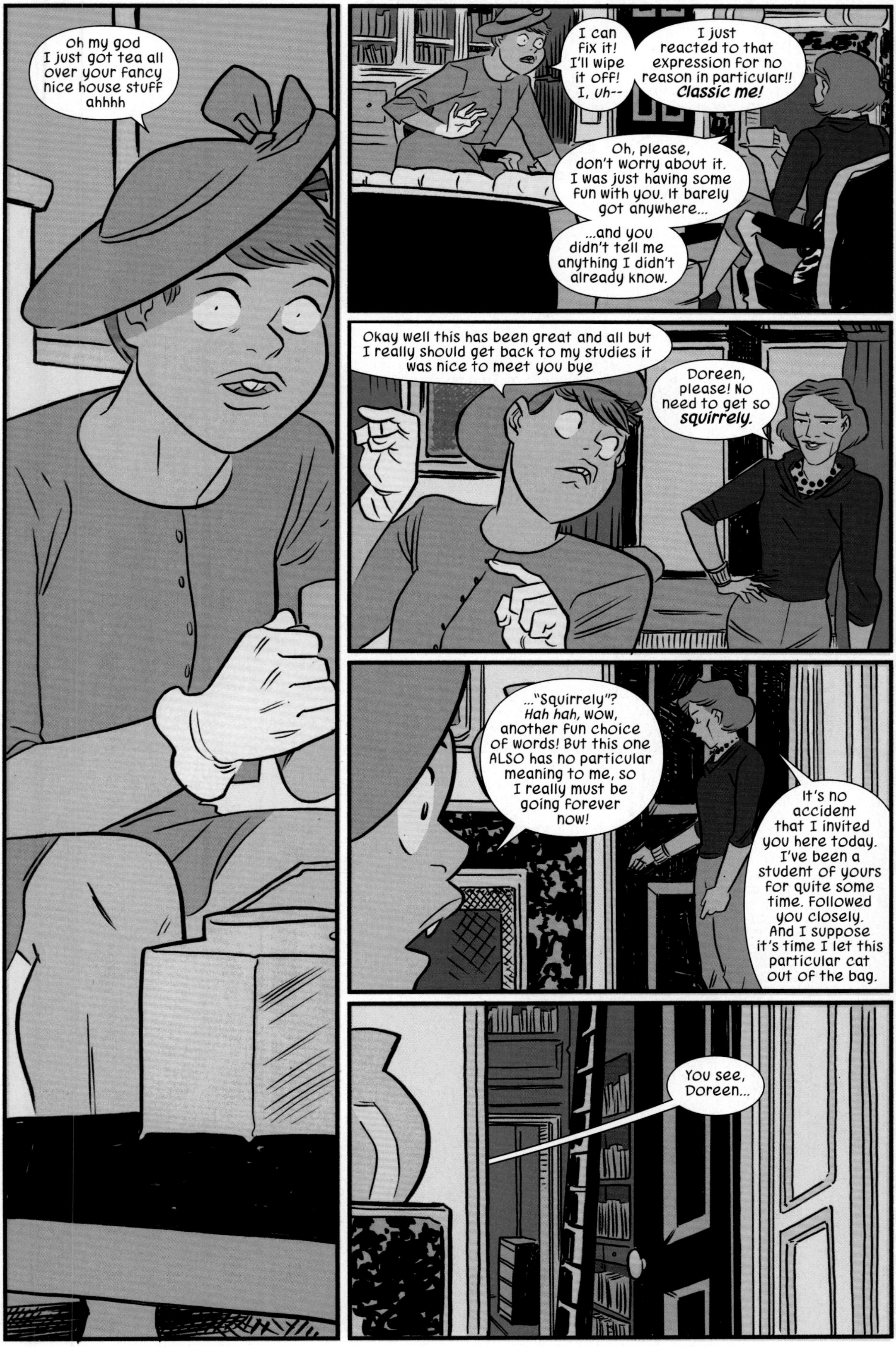
Oh my god I just got tea all over your fancy nice house stuff ahhhh
I can fix it! I'll wipe it off! I, uh--
I just reacted to that expression for no reason in particular!! Classic me!
Oh, please, don't worry about it. I was just having some fun with you. It barely got anywhere...
...and you didn't tell me anything I didn't already know.
Okay well this has been great and all but I really should get back to my studies it was nice to meet you bye
Doreen, please! No need to get so squirrely.
..."Squirrely"? Hah hah, wow, another fun choice of words! But this one ALSO has no particular meaning to me, so I really must be going forever now!
It's no accident that I invited you here today. I've been a student of yours for quite some time. Followed you closely. And I suppose it's time I let this particular cat out of the bag.
You see, Doreen...

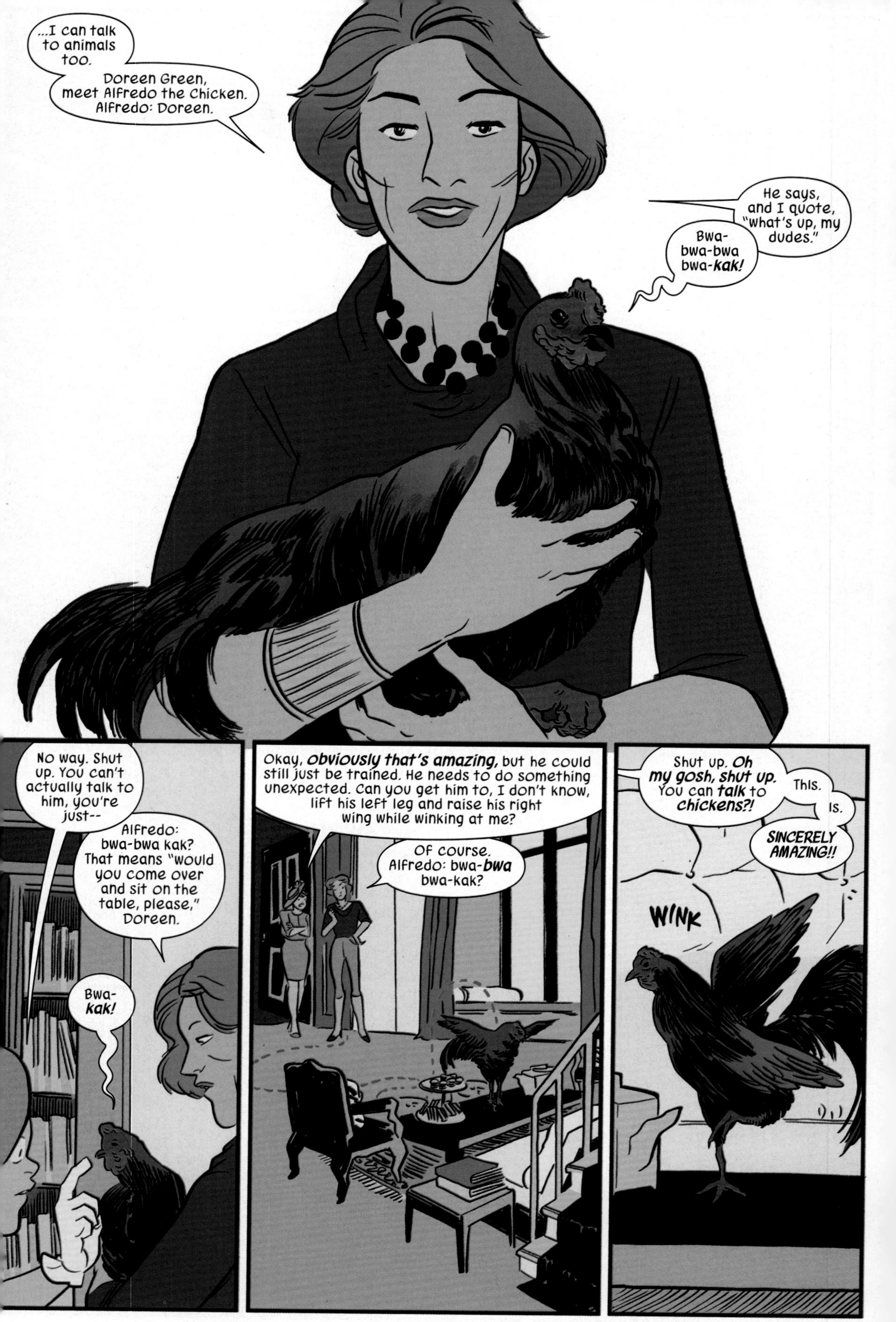
...I can talk to animals too.
Doreen Green, meet Alfredo the Chicken. Alfredo: Doreen.
He says, and I quote, "what's up, my dudes."
Bwa-bwa-bwa bwa-*kak!*
No way. Shut up. You can't actually talk to him, you're just--
Alfredo: bwa-bwa kak? That means "would you come over and sit on the table, please," Doreen.
Bwa-*kak!*
Okay, ***obviously that's amazing,*** but he could still just be trained. He needs to do something unexpected. Can you get him to, I don't know, lift his left leg and raise his right wing while winking at me?
Of course. Alfredo: bwa-***bwa*** bwa-kak?
Shut up. ***Oh my gosh, shut up.*** You can ***talk*** to ***chickens?!***
This.
Is.
SINCERELY AMAZING!!
WINK

This. Is. ***MAKING ME REALLY GLAD I ATTENDED AN OPTIONAL LECTURE THAT WE WEREN'T EVEN GETTING CREDIT FOR!!***

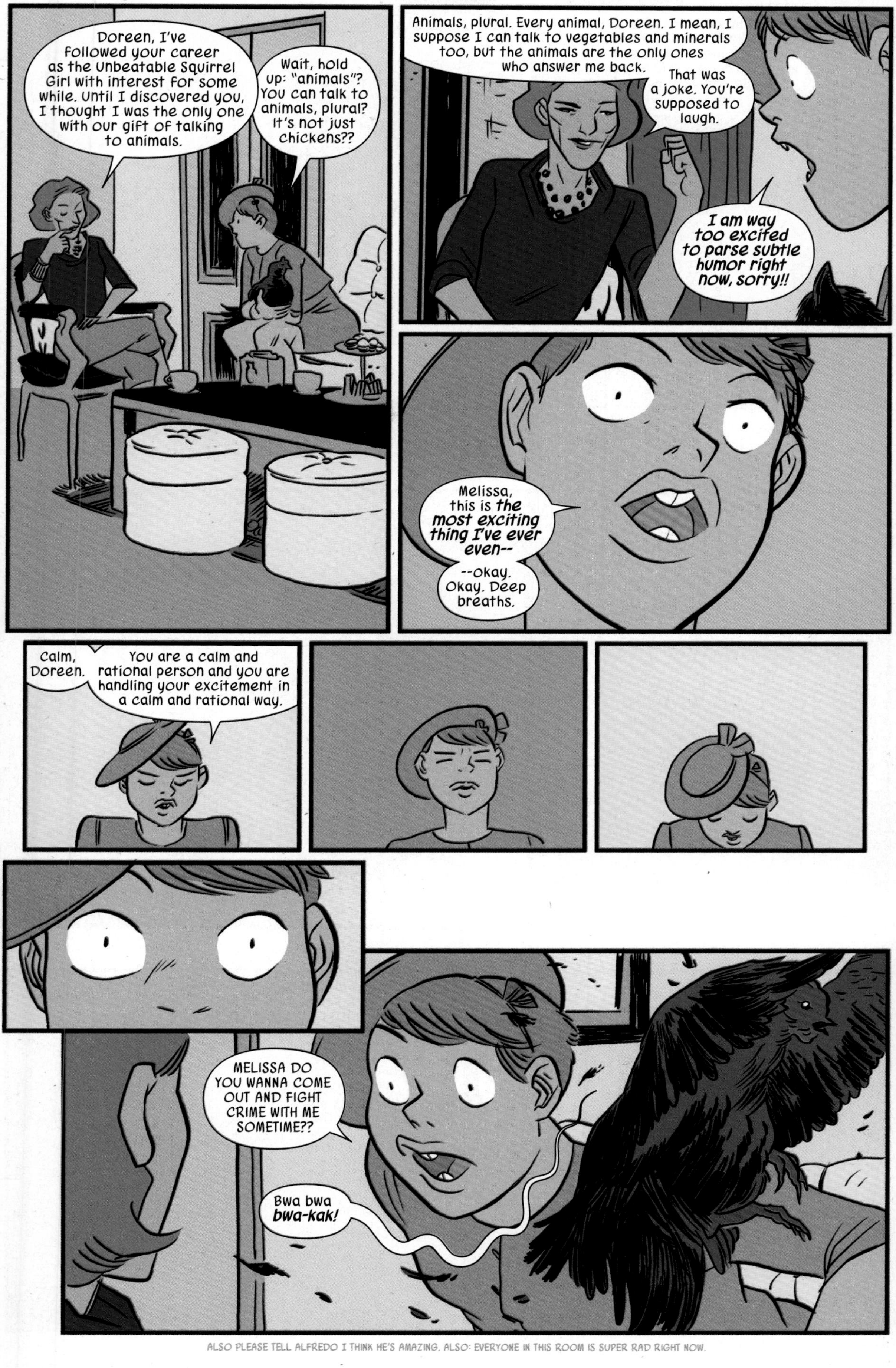

Doreen, I've followed your career as the Unbeatable Squirrel Girl with interest for some while. Until I discovered you, I thought I was the only one with our gift of talking to animals.
Wait, hold up: "animals"? You can talk to animals, plural? It's not just chickens??
Animals, plural. Every animal, Doreen. I mean, I suppose I can talk to vegetables and minerals too, but the animals are the only ones who answer me back.
That was a joke. You're supposed to laugh.
I am way too excited to parse subtle humor right now, sorry!!
Melissa, this is the most exciting thing I've ever even--
--Okay. Okay. Deep breaths.
Calm, Doreen.
You are a calm and rational person and you are handling your excitement in a calm and rational way.
MELISSA DO YOU WANNA COME OUT AND FIGHT CRIME WITH ME SOMETIME??
Bwa bwa bwa-kak!

ALSO PLEASE TELL ALFREDO I THINK HE'S AMAZING. ALSO: EVERYONE IN THIS ROOM IS SUPER RAD RIGHT NOW.

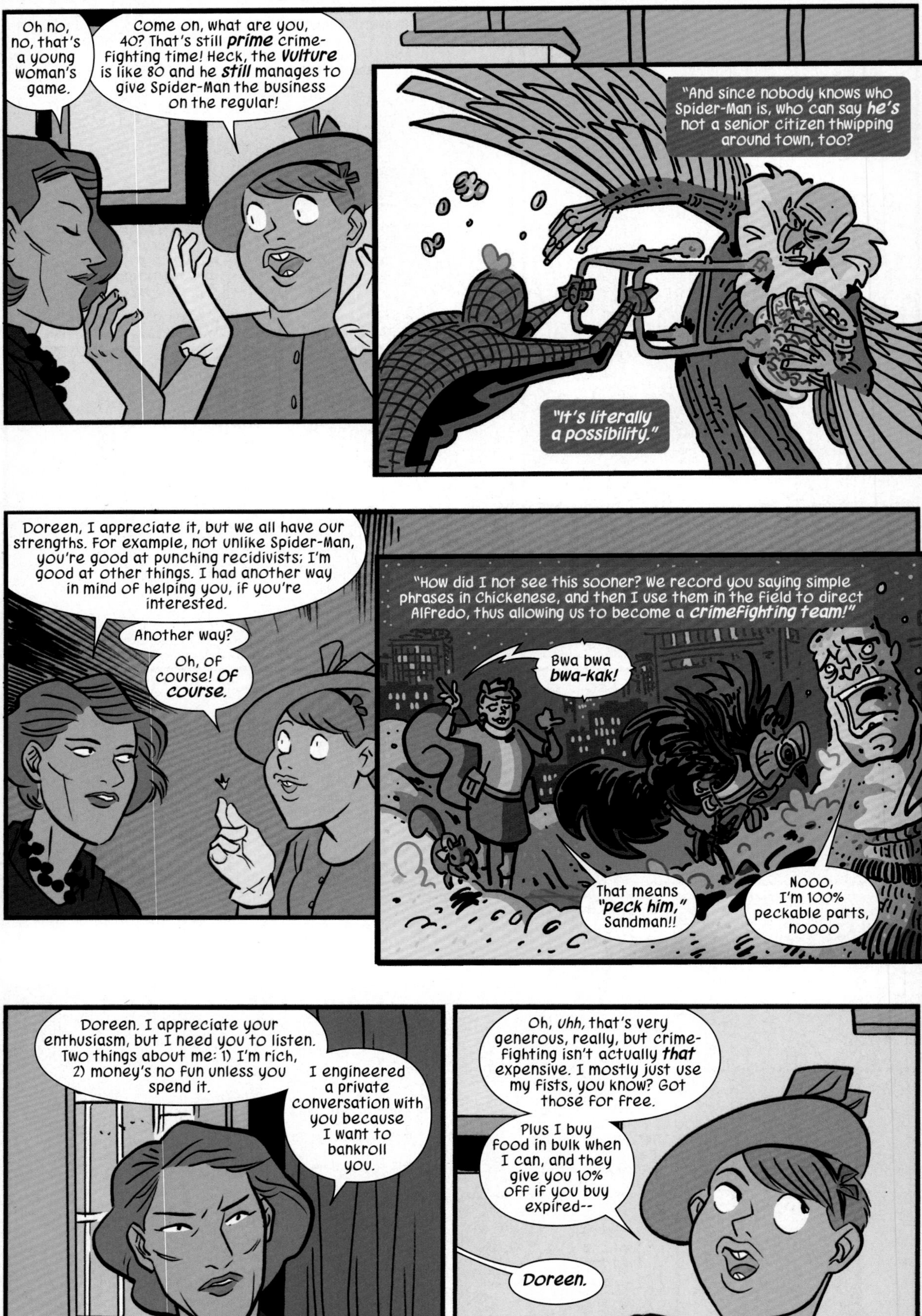
Oh no, no, that's a young woman's game.
Come on, what are you, 40? That's still prime crime-fighting time! Heck, the Vulture is like 80 and he still manages to give Spider-Man the business on the regular!
"And since nobody knows who Spider-Man is, who can say he's not a senior citizen thwipping around town, too?
"It's literally a possibility."
Doreen, I appreciate it, but we all have our strengths. For example, not unlike Spider-Man, you're good at punching recidivists; I'm good at other things. I had another way in mind of helping you, if you're interested.
Another way?
Oh, of course! Of course.
"How did I not see this sooner? We record you saying simple phrases in Chickenese, and then I use them in the field to direct Alfredo, thus allowing us to become a crimefighting team!"
Bwa bwa bwa-kak!
That means "peck him," Sandman!!
NOOO, I'm 100% peckable parts, NOOOO
Doreen. I appreciate your enthusiasm, but I need you to listen. Two things about me: 1) I'm rich, 2) money's no fun unless you spend it.
I engineered a private conversation with you because I want to bankroll you.
Oh, uhh, that's very generous, really, but crime-fighting isn't actually that expensive. I mostly just use my fists, you know? Got those for free.
Plus I buy food in bulk when I can, and they give you 10% off if you buy expired--
Doreen.

Sandman is a villain made entirely out of sand, and he's only slightly less vulnerable to Alfredo's pecking than Lady Kernels Of Corn, who is a villain I just made up! She's got an ear for crime but explodes under pressure! ***Did you know:*** she's the only (and therefore technically the greatest) character ever introduced in the little notes beneath a Marvel comic??

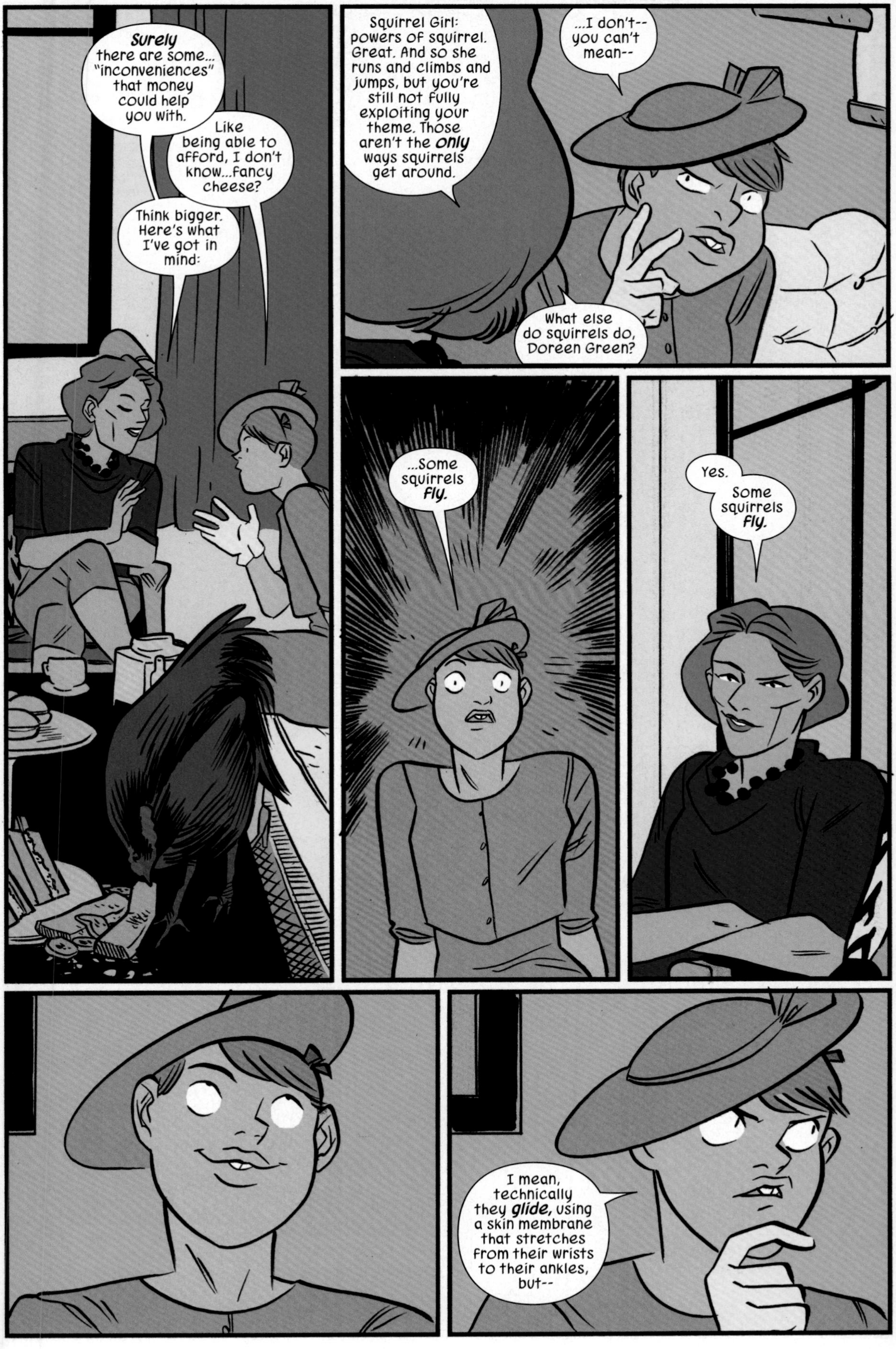
Surely there are some... "inconveniences" that money could help you with.
Like being able to afford, I don't know...fancy cheese?
Think bigger. Here's what I've got in mind:
Squirrel Girl: powers of squirrel. Great. And so she runs and climbs and jumps, but you're still not fully exploiting your theme. Those aren't the only ways squirrels get around.
...I don't-- you can't mean--
What else do squirrels do, Doreen Green?
...Some squirrels fly.
Yes.
Some squirrels fly.
I mean, technically they glide, using a skin membrane that stretches from their wrists to their ankles, but--

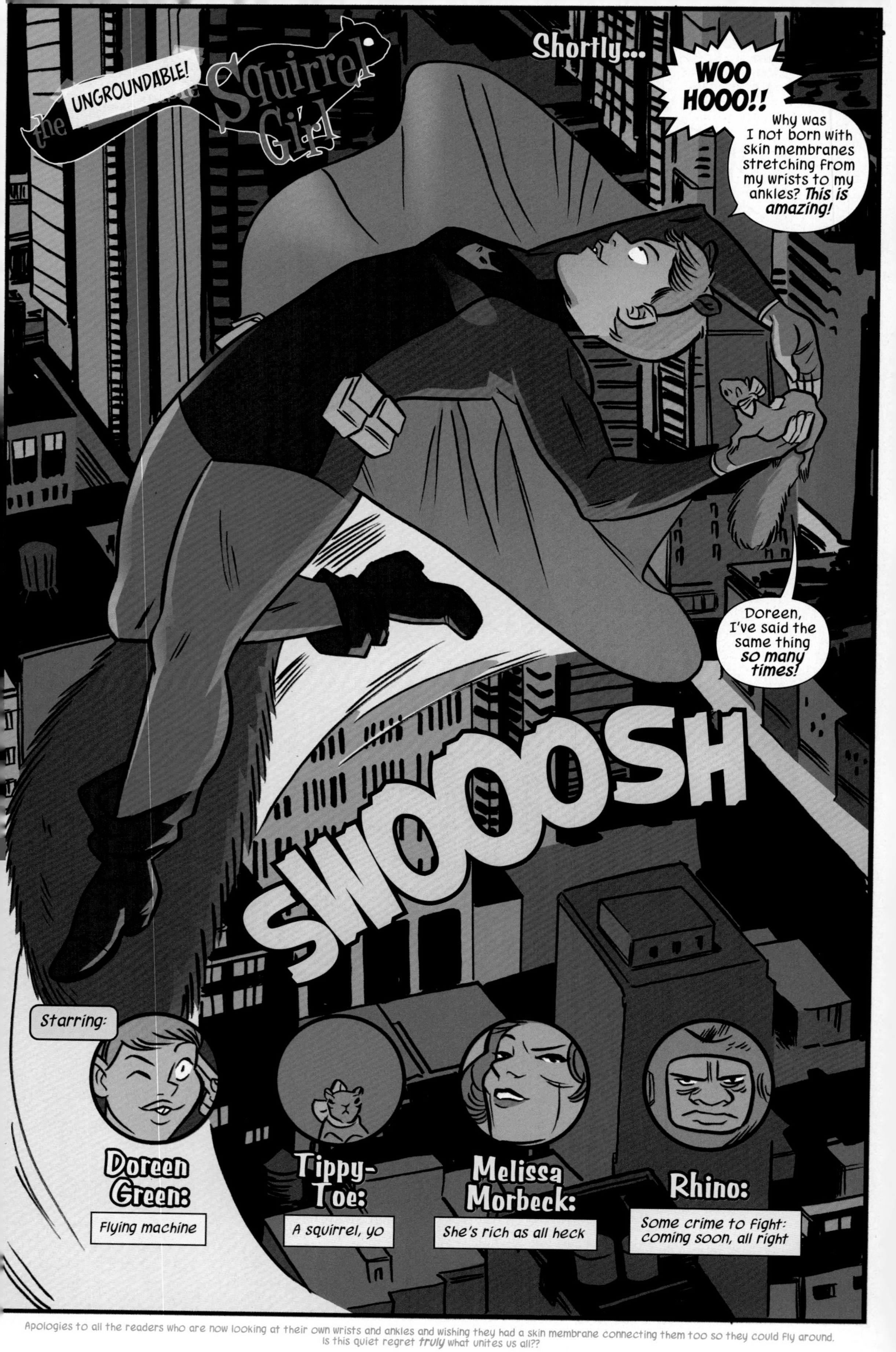
UNGROUNDABLE!
the Squirrel Girl
Shortly...
WOO HOOO!!
Why was I not born with skin membranes stretching from my wrists to my ankles? This is amazing!
Doreen, I've said the same thing so many times!
SWOOOSH
Starring:
Doreen Green:
Flying machine
Tippy-Toe:
A squirrel, yo
Melissa Morbeck:
She's rich as all heck
Rhino:
Some crime to fight: coming soon, all right

Apologies to all the readers who are now looking at their own wrists and ankles and wishing they had a skin membrane connecting them too so they could fly around. Is this quiet regret *truly* what unites us all??

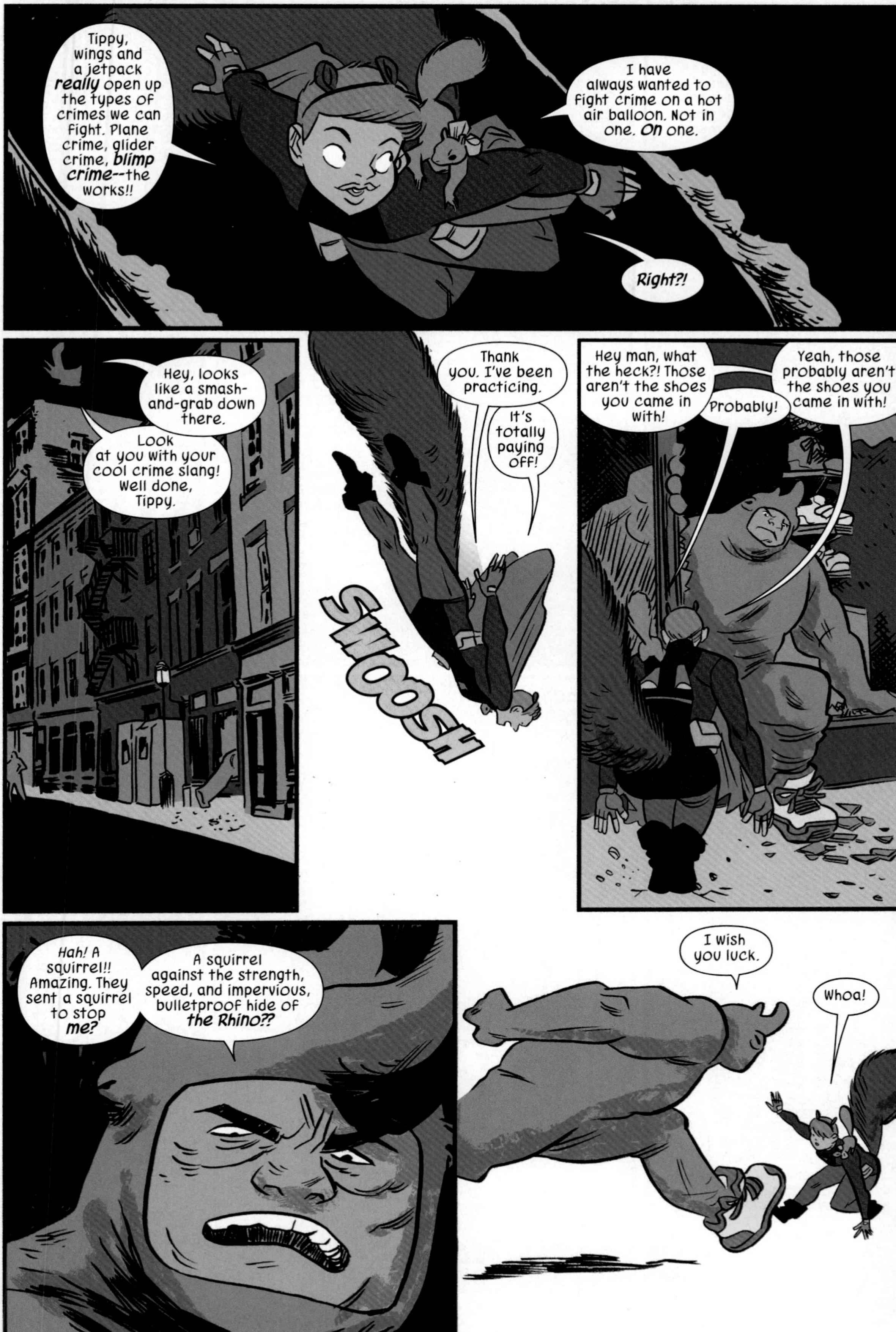
Tippy, wings and a jetpack *really* open up the types of crimes we can fight. Plane crime, glider crime, *blimp crime*--the works!!
I have always wanted to fight crime on a hot air balloon. Not in one. *On* one.
Right?!
Hey, looks like a smash-and-grab down there.
Look at you with your cool crime slang! Well done, Tippy.
Thank you. I've been practicing.
It's totally paying off!
SWOOSH
Hey man, what the heck?! Those aren't the shoes you came in with!
Probably!
Yeah, those probably aren't the shoes you came in with!
Hah! A squirrel!! Amazing. They sent a squirrel to stop *me?*
A squirrel against the strength, speed, and impervious, bulletproof hide of *the Rhino??*
I wish you luck.
Whoa!

Not pictured: all the criminals who just bought blimps to secure themselves from ground-level justice as they glance up, see Squirrel Girl flying by, then quickly search on their phones for "are blimps returnable for a full refund + it's an emergency."

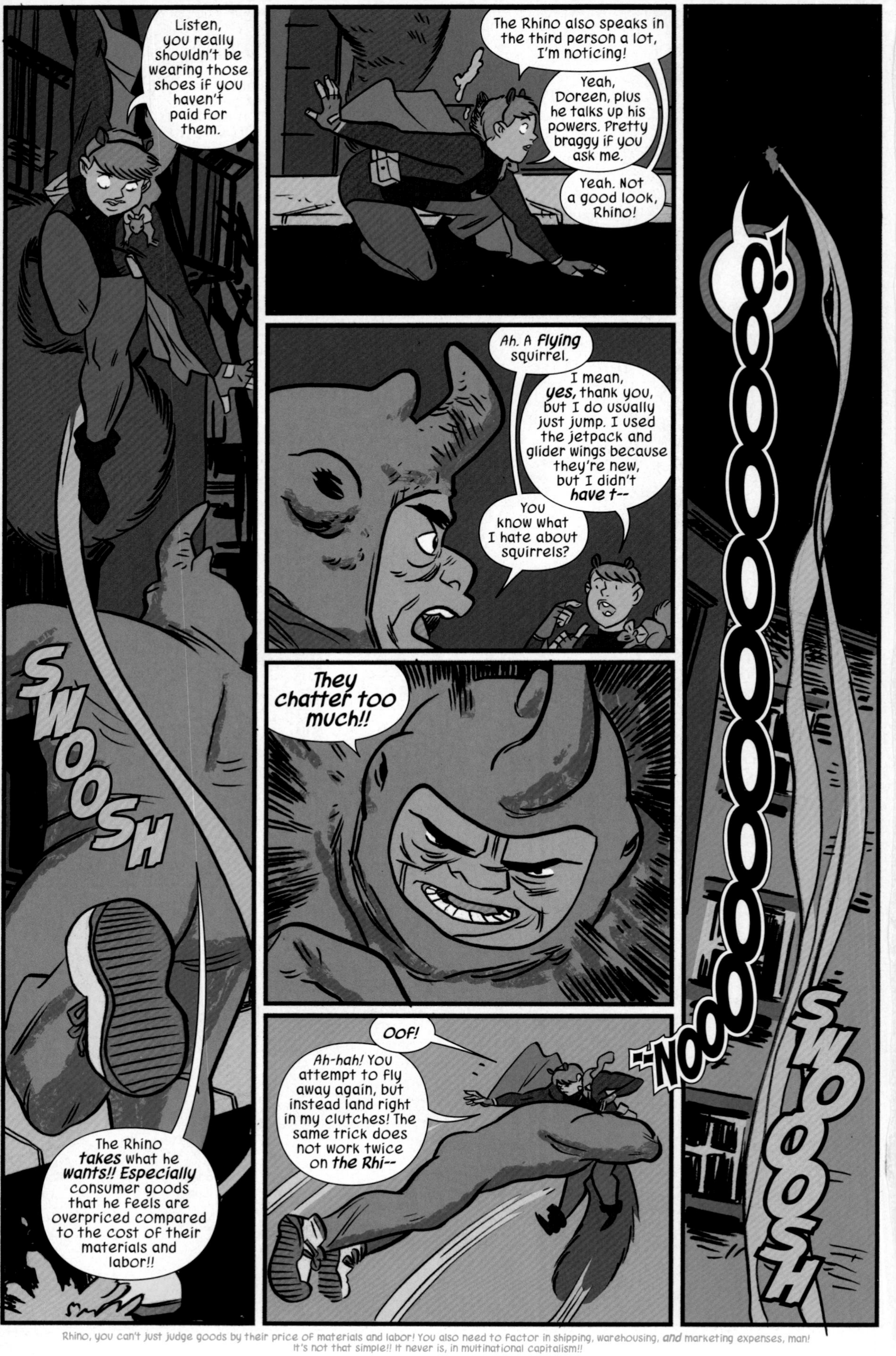

Listen, you really shouldn't be wearing those shoes if you haven't paid for them.
The Rhino also speaks in the third person a lot, I'm noticing!
Yeah, Doreen, plus he talks up his powers. Pretty braggy if you ask me.
Yeah. Not a good look, Rhino!
Ah. A **flying** squirrel.
I mean, ***yes,*** thank you, but I do usually just jump. I used the jetpack and glider wings because they're new, but I didn't ***have t--***
You know what I hate about squirrels?
They chatter too much!!
SWOOSH
The Rhino ***takes*** what he ***wants!! Especially*** consumer goods that he feels are overpriced compared to the cost of their materials and labor!!
OOF!
Ah-hah! You attempt to fly away again, but instead land right in my clutches! The same trick does not work twice on ***the Rhi--***
--NOOOOOOOOOOOOOOO!
SWOOOSH

Rhino, you can't just judge goods by their price of materials and labor! You also need to factor in shipping, warehousing, ***and*** marketing expenses, man! It's not that simple!! It never is, in multinational capitalism!!

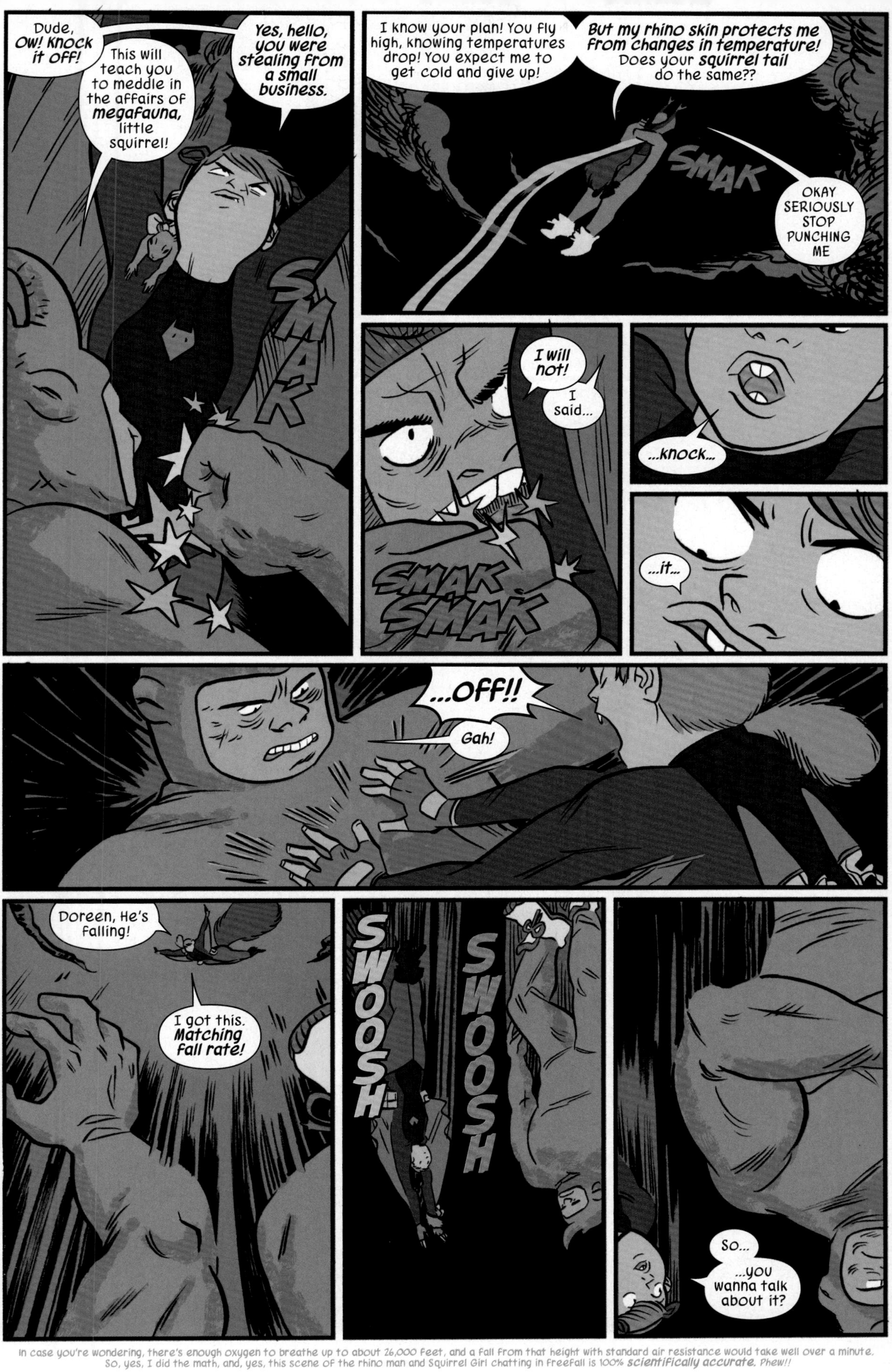
Dude, Ow! Knock it off!
This will teach you to meddle in the affairs of megafauna, little squirrel!
Yes, hello, you were stealing from a small business.
SMAK
I know your plan! You fly high, knowing temperatures drop! You expect me to get cold and give up!
But my rhino skin protects me from changes in temperature! Does your squirrel tail do the same??
SMAK
OKAY SERIOUSLY STOP PUNCHING ME
I will not!
I said...
SMAK SMAK
...knock...
...it...
...OFF!!
Gah!
Doreen, He's falling!
I got this. Matching fall rate!
SWOOSH
SWOOSH
So...
...you wanna talk about it?

In case you're wondering, there's enough oxygen to breathe up to about 26,000 feet, and a fall from that height with standard air resistance would take well over a minute. So, yes, I did the math, and, yes, this scene of the rhino man and Squirrel Girl chatting in freefall is 100% *scientifically accurate*. Phew!!

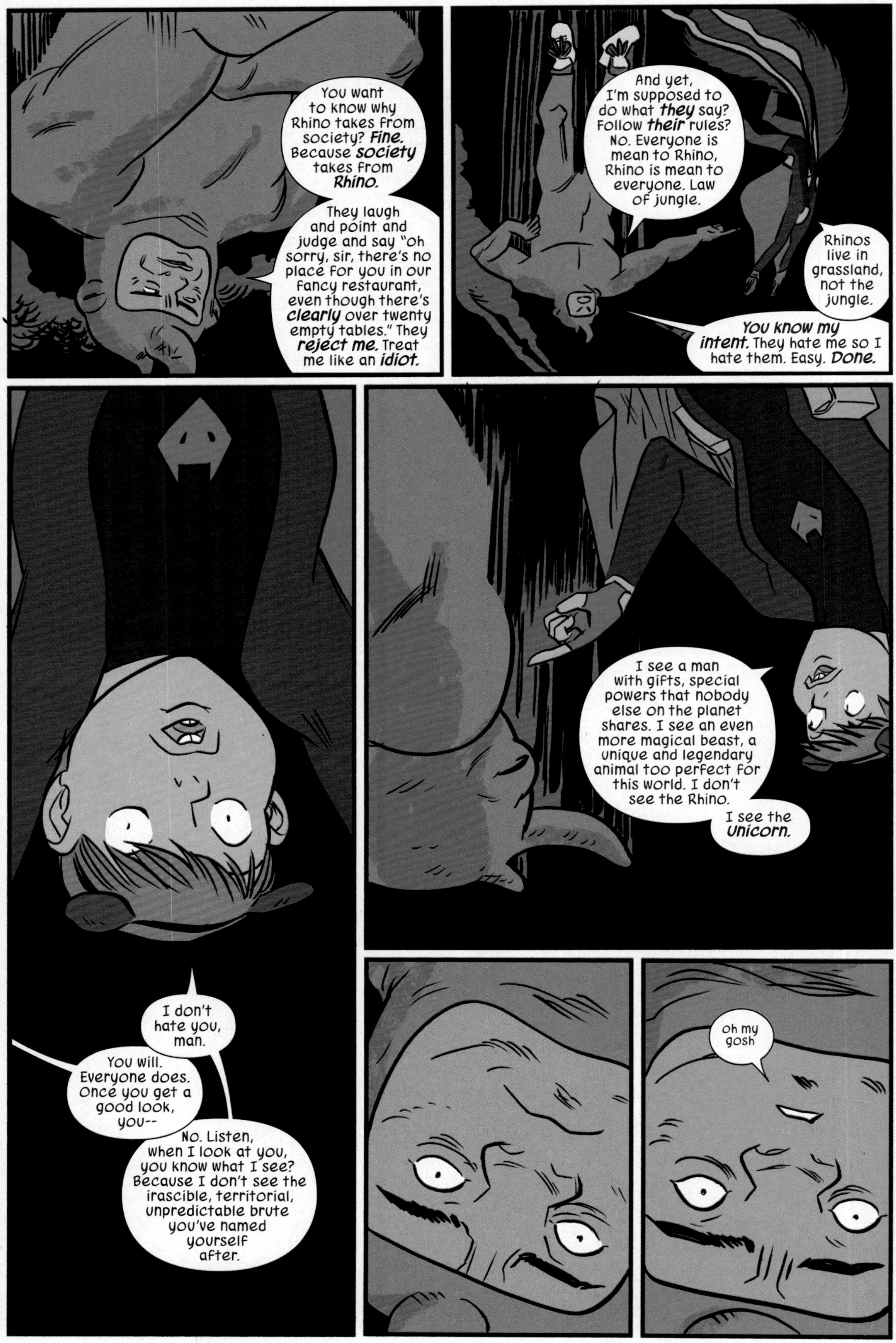
You want to know why Rhino takes from society? Fine. Because society takes from Rhino.
They laugh and point and judge and say "oh sorry, sir, there's no place for you in our fancy restaurant, even though there's clearly over twenty empty tables." They reject me. Treat me like an idiot.
And yet, I'm supposed to do what they say? Follow their rules? No. Everyone is mean to Rhino, Rhino is mean to everyone. Law of jungle.
Rhinos live in grassland, not the jungle.
You know my intent. They hate me so I hate them. Easy. Done.
I don't hate you, man.
You will. Everyone does. Once you get a good look, you--
No. Listen, when I look at you, you know what I see? Because I don't see the irascible, territorial, unpredictable brute you've named yourself after.
I see a man with gifts, special powers that nobody else on the planet shares. I see an even more magical beast, a unique and legendary animal too perfect for this world. I don't see the Rhino.
I see the Unicorn.
Oh my gosh

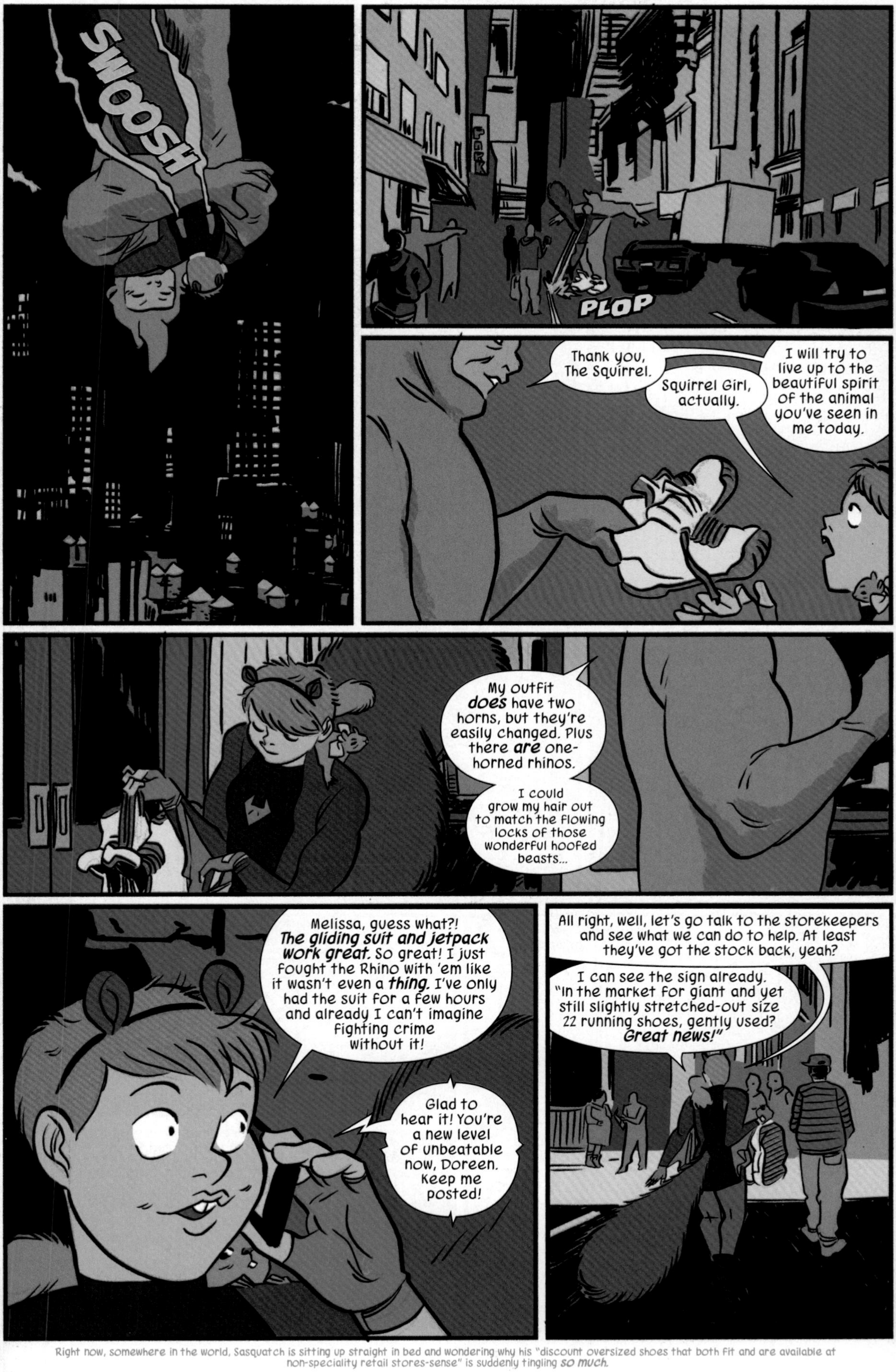
SWOOSH
PLOP
Thank you, The Squirrel.
Squirrel Girl, actually.
I will try to live up to the beautiful spirit of the animal you've seen in me today.
My outfit does have two horns, but they're easily changed. Plus there are one-horned rhinos.
I could grow my hair out to match the flowing locks of those wonderful hoofed beasts...
Melissa, guess what?! The gliding suit and jetpack work great. So great! I just fought the Rhino with 'em like it wasn't even a thing. I've only had the suit for a few hours and already I can't imagine fighting crime without it!
Glad to hear it! You're a new level of unbeatable now, Doreen. Keep me posted!
All right, well, let's go talk to the storekeepers and see what we can do to help. At least they've got the stock back, yeah?
I can see the sign already. "In the market for giant and yet still slightly stretched-out size 22 running shoes, gently used? Great news!"

Right now, somewhere in the world, Sasquatch is sitting up straight in bed and wondering why his "discount oversized shoes that both fit and are available at non-speciality retail stores-sense" is suddenly tingling *so much.*

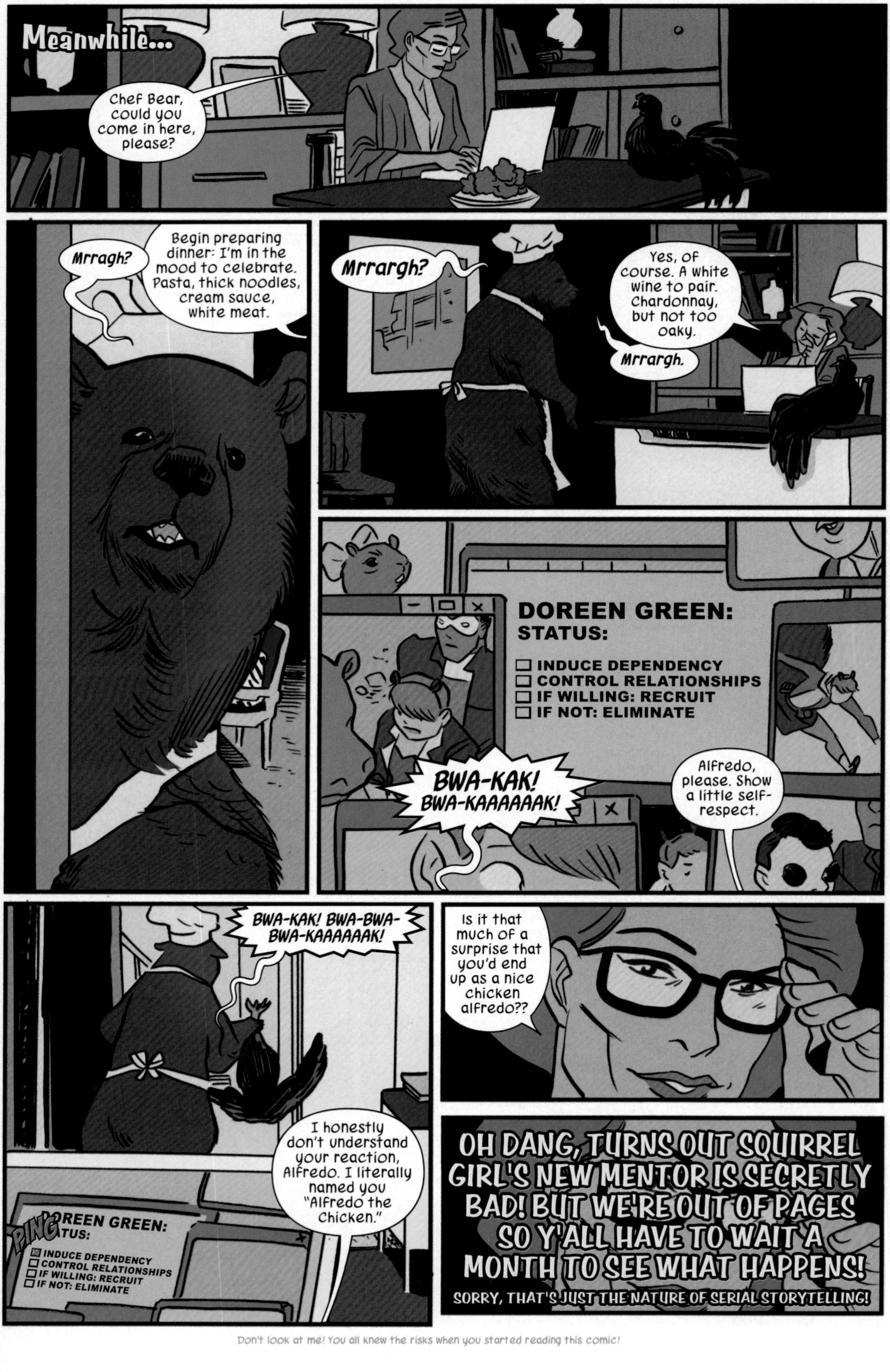
Meanwhile...
Chef Bear, could you come in here, please?
Mrragh?
Begin preparing dinner: I'm in the mood to celebrate. Pasta, thick noodles, cream sauce, white meat.
Mrrargh?
Yes, of course. A white wine to pair. Chardonnay, but not too oaky.
Mrrargh.
DOREEN GREEN:
STATUS:
INDUCE DEPENDENCY
CONTROL RELATIONSHIPS
IF WILLING: RECRUIT
IF NOT: ELIMINATE
BWA-KAK! BWA-KAAAAAAK!
Alfredo, please. Show a little self-respect.
BWA-KAK! BWA-BWA-BWA-KAAAAAAK!
I honestly don't understand your reaction, Alfredo. I literally named you "Alfredo the Chicken."
PING
INDUCE DEPENDENCY
CONTROL RELATIONSHIPS
IF WILLING: RECRUIT
IF NOT: ELIMINATE
Is it that much of a surprise that you'd end up as a nice chicken alfredo??
OH DANG, TURNS OUT SQUIRREL GIRL'S NEW MENTOR IS SECRETLY BAD! BUT WE'RE OUT OF PAGES SO Y'ALL HAVE TO WAIT A MONTH TO SEE WHAT HAPPENS!
SORRY, THAT'S JUST THE NATURE OF SERIAL STORYTELLING!

Don't look at me! You all knew the risks when you started reading this comic!

Letters From Nuts

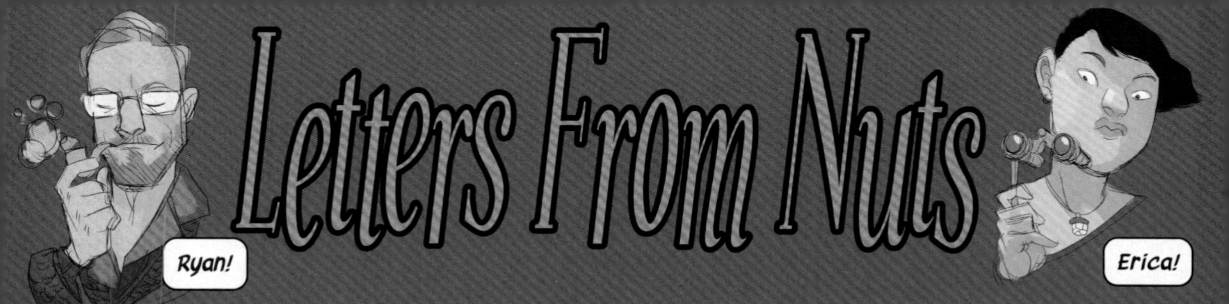
Ryan!
Erica!

Send letters to mheroes@marvel.com or 135 W 50th St, 7th Floor, New York, NY 10020 (Please mark "OKAY TO PRINT")

Hi guys,

Having read the SQUIRREL GIRL BEATS UP THE MARVEL UNIVERSE graphic novel (which was fantastic), I didn't expect it to become a reality!

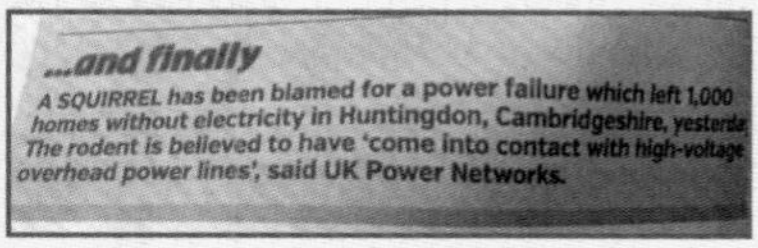

...and finally

A SQUIRREL has been blamed for a power failure which left 1,000 homes without electricity in Huntingdon, Cambridgeshire, yesterday. The rodent is believed to have 'come into contact with high-voltage overhead power lines', said UK Power Networks.

Keep up the great comic, but stop predicting the future okay?

Yours awesomely,
Cameron Leacock

RYAN: Allene gets around!! Which actually is weird, since she's supposed to be [SPOILERS REMOVED IN CASE YOU HAVEN'T READ THE BOOK YET].

ERICA: And that's just ONE squirrel. SO Y'ALL BETTER WATCH OUT.

Hi Ryan and Erica and Rico and co.!

I'm a Young Adult librarian, and I love to talk about Squirrel Girl when I visit schools. Every month, I give book talks at a junior high, and back in October, I decided that the only way I could improve on the experience of talking to teenagers about library books for forty-minute classes would be to do it...while dressed as Squirrel Girl! Attached are pictures.
Thank you for making my favorite comic!

Emily

P.S. I hope to meet you at C2E2 next year, Erica!

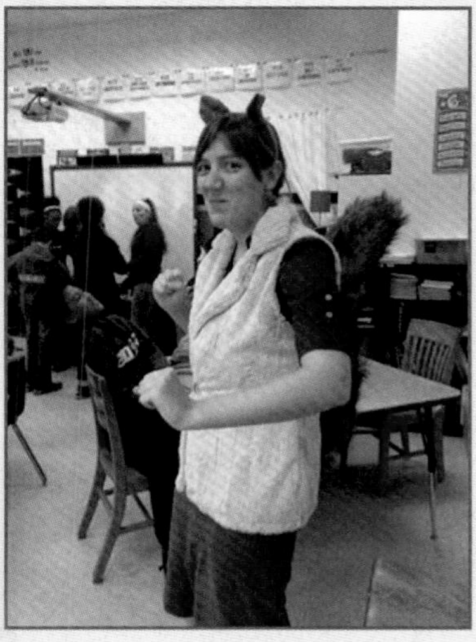

RYAN: I love a) that you do this and b) that you do this in costume! SO GREAT. My love of libraries and librarians is well-documented (in the pages of this very comic, no less) so I guess it's no surprise that I'm big into this!

ERICA: This is great! I was just thinking how warm you look (my heat is off for some reason) and I just remembered that we were talking about doing a winter-time costume for her. HM HM HM. Thanks for the reminder even if you didn't mean to do it!

Dear SQUIRREL GIRL nuts,

Thank you for your consistently delightful content in each issue of SQUIRREL GIRL! Luckily, I discovered THE UNBEATABLE SQUIRREL GIRL when it was still very new, and I've collected every issue since. I even more recently acquired an original 1991 X-MEN comic with the original appearance of Squirrel Girl, which will be framed and displayed in my home as a wonderful conversation starter.

This past summer, I put together my very own Squirrel Girl getup to wear to the Phoenix Comicon. As you can see, every effort was made to make the costume perfect. I made most of it with my own two hands. I had quite a few people excitedly comment on my costume, which means quite a few people would enjoy your attendance at a future PCC event. *wink wink* Pictured is me and a classmate of mine who has recently become a little nuts herself. Keep the gold coming!

Bonnie Mangum

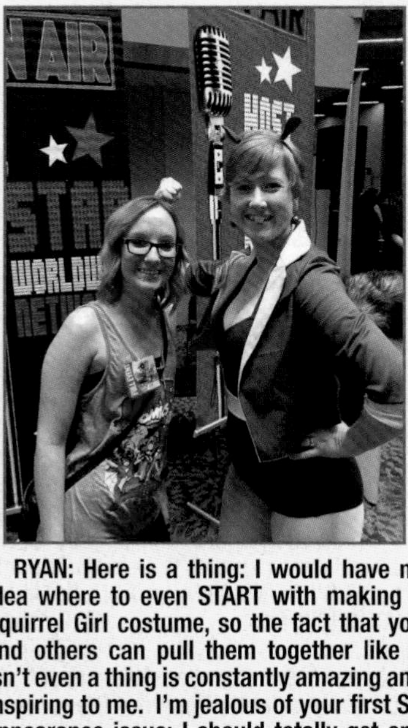

RYAN: Here is a thing: I would have no idea where to even START with making a Squirrel Girl costume, so the fact that you and others can pull them together like it isn't even a thing is constantly amazing and inspiring to me. I'm jealous of your first SG appearance issue: I should totally get one too! I've also never been to Phoenix, and maybe that should change??

ERICA: I love it! I remember either right before or right after the series launched, my friend who owns my local comic shop Hub Comics asked if I wanted to buy her original appearance because it was still crazy cheap at the time. I said no and now I really regret it. It costs a LOT MORE all of a sudden!

Dear UNBEATABLE SG Squad,

Hi. My name is Nora S, and I am 9 (almost 10!) years old. My dad introduced me to Squirrel Girl and I LOVE it SOOOOOO much. It is probably the FUNNIEST comic/book I have ever read! (And I read a lot.) In fact, I even dressed up as Squirrel Girl for Halloween! (I have included a picture below.)

Thank you for making such a MARVELous comic!

Sincerely,
Nora S.

P.S.: Squirrels Forever!

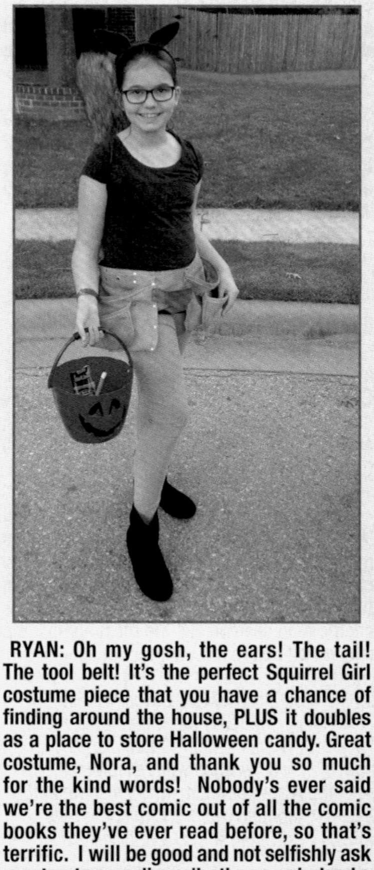

RYAN: Oh my gosh, the ears! The tail! The tool belt! It's the perfect Squirrel Girl costume piece that you have a chance of finding around the house, PLUS it doubles as a place to store Halloween candy. Great costume, Nora, and thank you so much for the kind words! Nobody's ever said we're the best comic out of all the comic books they've ever read before, so that's terrific. I will be good and not selfishly ask you to stop reading all other comic books now just so I can keep that good feeling forever. Thank you!

ERICA: I am for sure using that tool belt idea even though I don't have a place for it yet. You look great!

Dear Erica and Ryan,

I went to Comic Con in Chicago, and we went as our favorite heroes. I dressed up as Nancy Whitehead, my mom dressed up as my best friend Squirrel Girl, my brother Dillon went as Chipmunk Hunk, my auntie went as the Squirrel Army, my brother's friend went as Koi Boy, and we had a lot of fun and lots of people took pictures of us.

When are we going to meet Nancy's mom? Is Squirrel Girl going to like Nancy's mom as much as Nancy liked Doreen's mom? I LOVED Doreen's mom—that issue made me laugh so hard!!

Rose Collins, Milwaukee Wisconsin (age 12)

P.S. My brother wants to know if Chipmunk Hunk and Koi Boy will make more appearances.

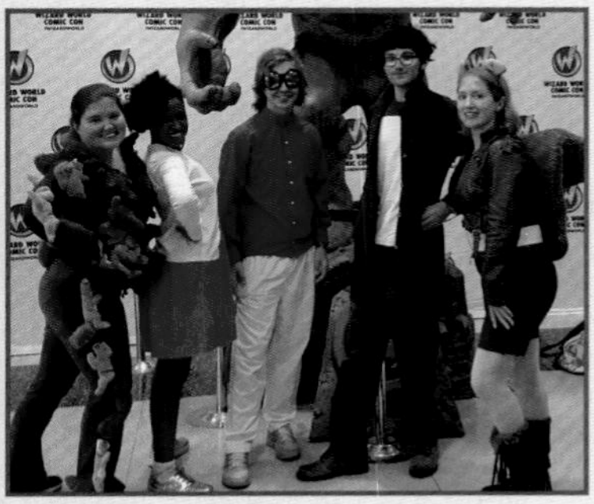

RYAN: AHHH, IT'S THE WHOLE CAST, I CAN BARELY HANDLE IT!! AMAZING. So, SO great. Also, I've never really thought about Nancy's parents! Erica, we're gonna have to talk about this!

ERICA: This is sooooo great. I can't believe there's a squirrel army costume out there now. Also, Ryan, I've been thinking about Nancy's parents so DON'T YOU WORRY.

Hi, Erica and Ryan,

I am in your debt: At my urging (read: nagging, but in a charming way) my not-a-comics-fan-but-definitely-a-computer-guy husband read THE UNBEATABLE SQUIRREL GIRL #11, laughed, loved it, and generally deemed it the bee's knees, the cat's pajamas, and the squirrel's muumuu (sorry, I'm still working on that one.).

It being the Festive Season, and at his urging (read: nagging, but like Cary Grant would do it), I would like to share with you the holiday carol I composed in Doreen's honor. It's to the tune of "O Christmas Tree" because a tree-centric tune seemed like the most appropriate leaping-off point for a Squirrel Girl song:

O Squirrel Girl, O Squirrel Girl,
You really are Unbeatable!
O Squirrel Girl, O Squirrel Girl,
For reasons well repeatable!
You leave your home to kick some butts,
And then return to eat some nuts.
O Squirrel Girl, O Squirrel Girl,
This pizza is reheatable!

O Squirrel Girl, O Squirrel Girl,
Your tail is truly bushy!
O Squirrel Girl, O Squirrel Girl,
I hope I don't sound pushy.
Whence come your powers? I dunno.
Your sidekick's name is Tippy-Toe.
O Squirrel Girl, O Squirrel Girl

I'm going to quit while I'm ahead without trying to find a good rhyme for bushy/pushy, lest I end up with something even worse than the repeatable pizza line in the first verse. *Fa-la-la-la-la, etceteraaaaaaaa!*

Thanks for a wonderful book.

Best,
Esther Friesner

RYAN: Esther, there is a proud tradition – starting in the first panel of our very first issue – of taking other songs and upgrading them so they're about Squirrel Girl now. I'm so glad that this tradition has now spread to non-me people!

ERICA: Oh man who else wants a pizza really badly right now? Is it just me? All the time?

Ryan, Erica & Team Squirrel,

I had a dream last night that I met Squirrel Girl and I was like say hi to Monkey Joe for me and she glared at me and I was like crap that was her squirrel that died her current squirrel is Tippy-Toe YOU SHOULD KNOW THAT GREG GET IT TOGETHER.

Also Dick Van Dyke was my uncle.

Greg Packnett
Madison, Wisconsin

RYAN: Greg, your subconscious has given you the gift of the opportunity of getting it together before you embarrass yourself in real life! Well done, Greg's subconscious! Also: Your uncle is a very talented performer.

ERICA: Weird side note: When I went to visit Ryan in Canada he took us to a science museum, which had an exhibit of Rowland Emett's inventions, including his work in CHITTY CHITTY BANG BANG. It's all coming full circle.

Okay, that's all for this month. But before we go, we've got a special treat! *New York Times* best-selling, award-winning, all-around butt-kicking authors Shannon Hale and Dean Hale have penned a BRAND-NEW SQUIRREL GIRL PROSE NOVEL for young adults — and it just hit shelves! You've seen her in college — but how did the bodaciously tailed and slightly buck-toothed Doreen survive the woes of middle school? BY BEING FREAKING UNBEATABLE, THAT'S HOW. Duh.

Here's some more info about it: Fourteen-year-old Doreen Green just moved from sunny California to the suburbs of New Jersey. She must start at a new school, make new friends, and continue to hide her furry tail. Yep, Doreen has the powers of . . . a SQUIRREL! After failing at several attempts to find her new BFF, Doreen feels lonely and trapped, liked a caged animal. Then one day Doreen uses her extraordinary powers to stop a group of troublemakers from causing mischief in the neighborhood, and her whole life changes. Everyone at school is talking about the mystery hero who saved the day! Doreen contemplates becoming a full-fledged super hero, and thus, Squirrel Girl is born! She saves cats from trees, keeps the sidewalks clean, and dissuades vandalism. All is well until a real-life super villain steps out of the shadows and declares Squirrel Girl his archenemy. Can Doreen balance being a teenager and a super hero? Or will she go . . . NUTS?

THE UNBEATABLE SQUIRREL GIRL: SQUIRREL MEETS WORLD novel is on-sale now!

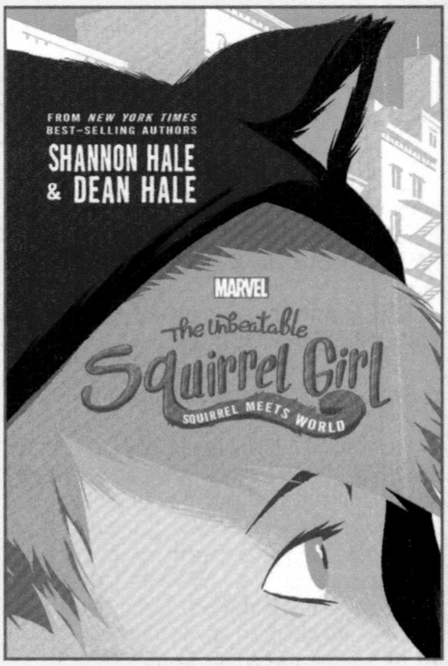
FROM NEW YORK TIMES BEST-SELLING AUTHORS
SHANNON HALE & DEAN HALE
MARVEL
The Unbeatable Squirrel Girl
SQUIRREL MEETS WORLD

Next Issue:

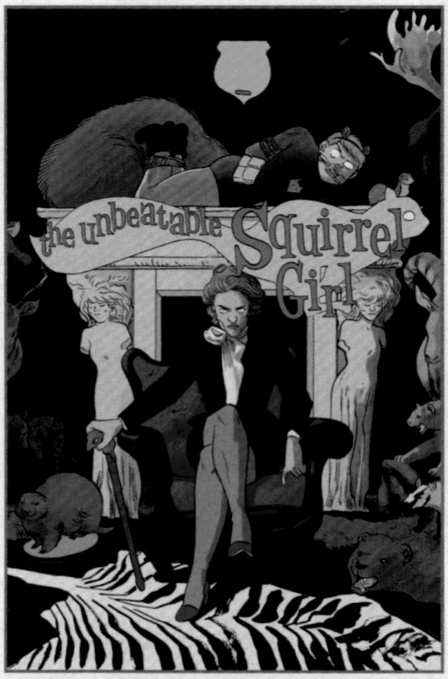
the unbeatable Squirrel Girl

Attention, Squirrel Scouts! Make sure to check out our production blog, **unbeatablesquirrelgirl.tumblr.com**, where we post behind-the-scenes stuff on how the book gets made, along with all sorts of cool things *you* make: fanart, cosplay, whatever!

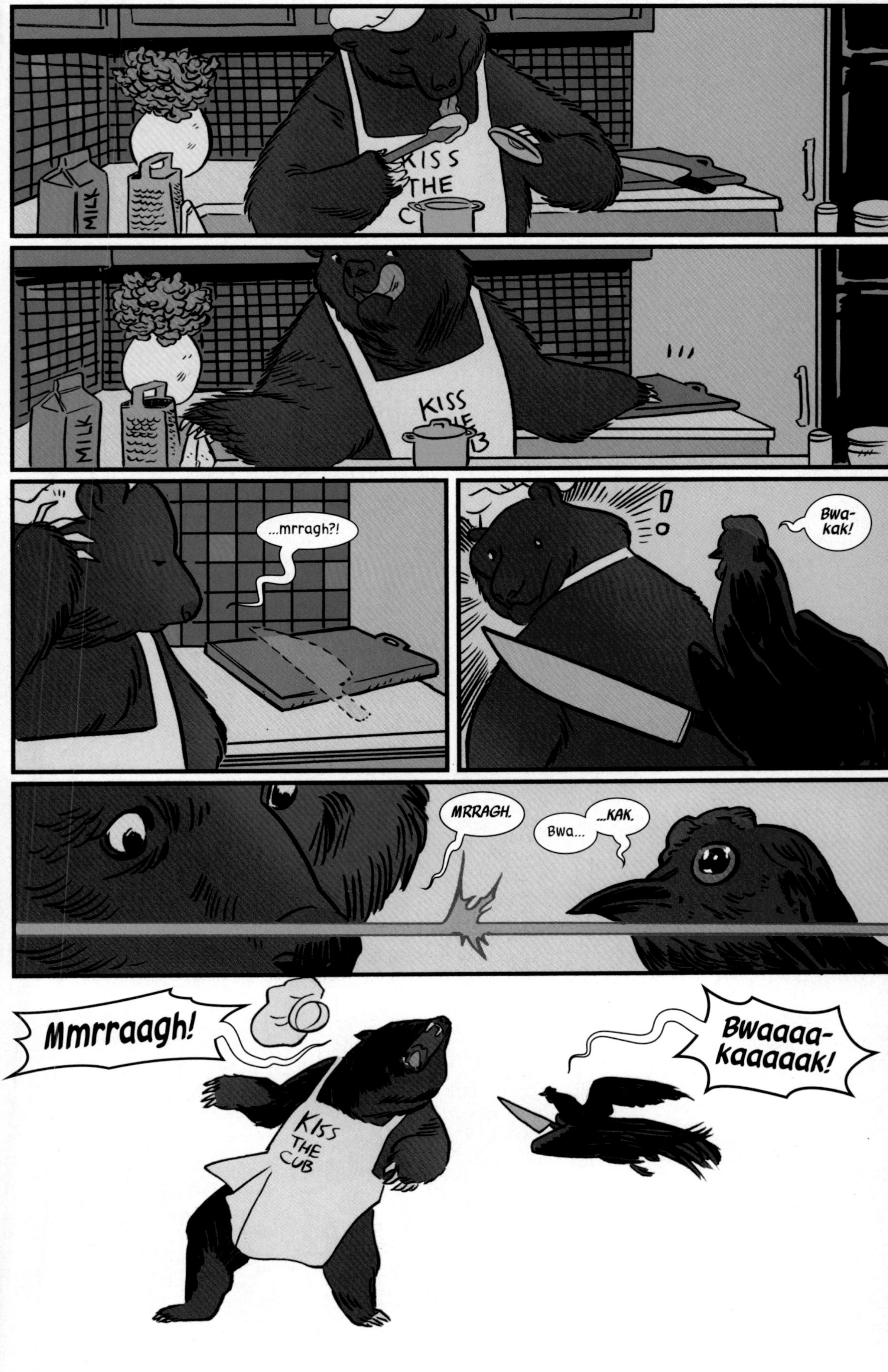
KISS THE C
KISS THE
...mrragh?!
Bwa-
kak!
MRRAGH.
Bwa...
...KAK.
Mmrraagh!
Bwaaaa-
kaaaaak!
KISS THE CUB

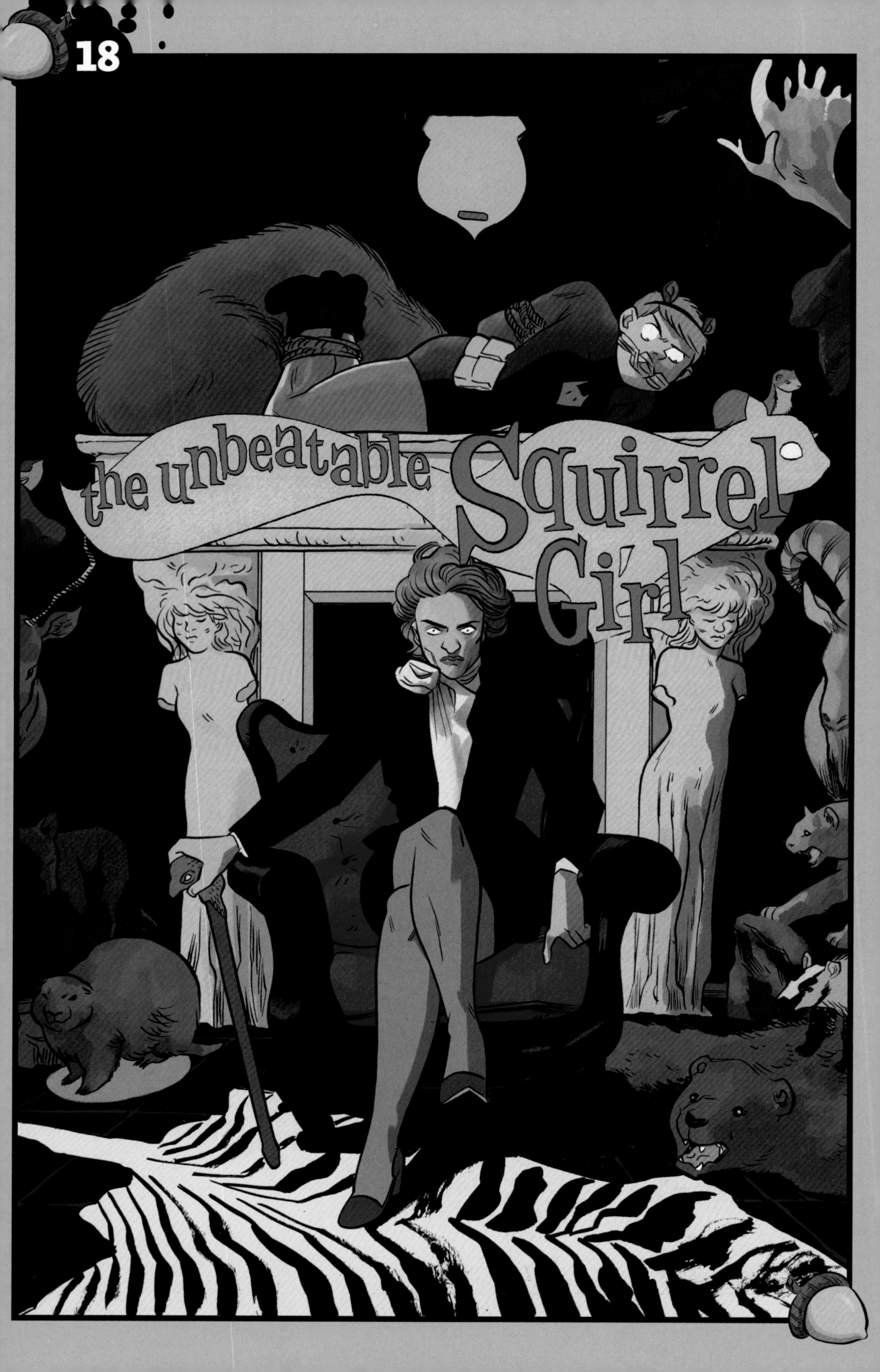
18
the unbeatable Squirrel Girl

Doreen Green isn't just a second-year computer science student: she secretly also has all the powers of both squirrel and girl! She uses her amazing abilities to fight crime **and** be as awesome as possible. You know her as...The Unbeatable Squirrel Girl! Find out what she's been up to, with...

Squirrel Girl in a nutshell

Tony Stark @starkmantony ✓
@unbeatablesg Hey just a heads up: there was a really big super hero fight, a "civil war" if you will. It was definitely a good idea, buuut…

Tony Stark @starkmantony ✓
@unbeatablesg …at the end I got knocked into a coma. Which is NORMALLY BAD, I admit. But I had already uploaded my brain to a computer!

Tony Stark @starkmantony ✓
@unbeatablesg So I'm an AI now, which is nice. Cheated death, but that's no big deal for geniuses like me.

Tony Stark @starkmantony ✓
@unbeatablesg It feels about the same, but I'm a bit better at math questions. Anyway, just wanted to let you know!

Squirrel Girl @unbeatablesg
@starkmantony haha good one Tony!! What's ten times ten?

Tony Stark @starkmantony ✓
@unbeatablesg 100. ...Which I also knew before I was an AI, Squirrel Girl.

Tony Stark @starkmantony ✓
@unbeatablesg Which, again, is what I am now. Because I uploaded my brain to a computer. IT'S KIND OF A BIG DEAL.

Tony Stark @starkmantony ✓
@unbeatablesg Maybe that should be the focus here instead of brain teasers???

Squirrel Girl @unbeatablesg
@starkmantony Wait wait wait. Are you seriously telling me, right here, right now...

Squirrel Girl @unbeatablesg
@starkmantony ...that if I show you a "prove you're a human" picture with distorted letters on a crazy background it'll BLOW YOUR MIND?????

Squirrel Girl @unbeatablesg
@starkmantony

SQUIRREL GIRL RULES

Tony Stark @starkmantony ✓
@unbeatablesg ...No. I'm still me. Just an AI now. I can still log into my email.

Squirrel Girl @unbeatablesg
@starkmantony Tony you doing pranks is frankly adorable but if you were really an AI I could put you on my phone and have Pocket Pal Tony!!

Squirrel Girl @unbeatablesg
@starkmantony But I just checked and that is not the case so NICE TRY, MY DUDE.

Tony Stark @starkmantony ✓
@unbeatablesg ...That's...actually not a bad idea. I'll get R&D right on it.

Squirrel Girl @unbeatablesg
Attention to both the criminally insane and the casual weekend criminals alike! I CAN FLY NOW.

Squirrel Girl @unbeatablesg
That's right! I got a FLYING SQUIRREL SUIT, so y'all better GO EASY on the friggin' SKY CRIME, because I am UP THERE, ready to stop it!!

Squirrel Girl @unbeatablesg
Oh! I have slipped the surly bonds of Earth / And danced the skies on high-tech gliding wings with a jetpack strapped to my back

Squirrel Girl @unbeatablesg
And, with silent lifting mind I'll climb / The high untrespassed sanctity of space / Put out my hand, and punch the face of Crime.

Nancy W. @sewwiththeflo
@unbeatablesg Quasi-quoting the poetry of John Gillespie Magee, Junior. Sure to strike fear into the hearts of the criminal lot.

Squirrel Girl @unbeatablesg
@sewwiththeflo Um excuse me, any of MY arch-criminals who follow me on social media are getting ENLIGHTENED

search! 🔍

#flyingsquirrelgirl

#greatpower

#greatresponsibility

#chefbear

#alfredothechicken

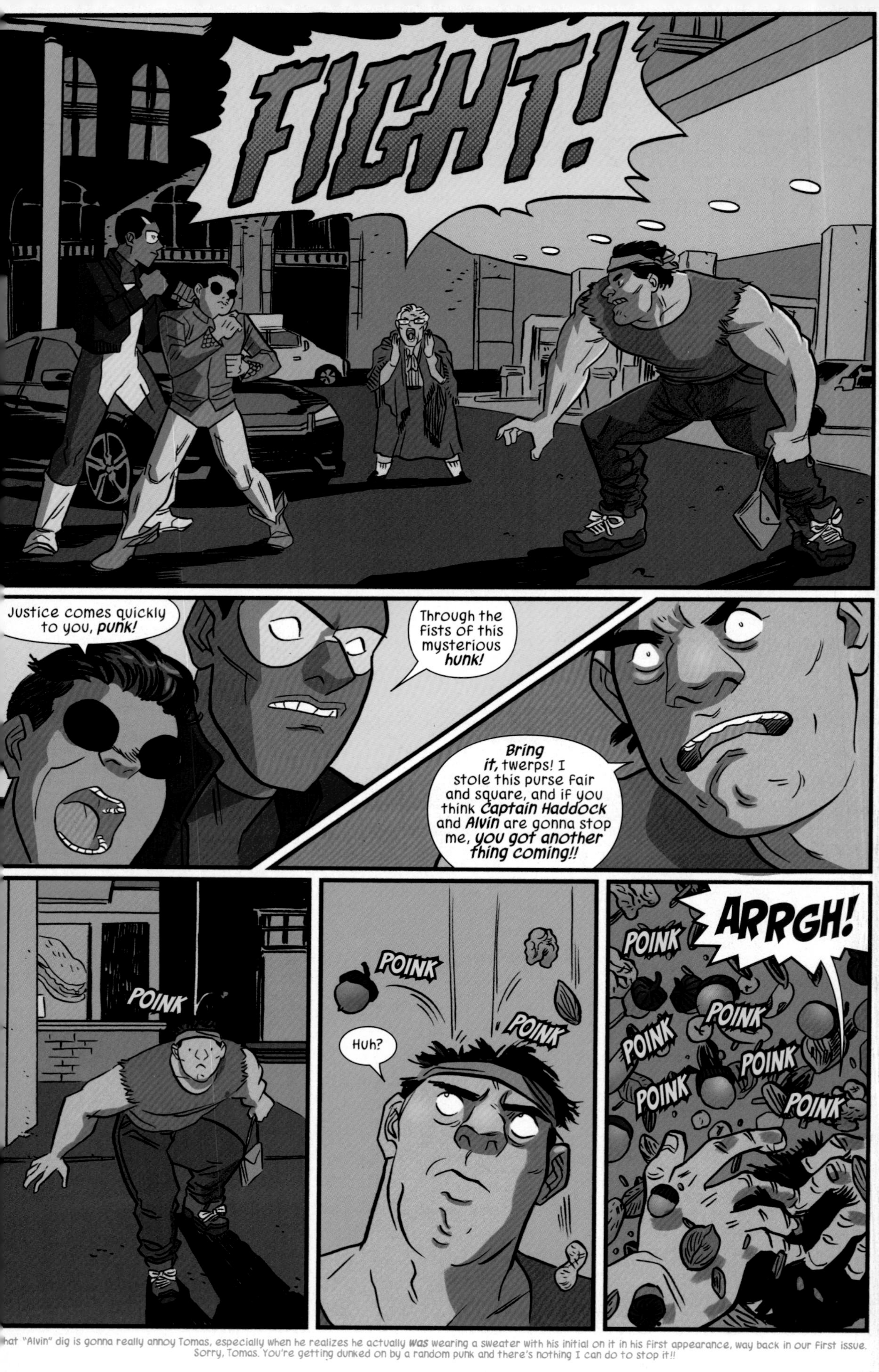
FIGHT!
Justice comes quickly to you, punk!
Through the fists of this mysterious hunk!
Bring it, twerps! I stole this purse fair and square, and if you think Captain Haddock and Alvin are gonna stop me, you got another thing coming!!
POINK
POINK
POINK
Huh?
ARRGH!
POINK
POINK
POINK
POINK
POINK
POINK

hat "Alvin" dig is gonna really annoy Tomas, especially when he realizes he actually *was* wearing a sweater with his initial on it in his first appearance, way back in our first issue. Sorry, Tomas. You're getting dunked on by a random punk and there's nothing I can do to stop it!!

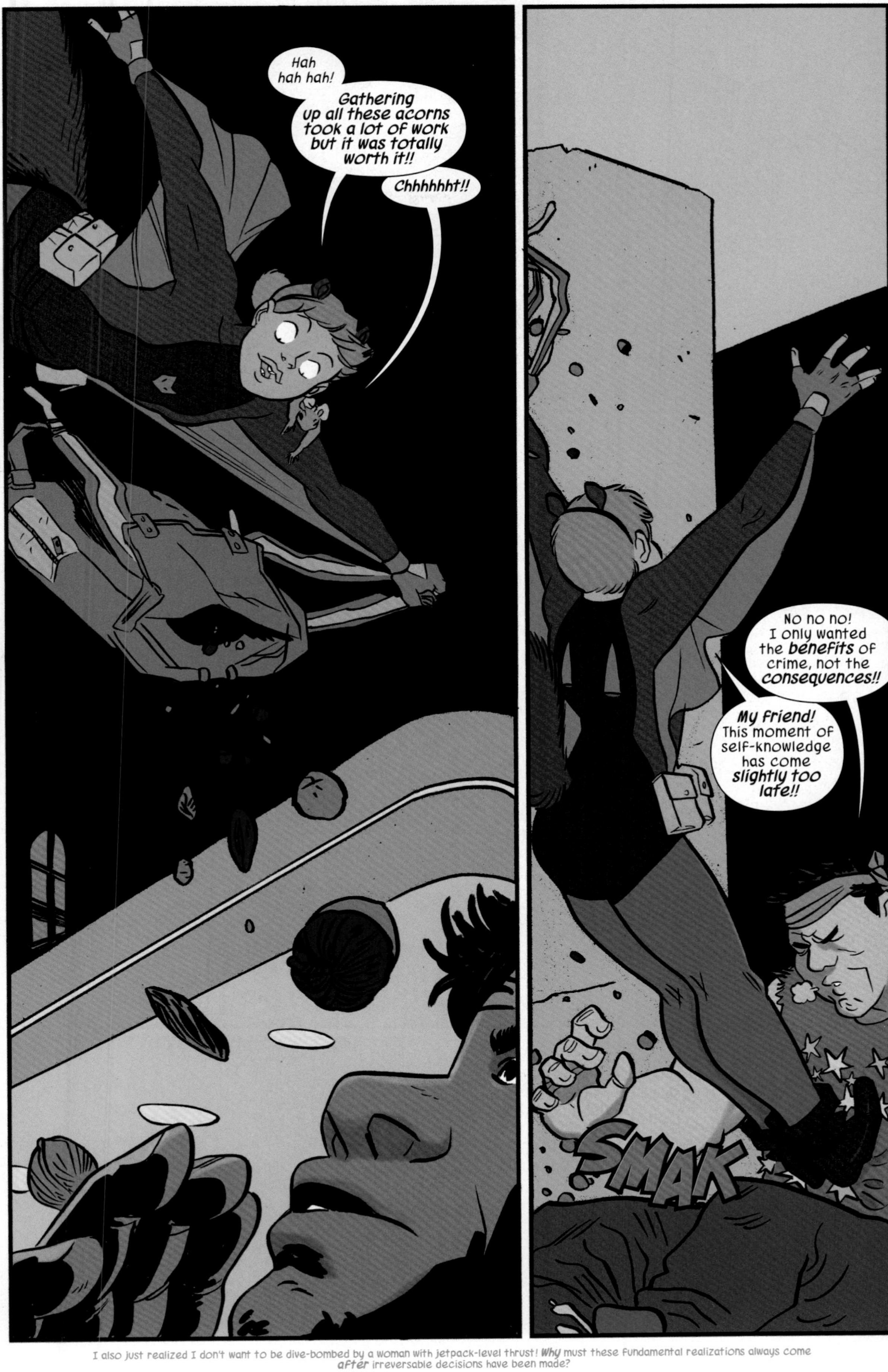
Hah hah hah!
Gathering up all these acorns took a lot of work but it was totally worth it!!
Chhhhhht!!
No no no! I only wanted the benefits of crime, not the consequences!!
My friend! This moment of self-knowledge has come slightly too late!!
SMAK

I also just realized I don't want to be dive-bombed by a woman with jetpack-level thrust! *Why* must these fundamental realizations always come *after* irreversable decisions have been made?

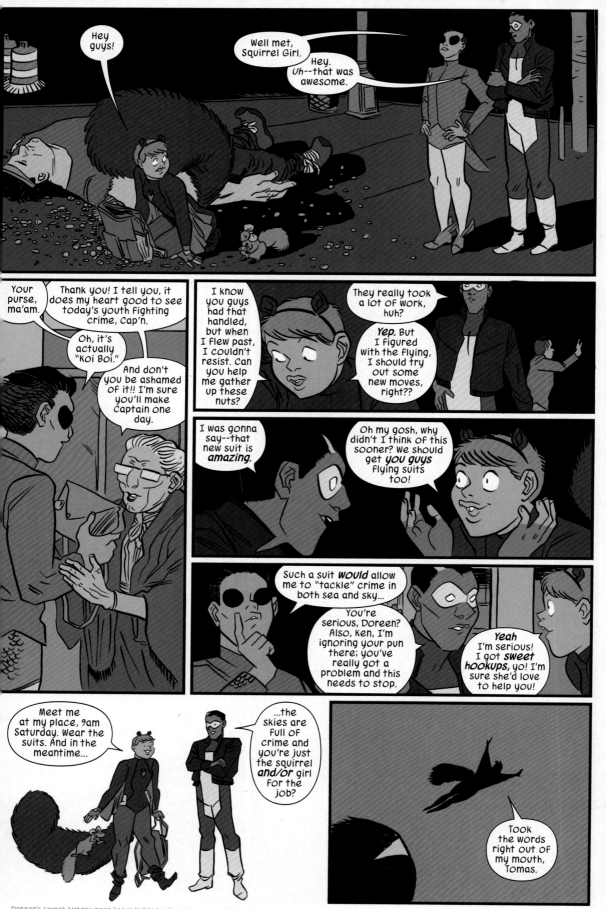

Hey guys!

Well met, Squirrel Girl.

Hey. Uh--that was awesome.

Your purse, ma'am.

Thank you! I tell you, it does my heart good to see today's youth fighting crime, Cap'n.

Oh, it's actually "Koi Boi."

And don't you be ashamed of it!! I'm sure you'll make Captain one day.

I know you guys had that handled, but when I flew past, I couldn't resist. Can you help me gather up these nuts?

They really took a lot of work, huh?

Yep. But I figured with the flying, I should try out some new moves, right??

I was gonna say--that new suit is amazing.

Oh my gosh, why didn't I think of this sooner? We should get you guys flying suits too!

Such a suit WOULD allow me to "tackle" crime in both sea and sky...

You're serious, Doreen? Also, Ken, I'm ignoring your pun there; you've really got a problem and this needs to stop.

Yeah I'm serious! I got sweet hookups, yo! I'm sure she'd love to help you!

Meet me at my place, 9am Saturday. Wear the suits. And in the meantime...

...the skies are full of crime and you're just the squirrel and/or girl for the job?

Took the words right out of my mouth, Tomas.

Doreen's search history goes "cool things to drop on someone's head," "cool things to drop on someone's head--anvils," "cool but also cheap and nonfatal things to drop on someone's head," and finally, "how long it'd take me to get squirrels to gather up a bunch of nuts, wait nevermind I know this, I don't even know why I'm still typing this or hitting enter."

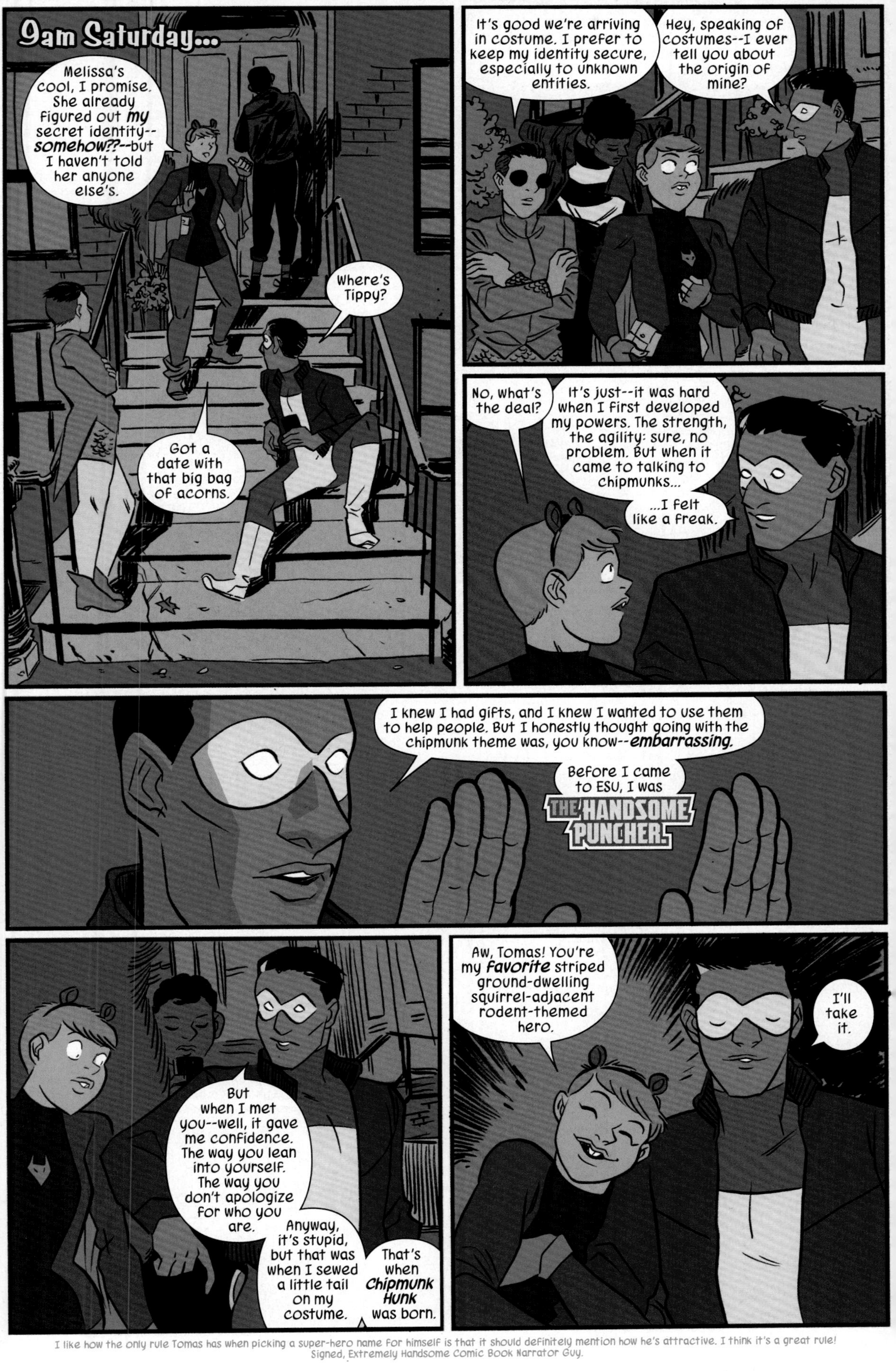

9am Saturday...
Melissa's cool, I promise. She already figured out my secret identity--somehow??--but I haven't told her anyone else's.
Where's Tippy?
Got a date with that big bag of acorns.
It's good we're arriving in costume. I prefer to keep my identity secure, especially to unknown entities.
Hey, speaking of costumes--I ever tell you about the origin of mine?
No, what's the deal?
It's just--it was hard when I first developed my powers. The strength, the agility: sure, no problem. But when it came to talking to chipmunks...
...I felt like a freak.
I knew I had gifts, and I knew I wanted to use them to help people. But I honestly thought going with the chipmunk theme was, you know--embarrassing.
Before I came to ESU, I was
THE HANDSOME PUNCHER.
But when I met you--well, it gave me confidence. The way you lean into yourself. The way you don't apologize for who you are.
Anyway, it's stupid, but that was when I sewed a little tail on my costume.
That's when Chipmunk Hunk was born.
Aw, Tomas! You're my favorite striped ground-dwelling squirrel-adjacent rodent-themed hero.
I'll take it.

I like how the only rule Tomas has when picking a super-hero name for himself is that it should definitely mention how he's attractive. I think it's a great rule!
Signed, Extremely Handsome Comic Book Narrator Guy.

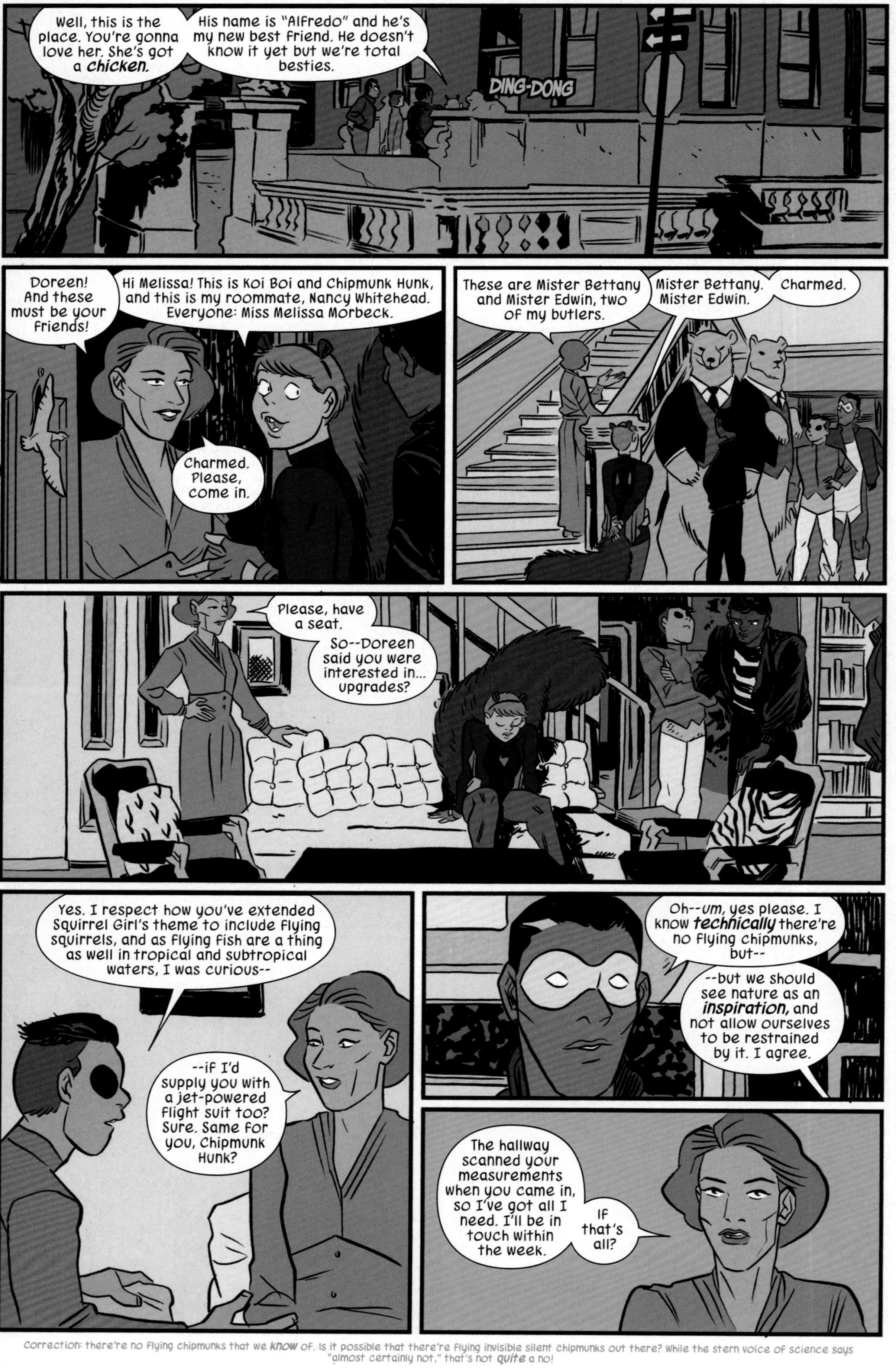
Well, this is the place. You're gonna love her. She's got a *chicken.*
His name is "Alfredo" and he's my new best friend. He doesn't know it yet but we're total besties.
DING-DONG
Doreen! And these must be your friends!
Hi Melissa! This is Koi Boi and Chipmunk Hunk, and this is my roommate, Nancy Whitehead. Everyone: Miss Melissa Morbeck.
Charmed. Please, come in.
These are Mister Bettany and Mister Edwin, two of my butlers.
Mister Bettany. Mister Edwin.
Charmed.
Please, have a seat.
So--Doreen said you were interested in... upgrades?
Yes. I respect how you've extended Squirrel Girl's theme to include flying squirrels, and as flying fish are a thing as well in tropical and subtropical waters, I was curious--
--if I'd supply you with a jet-powered flight suit too? Sure. Same for you, Chipmunk Hunk?
Oh--*um,* yes please. I know *technically* there're no flying chipmunks, but--
--but we should see nature as an *inspiration,* and not allow ourselves to be restrained by it. I agree.
The hallway scanned your measurements when you came in, so I've got all I need. I'll be in touch within the week.
If that's all?

Correction: there're no flying chipmunks that we *know* of. Is it possible that there're flying invisible silent chipmunks out there? While the stern voice of science says "almost certainly not," that's not *quite* a no!

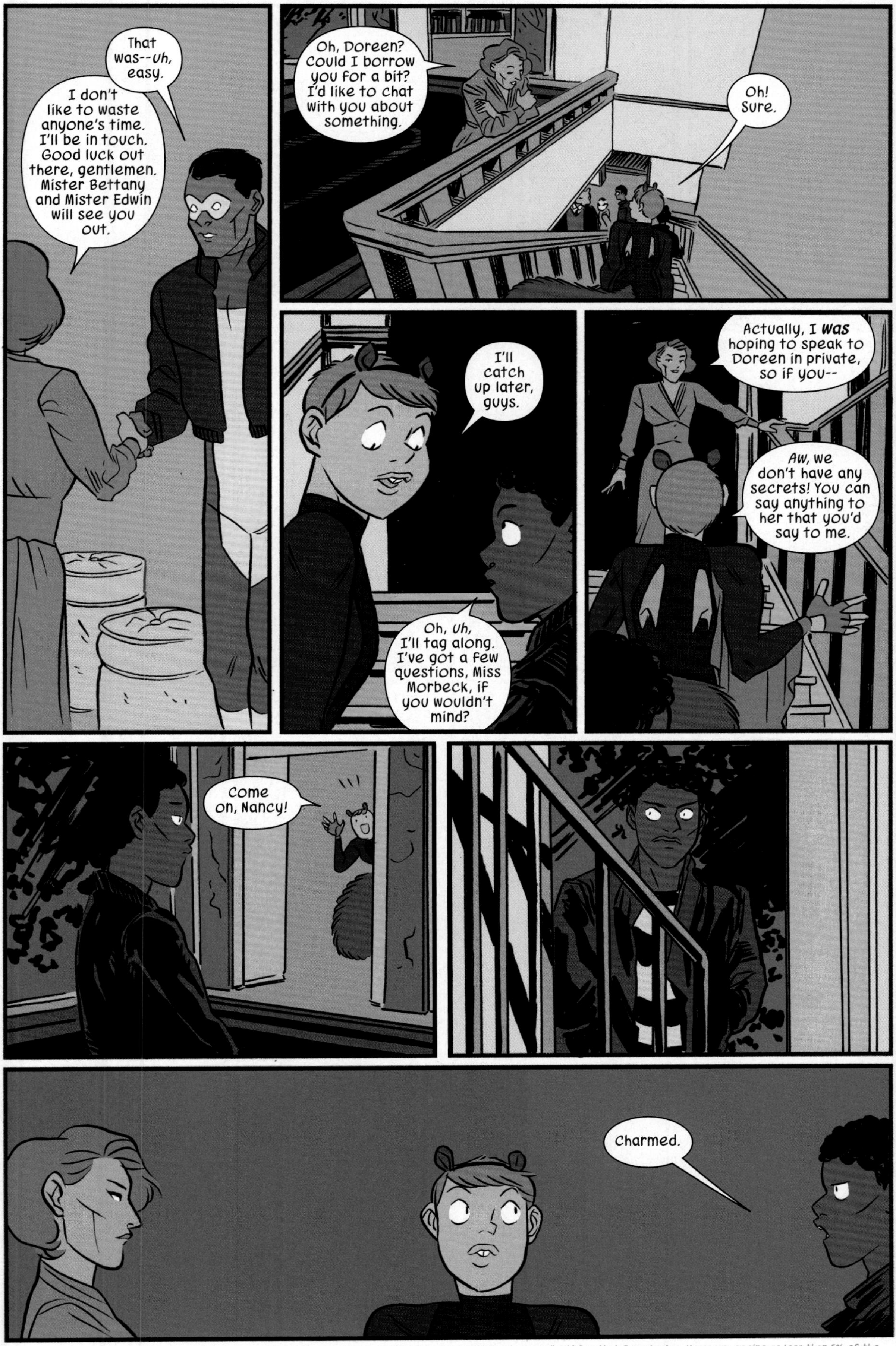
That was--uh, easy.
I don't like to waste anyone's time. I'll be in touch. Good luck out there, gentlemen. Mister Bettany and Mister Edwin will see you out.
Oh, Doreen? Could I borrow you for a bit? I'd like to chat with you about something.
Oh! Sure.
I'll catch up later, guys.
Oh, uh, I'll tag along. I've got a few questions, Miss Morbeck, if you wouldn't mind?
Actually, I *was* hoping to speak to Doreen in private, so if you--
Aw, we don't have any secrets! You can say anything to her that you'd say to me.
Come on, Nancy!
Charmed.

It has come to my attention that I *may* have oversold the possibility of "Flying invisible silent chipmunks," and for that I apologize. However, seeing as less than 5% of the ocean's floor has been explored, the possibility of "Flying invisible silent ***deep-sea*** chipmunks" remains enticingly open!!

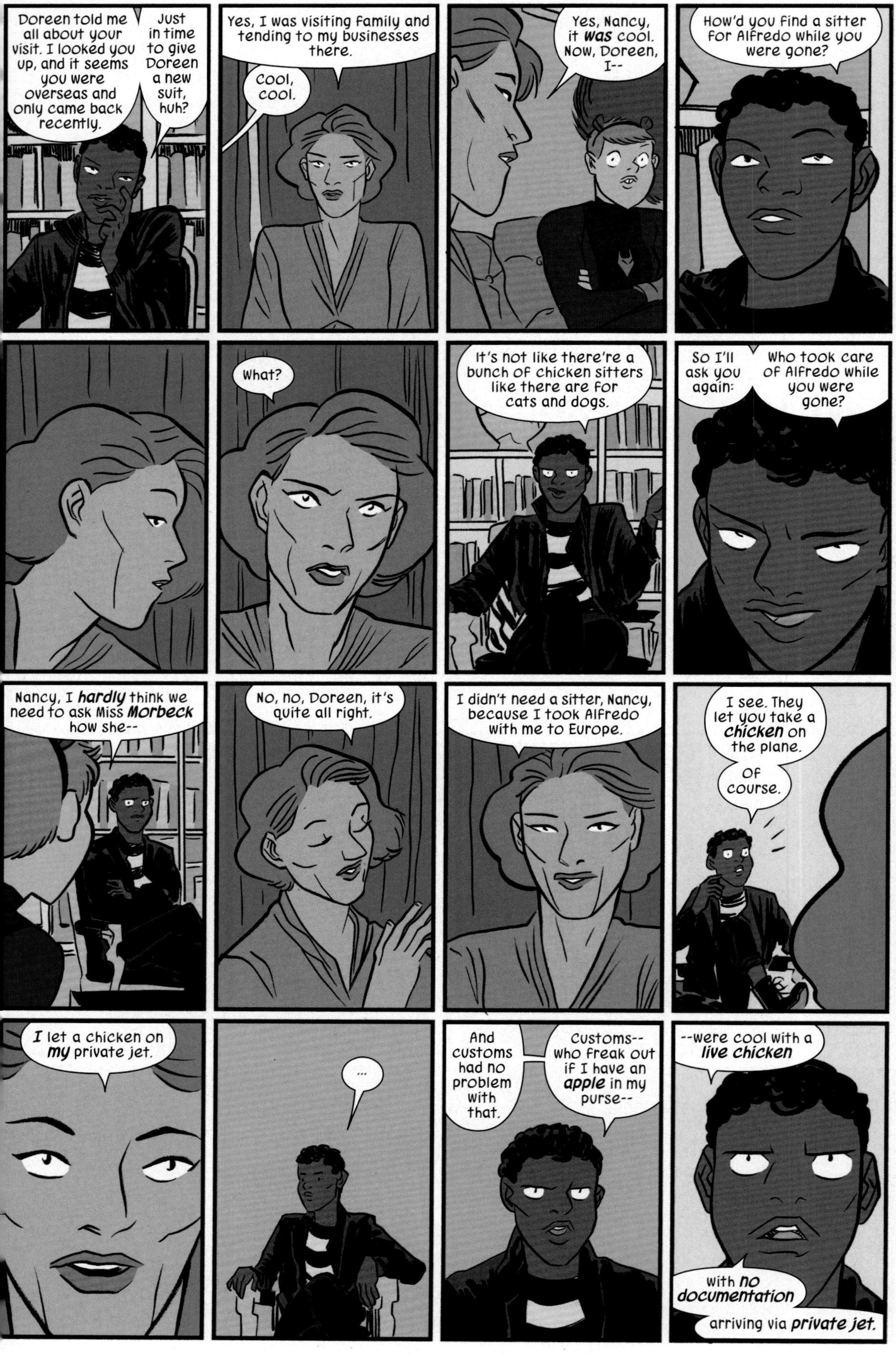
Doreen told me all about your visit. I looked you up, and it seems you were overseas and only came back recently.
Just in time to give Doreen a new suit, huh?
Yes, I was visiting family and tending to my businesses there.
Cool, cool.
Yes, Nancy, it *was* cool. Now, Doreen, I--
How'd you find a sitter for Alfredo while you were gone?
What?
It's not like there're a bunch of chicken sitters like there are for cats and dogs.
So I'll ask you again:
Who took care of Alfredo while you were gone?
Nancy, I *hardly* think we need to ask Miss *Morbeck* how she--
No, no, Doreen, it's quite all right.
I didn't need a sitter, Nancy, because I took Alfredo with me to Europe.
I see. They let you take a *chicken* on the plane.
Of course.
I let a chicken on *my* private jet.
...
And customs had no problem with that.
Customs-- who freak out if I have an *apple* in my purse--
--were cool with a *live chicken*
with *no documentation*
arriving via *private jet.*

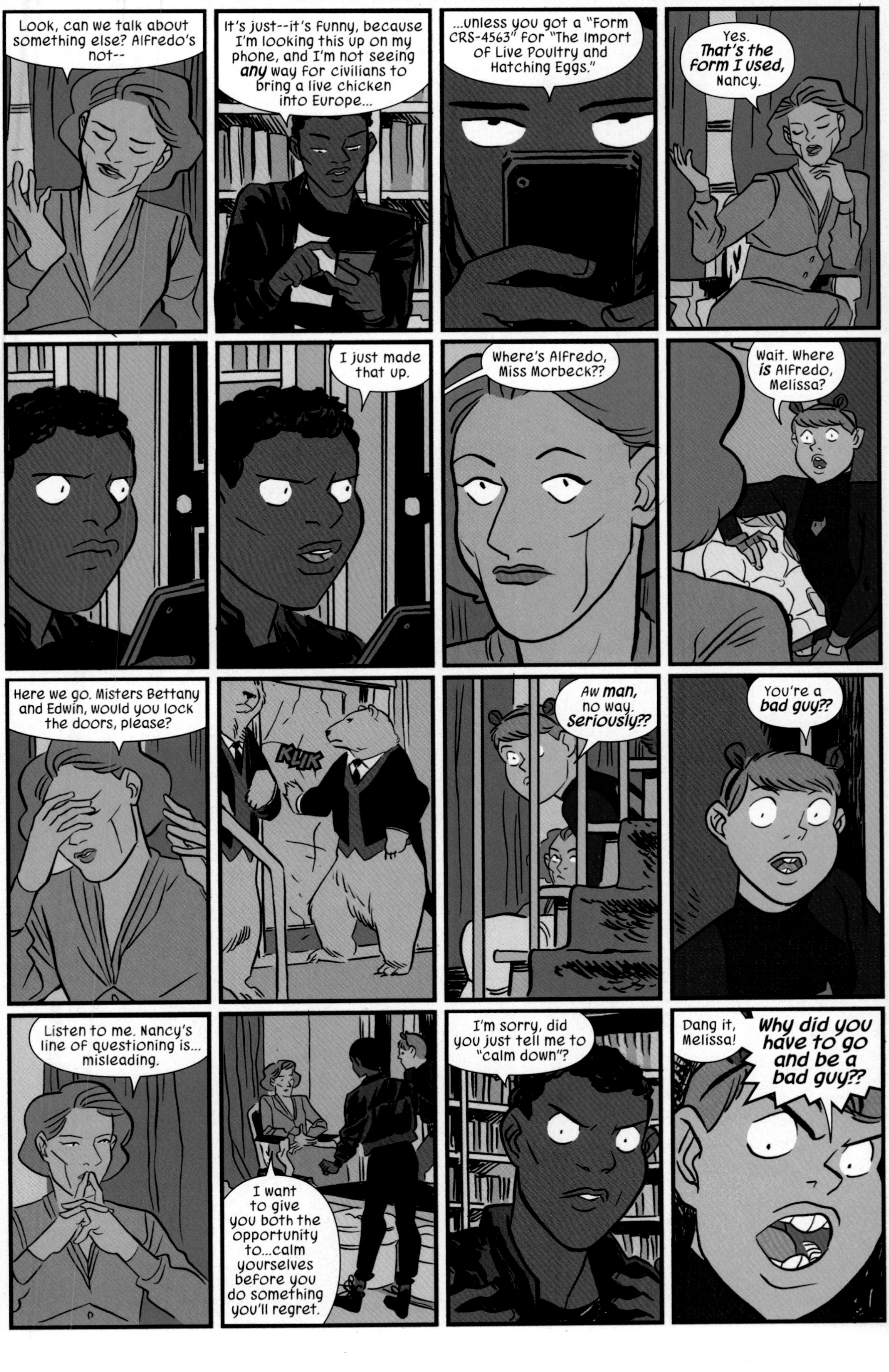
Look, can we talk about something else? Alfredo's not--
It's just--it's funny, because I'm looking this up on my phone, and I'm not seeing any way for civilians to bring a live chicken into Europe...
...unless you got a "Form CRS-4563" for "The Import of Live Poultry and Hatching Eggs."
Yes. That's the form I used, Nancy.
I just made that up.
Where's Alfredo, Miss Morbeck??
Wait. Where is Alfredo, Melissa?
Here we go. Misters Bettany and Edwin, would you lock the doors, please?
KLIK
Aw man, no way. Seriously??
You're a bad guy??
Listen to me. Nancy's line of questioning is... misleading.
I want to give you both the opportunity to...calm yourselves before you do something you'll regret.
I'm sorry, did you just tell me to "calm down"?
Dang it, Melissa!
Why did you have to go and be a bad guy??

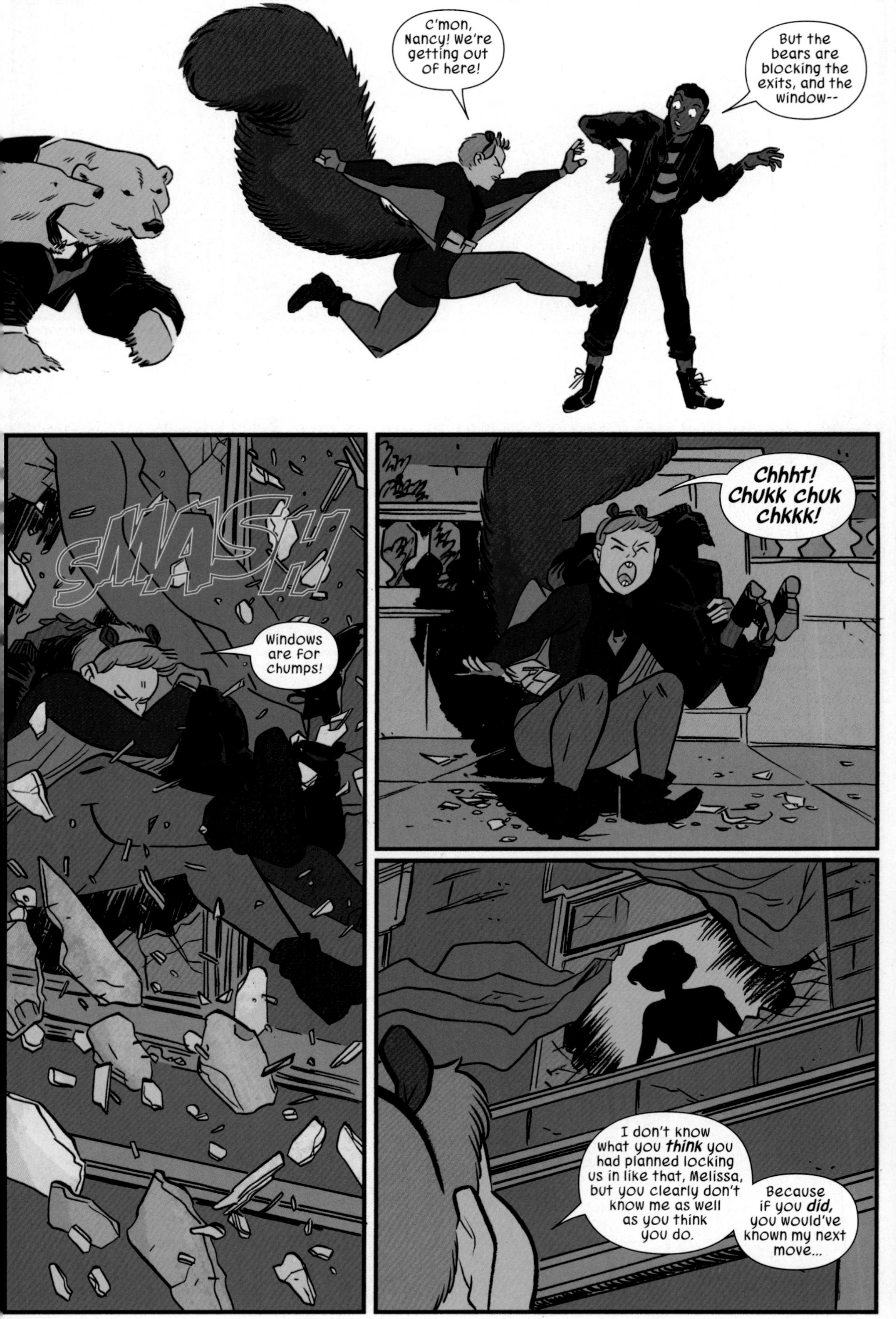
C'mon, Nancy! We're getting out of here!
But the bears are blocking the exits, and the window--
SMASH
Windows are for chumps!
Chhht! Chukk chuk chkkk!
I don't know what you *think* you had planned locking us in like that, Melissa, but you clearly don't know me as well as you think you do.
Because if you *did,* you would've known my next move...

Is it calling in every squirrel on campus? I really hope it's calling in every squirrel on campus.

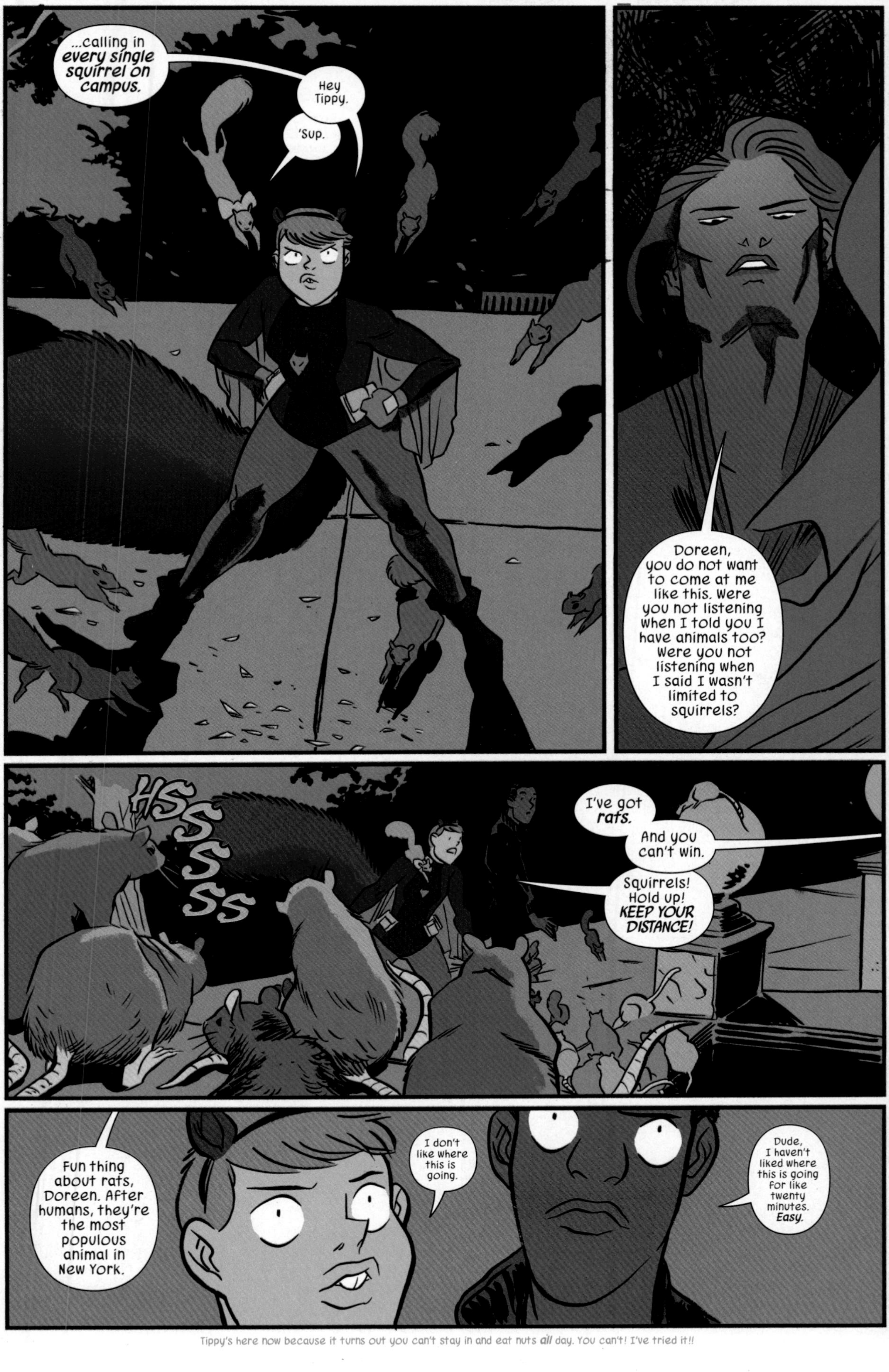

...calling in *every single squirrel on campus.*
Hey Tippy.
'Sup.
Doreen, you do not want to come at me like this. Were you not listening when I told you I have animals too? Were you not listening when I said I wasn't limited to squirrels?
HSSSSSS
I've got **rats.**
And you can't win.
Squirrels! Hold up! ***KEEP YOUR DISTANCE!***
Fun thing about rats, Doreen. After humans, they're the most populous animal in New York.
I don't like where this is going.
Dude, I haven't liked where this is going for like twenty minutes. *Easy.*

Tippy's here now because it turns out you can't stay in and eat nuts *all* day. You can't! I've tried it!!

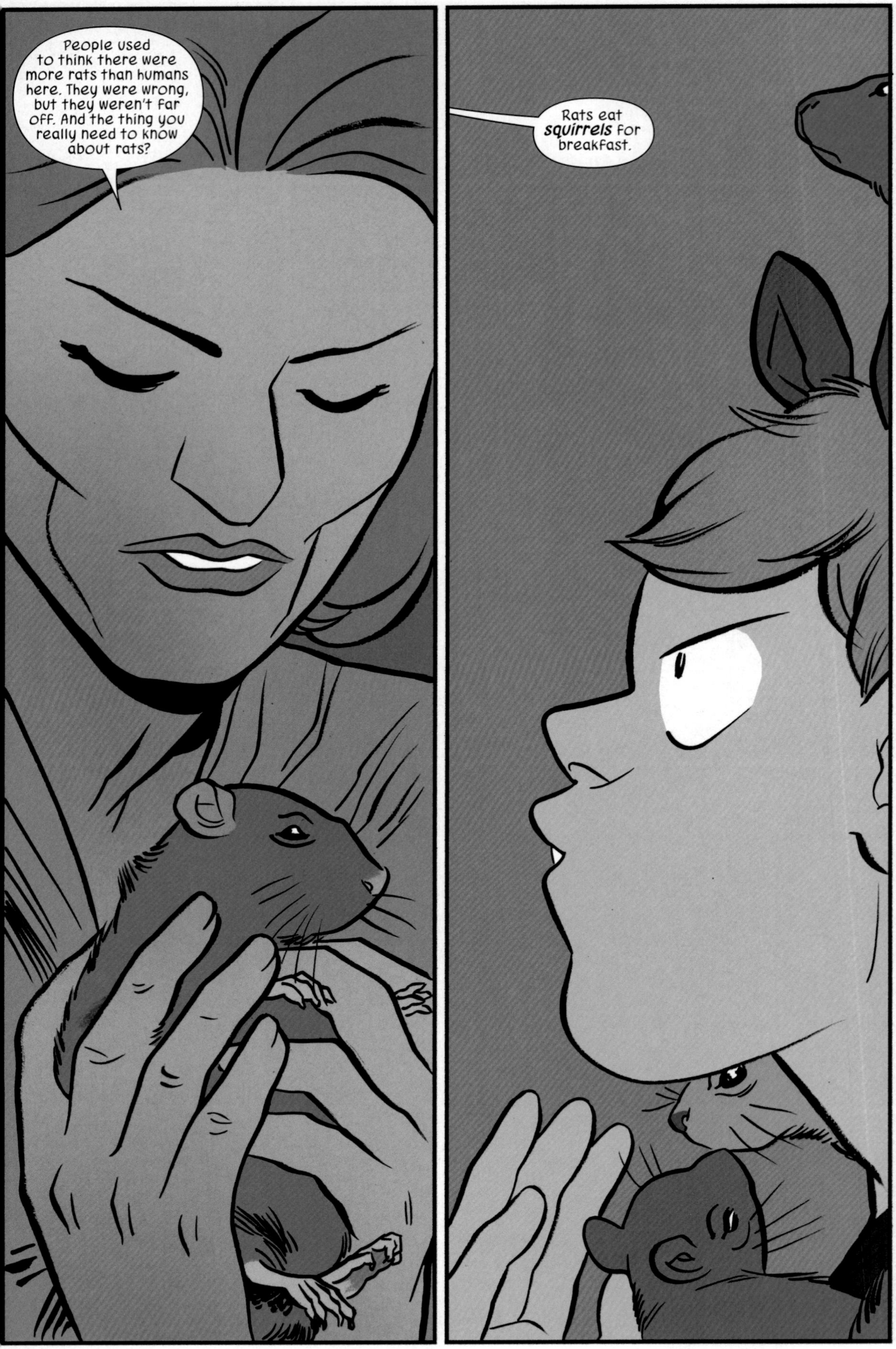
People used to think there were more rats than humans here. They were wrong, but they weren't far off. And the thing you really need to know about rats?
Rats eat **squirrels** for breakfast.

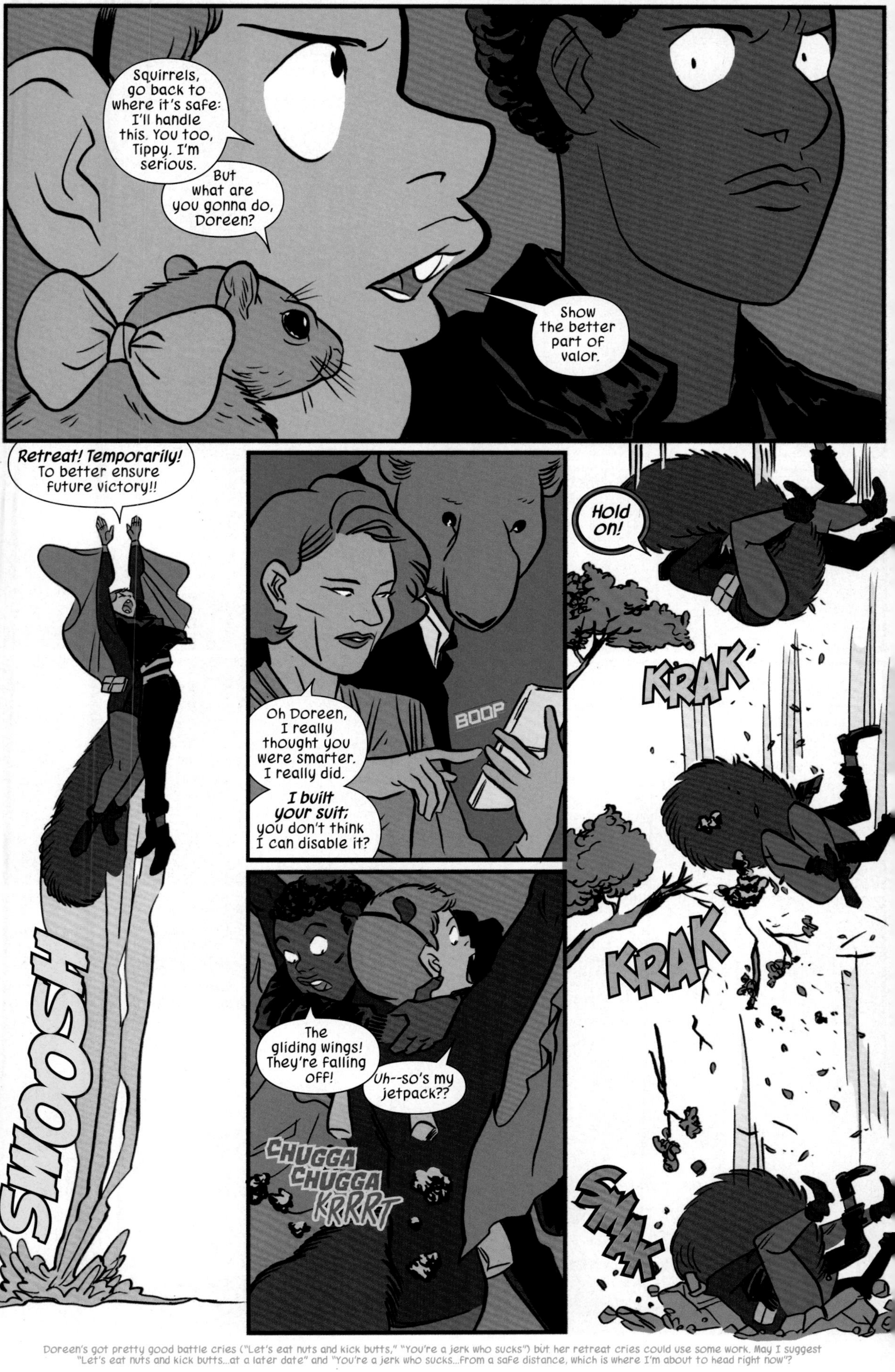
Squirrels, go back to where it's safe: I'll handle this. You too, Tippy. I'm serious.
But what are you gonna do, Doreen?
Show the better part of valor.
Retreat! Temporarily! To better ensure future victory!!
SWOOSH
BOOP
Oh Doreen, I really thought you were smarter. I really did.
I built your suit; you don't think I can disable it?
The gliding wings! They're falling off!
Uh--so's my jetpack??
CHUGGA CHUGGA KRRRT
Hold on!
KRAK
KRAK
SMAK

Doreen's got pretty good battle cries ("Let's eat nuts and kick butts," "You're a jerk who sucks") but her retreat cries could use some work. May I suggest "Let's eat nuts and kick butts...at a later date" and "You're a jerk who sucks...from a safe distance, which is where I'm about to head right now"?

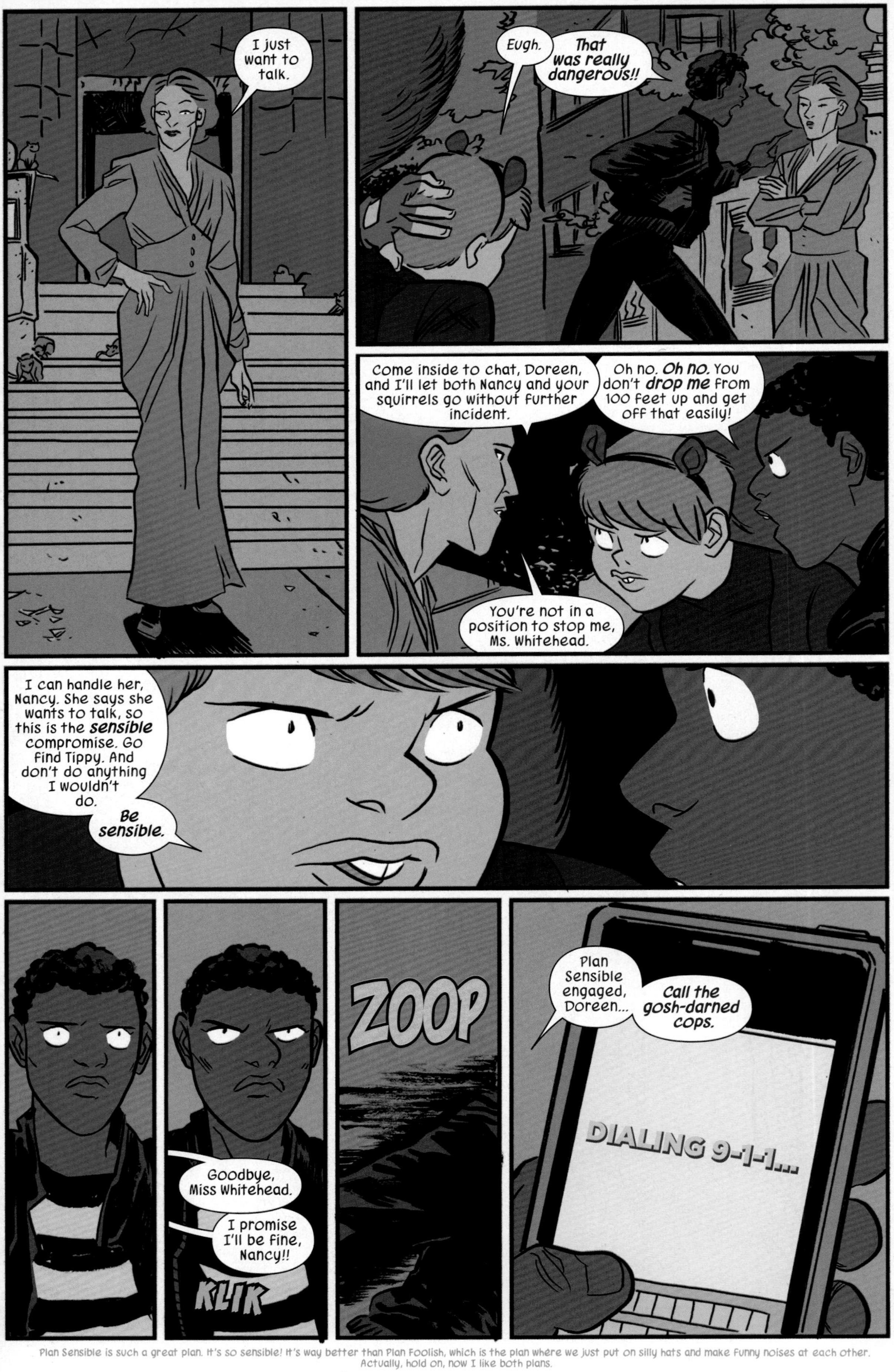
I just want to talk.
Eugh.
That was really dangerous!!
Come inside to chat, Doreen, and I'll let both Nancy and your squirrels go without further incident.
Oh no. Oh no. You don't drop me from 100 feet up and get off that easily!
You're not in a position to stop me, Ms. Whitehead.
I can handle her, Nancy. She says she wants to talk, so this is the sensible compromise. Go find Tippy. And don't do anything I wouldn't do.
Be sensible.
Goodbye, Miss Whitehead.
I promise I'll be fine, Nancy!!
KLIK
ZOOP
Plan Sensible engaged, Doreen...
Call the gosh-darned cops.
DIALING 9-1-1...

Plan Sensible is such a great plan. It's so sensible! It's way better than Plan Foolish, which is the plan where we just put on silly hats and make funny noises at each other. Actually, hold on, now I like both plans.

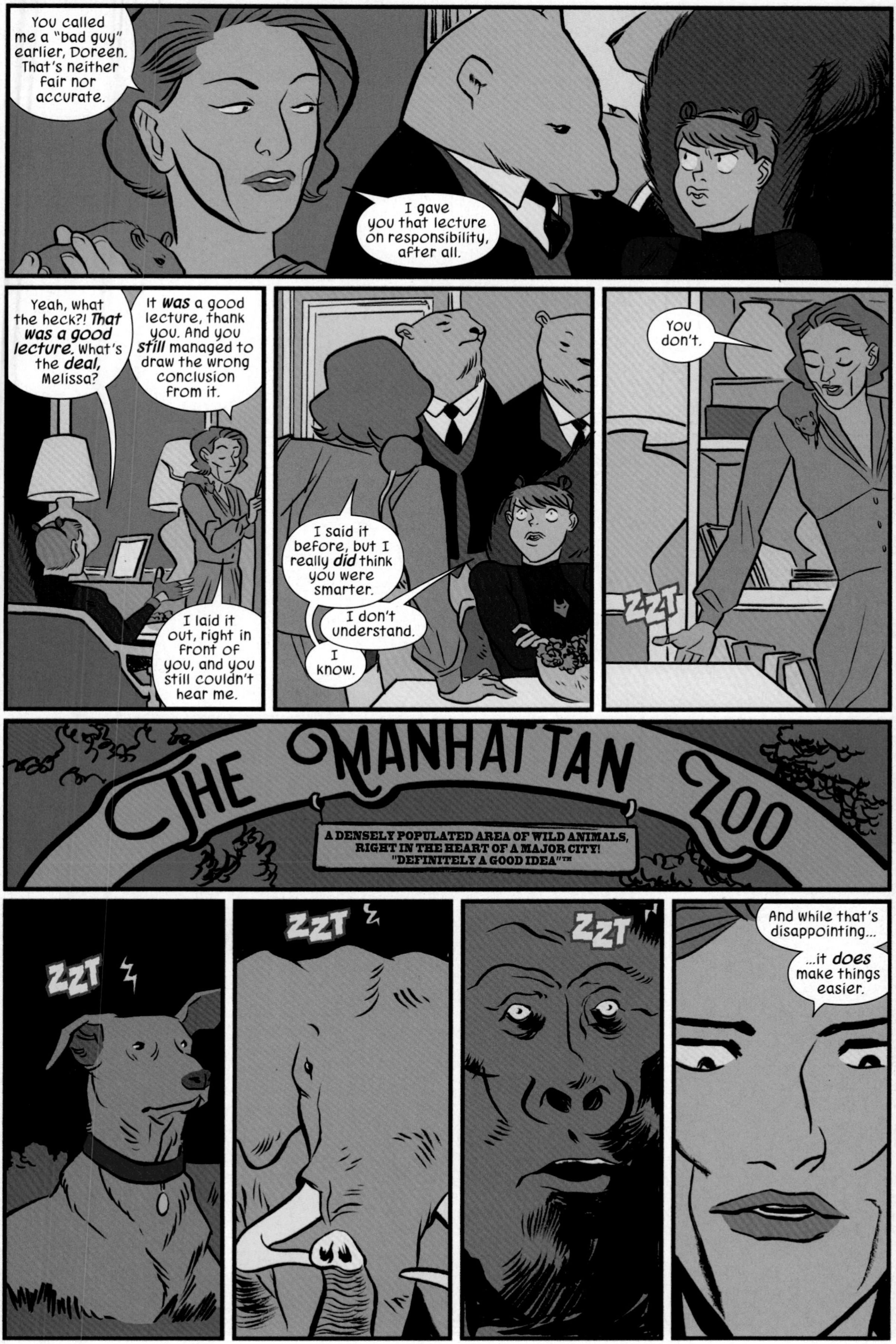
You called me a "bad guy" earlier, Doreen. That's neither fair nor accurate.
I gave you that lecture on responsibility, after all.
Yeah, what the heck?! That was a good lecture. What's the deal, Melissa?
It was a good lecture, thank you. And you still managed to draw the wrong conclusion from it.
I laid it out, right in front of you, and you still couldn't hear me.
I said it before, but I really did think you were smarter.
I don't understand.
I know.
You don't.
ZZT
THE MANHATTAN ZOO
A DENSELY POPULATED AREA OF WILD ANIMALS, RIGHT IN THE HEART OF A MAJOR CITY! "DEFINITELY A GOOD IDEA"™
ZZT
ZZT
ZZT
And while that's disappointing...
...it does make things easier.

The Manhattan Zoo: For When You Look At a Densely Populated Urban Area And Think, "This Is Fine, But It Would Be Even Better If It Had Venemous Spiders Stored In It Somewhere"™

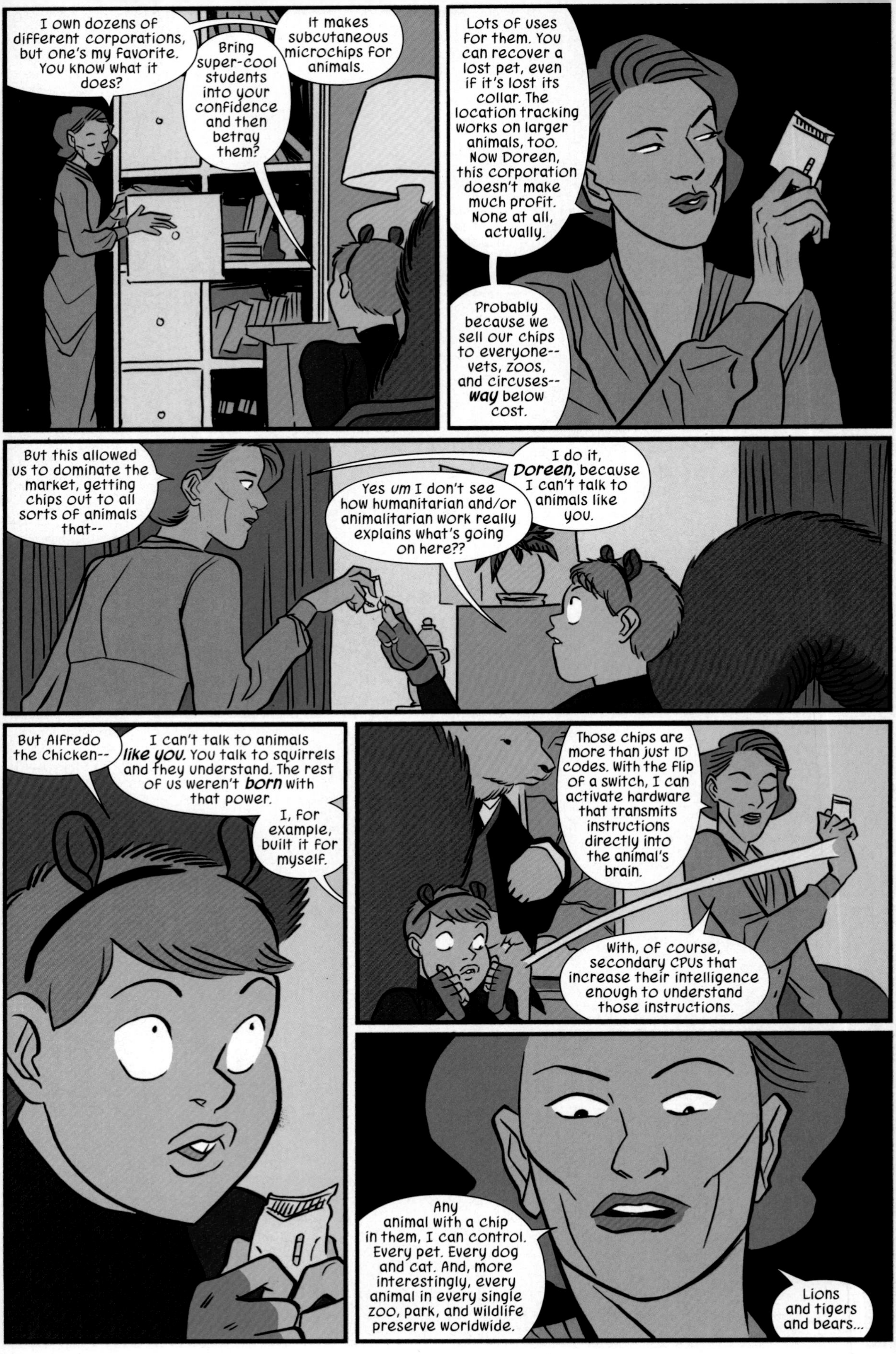
I own dozens of different corporations, but one's my favorite. You know what it does?
Bring super-cool students into your confidence and then betray them?
It makes subcutaneous microchips for animals.
Lots of uses for them. You can recover a lost pet, even if it's lost its collar. The location tracking works on larger animals, too. Now Doreen, this corporation doesn't make much profit. None at all, actually.
Probably because we sell our chips to everyone--vets, zoos, and circuses--*way* below cost.
But this allowed us to dominate the market, getting chips out to all sorts of animals that--
Yes *um* I don't see how humanitarian and/or animalitarian work really explains what's going on here??
I do it, *Doreen,* because I can't talk to animals like you.
But Alfredo the Chicken--
I can't talk to animals *like you.* You talk to squirrels and they understand. The rest of us weren't *born* with that power.
I, for example, built it for myself.
Those chips are more than just ID codes. With the flip of a switch, I can activate hardware that transmits instructions directly into the animal's brain.
With, of course, secondary CPUs that increase their intelligence enough to understand those instructions.
Any animal with a chip in them, I can control. Every pet. Every dog and cat. And, more interestingly, every animal in every single zoo, park, and wildlife preserve worldwide.
Lions and tigers and bears...

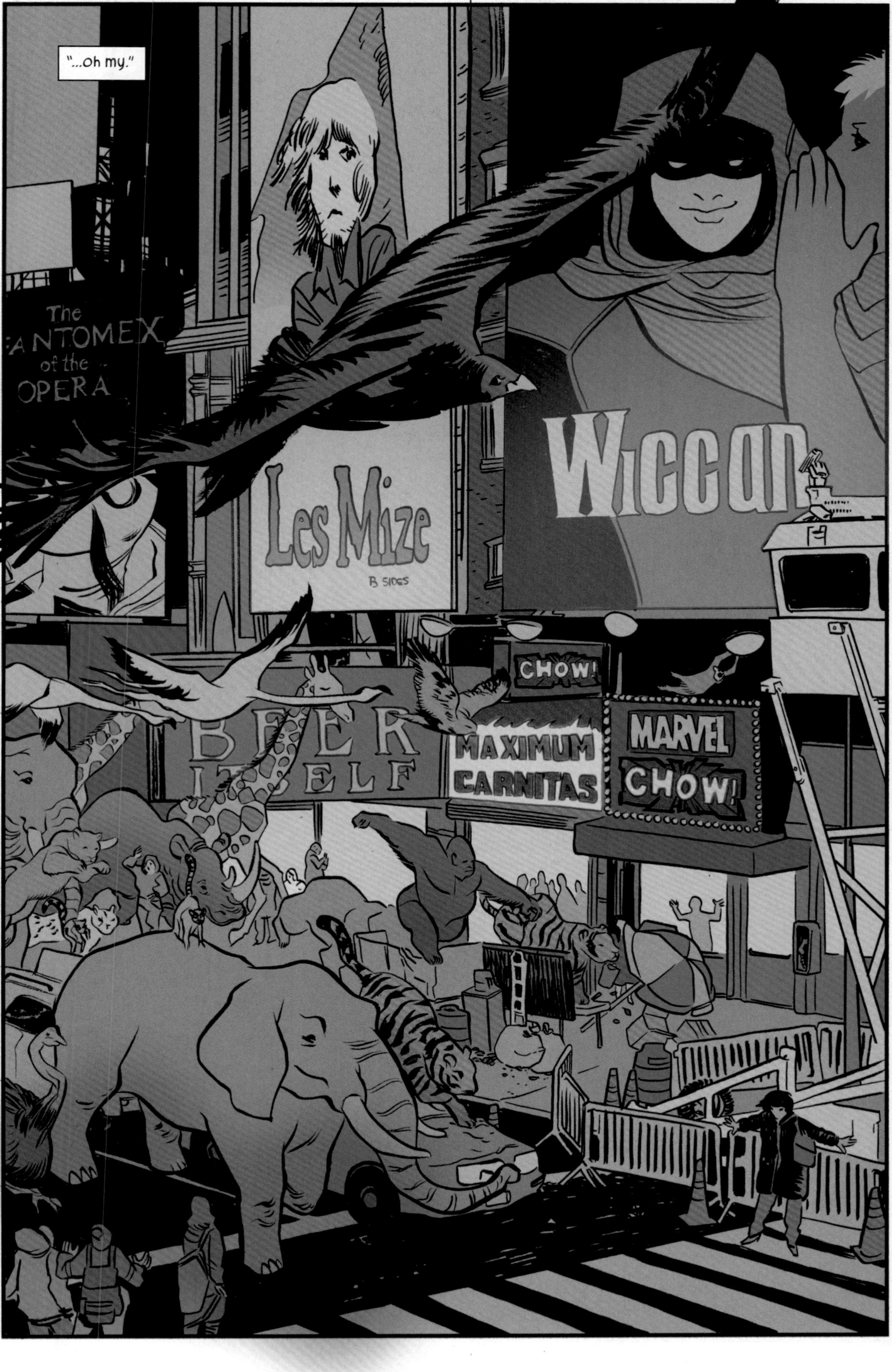
"...oh my."
The FANTOMEX of the OPERA
Les Mize
B SIDES
Wiccan
CHOW!
BEER ITSELF
MAXIMUM CARNITAS
MARVEL CHOW!

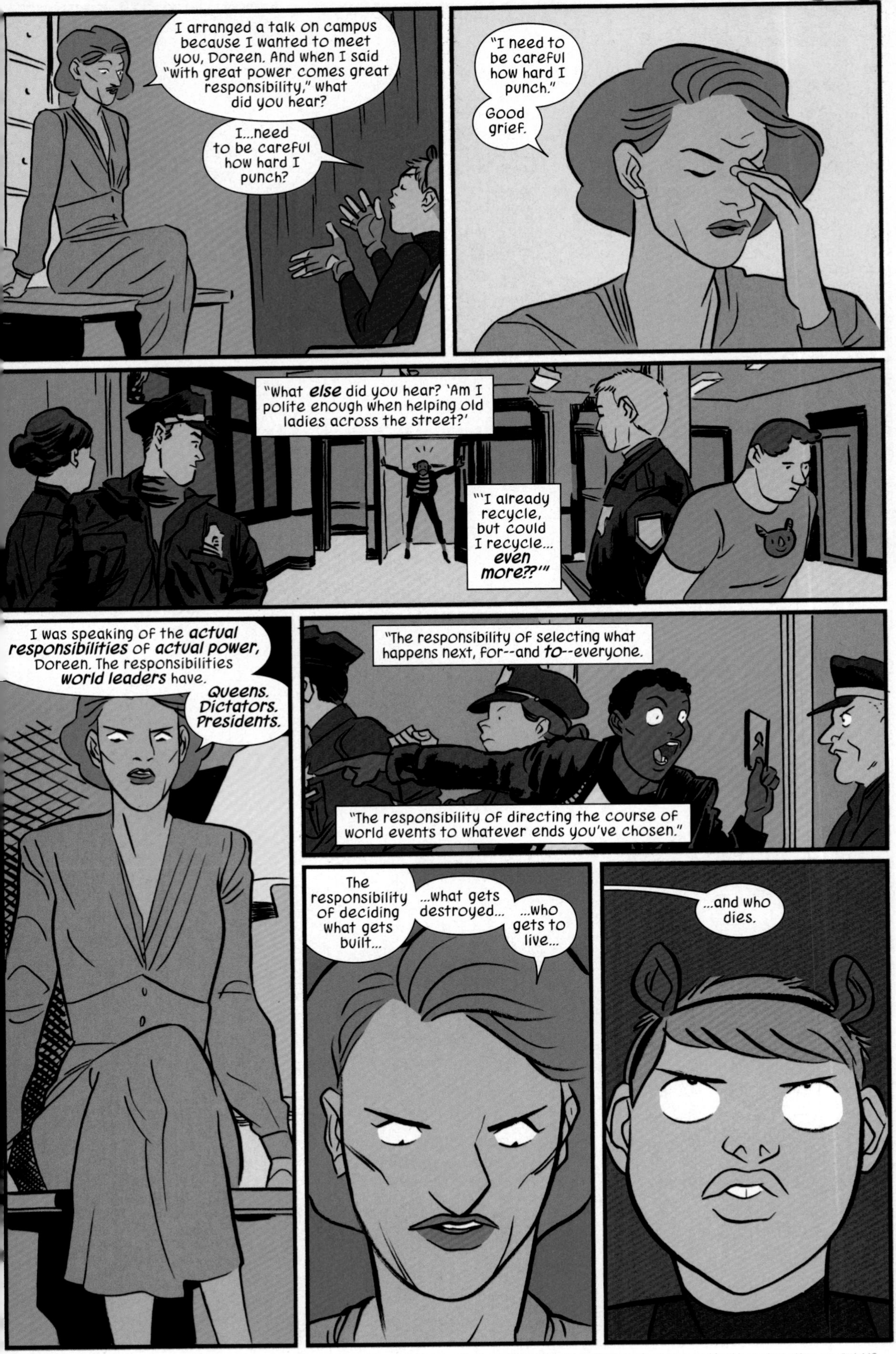
I arranged a talk on campus because I wanted to meet you, Doreen. And when I said "with great power comes great responsibility," what did you hear?
I...need to be careful how hard I punch?
"I need to be careful how hard I punch."
Good grief.
"What *else* did you hear? 'Am I polite enough when helping old ladies across the street?'
"'I already recycle, but could I recycle... *even more??*'"
I was speaking of the *actual responsibilities* of *actual power,* Doreen. The responsibilities *world leaders* have.
Queens. Dictators. Presidents.
"The responsibility of selecting what happens next, for--and *to*--everyone.
"The responsibility of directing the course of world events to whatever ends you've chosen."
The responsibility of deciding what gets built...
...what gets destroyed...
...who gets to live...
...and who dies.

Nobody tell Peter Parker about this concerning new reading of his mantra. Dude's got enough problems without having to radically reconsider his central ethos, am I right?

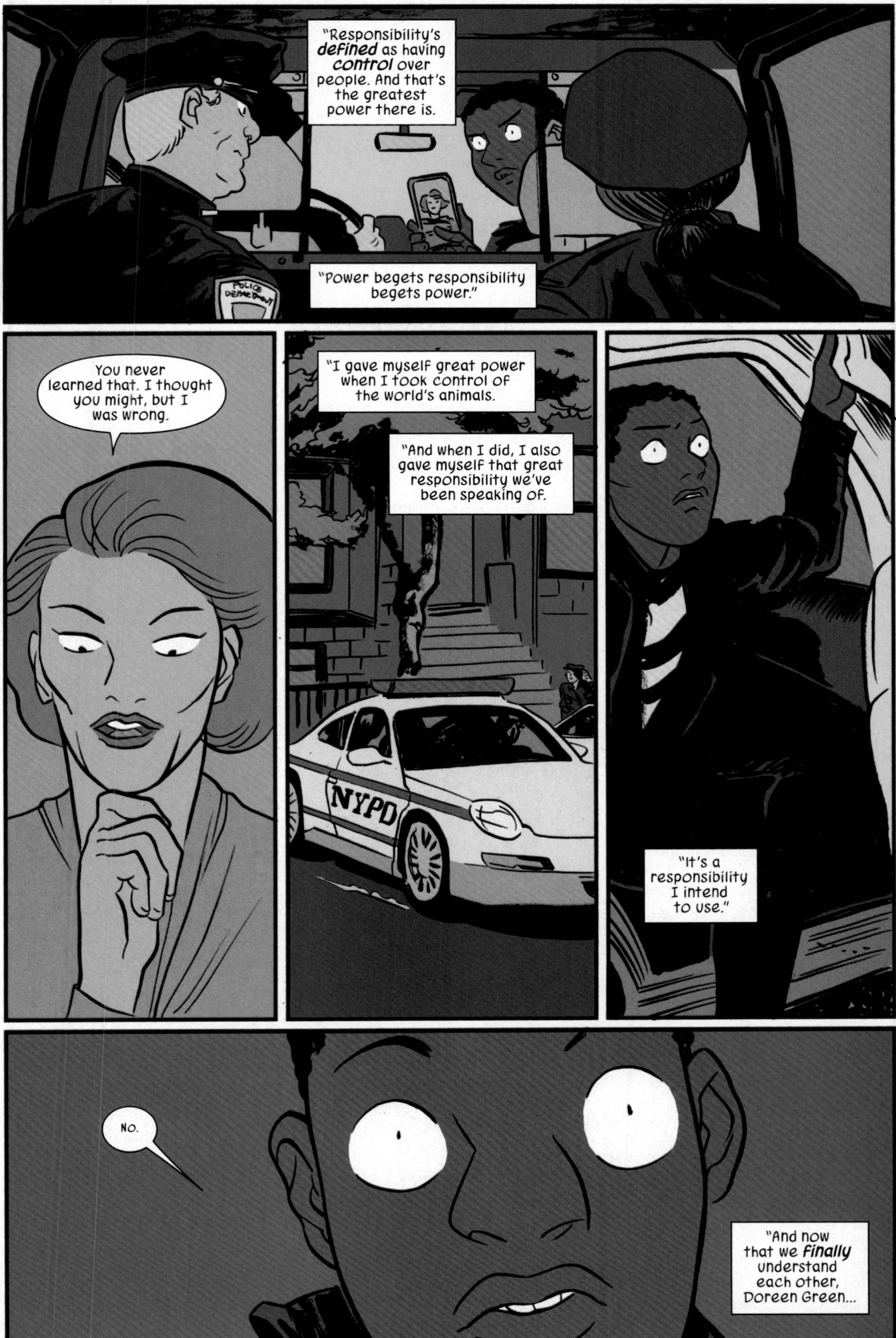
"Responsibility's *defined* as having *control* over people. And that's the greatest power there is.
"Power begets responsibility begets power."
POLICE DEPARTMENT
You never learned that. I thought you might, but I was wrong.
"I gave myself great power when I took control of the world's animals.
"And when I did, I also gave myself that great responsibility we've been speaking of.
NYPD
"It's a responsibility I intend to use."
NO.
"And now that we *finally* understand each other, Doreen Green...

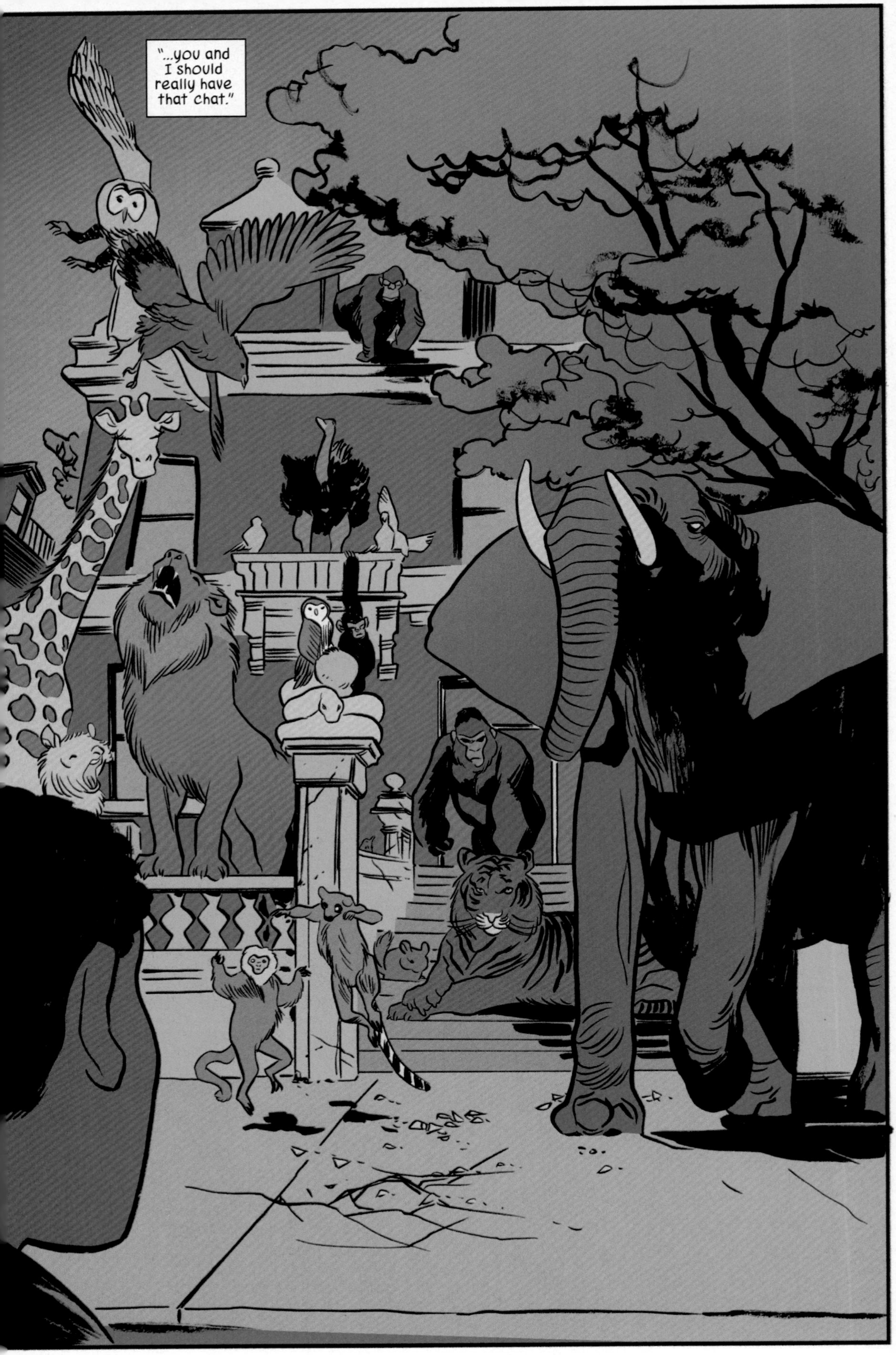
"...you and I should really have that chat."

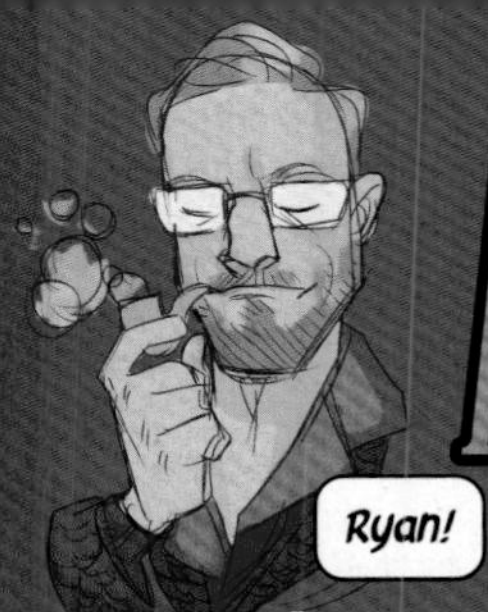
Ryan!

Letters From Nuts

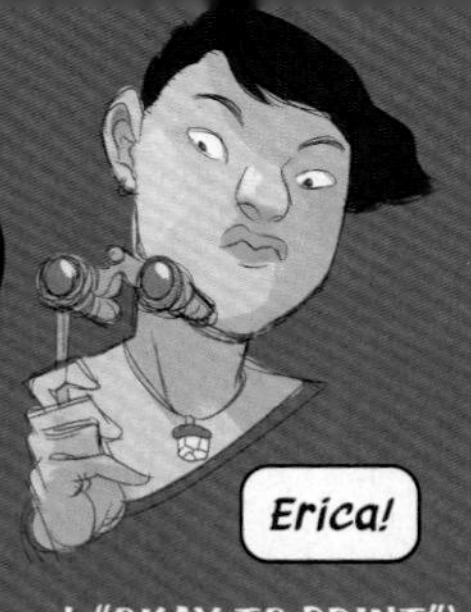
Erica!

Send letters to mheroes@marvel.com or 135 W 50th St, 7th Floor, New York, NY 10020 (Please mark "OKAY TO PRINT")

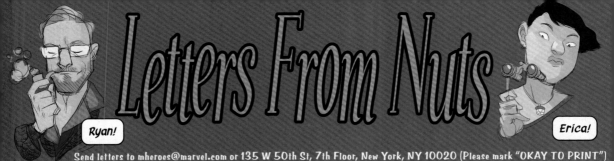

Hi Ryan and Erica!

I'm a huge SG fan, and after rereading all of the series yesterday and today (my last days of freedom before the semester starts up tomorrow), I felt inspired to draw this, and I wanted to share! Thank you so much for making such an amazing and funny heroine. I'm also a college student in engineering, so I really identify with a super heroine in college studying computer science!

Emma

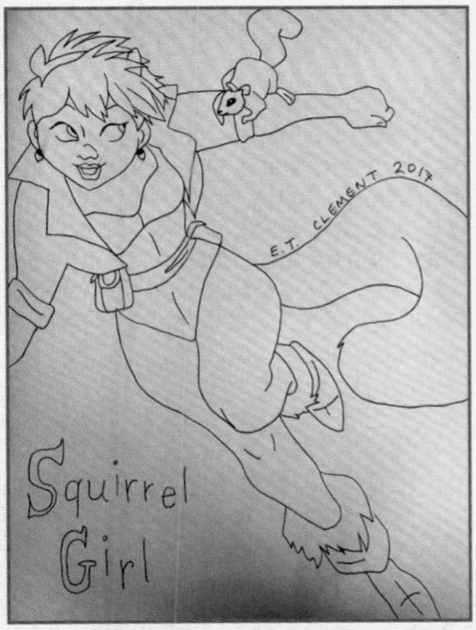
E.T. CLEMENT 2017
Squirrel Girl

RYAN: Thanks, Emma! Great job on the art too! I was kinda close to going into computer engineering (my dad is an electrical engineer), but the computer engineering courses I took showed me that I was better at abstract ideas about computation than the actual implementation. But I was really glad I took the courses, because they made me feel like if I had to build a computer from scratch, I'd at least have SOMEWHAT of an idea of what I was doing?

ERICA: I LOVE IT. I'm glad we could make your last day of break a good time.

Ryan and Erica,

I'm 13, and I'm a huge fan of the series. My older brother, Roni, the arrogant computer science student who wrote the pseudocode letter published in issue #16, had already started teaching me about CS when I read issue #11. So, with your and his help, here's my review of USG #16 in the form of flattering pseudocode:

```
IF (they announce a 25th anniversary){
 I_want_to_read_it_immediately();
}
I_start_reading_it();
I_am_literally_laughing_out_loud();
IF (I do not stop laughing){
 My_family_asks_me_to_be_quiet();
}
WHILE (seeing Doreen as a kid){
 She_is_too_cute();
 I_want_a_series_about_her();
}
IF (Will Murray writes a part){
 I_am_surprised();
 WHILE (reading it){
 I_do_not_want_it_to_end();
 }
}
IF (I finish reading){
 veni_vidi_lovediti();
 It_is_my_favorite_issue();
 I_want_SG_as_Avengers_leader();
}
```

Oof, that's not easy...
Ryan, I hope that, as "a guy who knows things," you'll approve my pseudocode. Erica, I hope that you'll enjoy my sorcery.

Adam Kaufman

P.S. Actually, I began reading USG before my brother, so I was upset when he got his letter published first.

P.P.S. Hey, Roni here! It made my day when I saw my letter was in the special issue, but I also noticed I had made a mistake! I forgot a closing bracket at the end! So, I apologize and I ask every reader to correct it. Grab a pen and add the bracket at the end. Thank you. By the way, Adam, did you just call me arrogant?!

RYAN: Pseudocode: APPROVED. And everyone, yes, please update your past issues appropriately. Finally: a niggling syntax error that I'm NOT responsible for!! The 25th anniversary issue was a lot of fun, and I really enjoyed hanging out with 5-, 10-, and 15-year-old Doreen. (Also 25-year-old Doreen, which is TECHNICALLY a spoiler, but if that spoils you why are you reading comic books out of order? In this comic, we respect the "sequential" part of "sequential art"!!) I think you should continue your brotherly arguments over "who is the most x" in other comic books too. Argue over who is the smartest in the letters page of MOON GIRL AND DEVIL DINOSAUR! Argue who is the strongest in the letters page of THE TOTALLY AWESOME HULK! Argue over who is the best at petting cats in the letters page of HELLCAT! I see zero flaws in this plan.

ERICA: Oh no code. One of these days I'll sneak in a bunch of art history references so that Ryan can be the one out of the loop. Mwahaha.

Dear Erica and Ryan,

I just wanted to drop a quick line and thank you for all the great work you have been doing on UNBEATABLE SQUIRREL GIRL. It is a constant beacon of optimism I get to look forward to every month.

Man, do we need Squirrel Girl. It's been a difficult year, packed to the brim with a lot of anxiety and apprehension and uncertainty. Yet, whenever I find myself at odds with others who have differing viewpoints, I always think back to how Doreen handles conflict. Having conviction, looking for common ground, and accepting the truth of other's "lived experiences" (USG #9) are all lessons we can learn from the unbeatable super heroine.

Really appreciate the work you guys are doing, and I hope you keep it up.

Manuel

RYAN: Thank you, Manuel! I do like how optimistic Doreen is, and I think it's a point of view that's especially hopeful when things look bleak.

ERICA: It's been really important to me for the same reason. I'm glad that we've had the chance to share these stories, and it's always good to hear that it's helping other people.

Dear Team Squirrel Girl,

My 10- and 13-year-old sons and I love your comic. When I don't read it quickly enough, they follow me around with it, brandishing it menacingly and saying, "We want to share the jokes, Mom. Read it now!"

But one thing gets in the way of my enjoyment. I am 48 and wear bifocals, and I still struggle to read the tiny beige type at the bottom of the pages. I love the tiny beige type at the bottom of the pages. I love the tiny type! It's full of funniness! But reading USG sometimes gives me a literal headache. Can you help a gal out?

Please, can you make the ink darker so it contrasts more and is easier to read? And if there's a possibility that you could make it even a squirrel's hair bigger, that'd be cool too. I might still need to get out a magnifying glass to aid my aging eyes, but darker ink would help a lot for those of us readers with older peepers.

I also had two questions about issue #16: Is the corgi when Doreen is 10 related to the corgis (mer- and otherwise) from MOCKINGBIRD?

Then, when she's 20, she says that she saved Iron Man before she helped the Hulk. Did I miss that happening?

Many thanks for the terrific book, and hopes for many more years of Doreen and team.

Kristin Boldon
Minneapolis, MN

RYAN: You did miss that happening! But that's forgivable, because it's from a story that came out 25 years ago! In Squirrel Girl's first appearance she saved Iron Man from Doctor Doom, and the two of them have been pals ever since. (Iron Man and Doreen, I mean. The relationship between Doom and Doreen is a bit more complicated.) I do like that the text at the bottom is small – it makes it like a fun surprise – but we might be able to make it more readable! As for the corgi, I will defer to Erica, the Corgi Expert on this team.

ERICA: The corgi doesn't have to do with anything except that Ryan wrote in the script that it's a big vicious dog and I thought: 1. A corgi would be funnier and 2. I don't want to perpetuate any bully-breed myths.

P.S. Ryan, the text doesn't have to be that big of a secret.

Hello SQUIRREL GIRL writers,

I've noticed something...wrong.

In the letters page to #13, Erica tells us that "As a vegetarian, Doreen would have to be fairly conscious of her diet...[Squirrels] also need fungi, greens, fruits and insects ... So Doreen's vegetarianism is less about being like a squirrel and more about realizing that animals are sentient."

Okay, fair enough.

BUT, in GREAT LAKES AVENGERS #1, Doreen is seen eating lobster. You can even see the claw sticking out of her mouth.

Was it a lapse? Does she make an exception for seafood? (Many people do, and call themselves vegetarian.) Was it a shapeshifter in disguise? Why does somebody with the powers of a squirrel get bored in the woods? Maybe an android version of her?

Mik Bennett
Canberra, Australia

P.S. Sorry, issue 01011 doesn't contain the story of how I learned to count in binary on my fingers—I learned that from a girl when I was in, uh, grade 11 or 12. I actually go from thumb to pinky, where SG goes pinky to thumb. Either way, be very careful around the number 4.

RYAN: My pal Zac Gorman wrote that comic, so you'd have to ask him how to explain this APPARENT DISCREPANCY. But if I were to hazard a guess, I would say Zac would definitely 100% say that Doreen was actually eating a soy faux-lobster confit which was coated in a hard nut-derived shell colored red with vegetable-derived inks. Does this food exist in real life? Sadly, not yet. But given that there is already a market for vegetarian food that can pass as meat (I'm looking at you, veggie ground round), are we truly that far off from a vegetarian "lobster" whose claws you can stuff into your mouth? All I can say is: HOPEFULLY NOT.

ERICA: ZAAAAAAAAAAC!

Hello, Squirrel Girl Team!

I'm a reading tutor, and I've been sharing THE UNBEATABLE SQUIRREL GIRL with one of my little students as her end-of-lesson treat. She wanted to send you a note about how much she loves Squirrel Girl, but please be aware that the note is from her alter ego — a super hero with "all the powers" named SuperZoe! who fights a new villain every day. Thanks for all your great work, and the fun you've given us.

Best,
Ellie

(Here is SuperZoe!'s letter. All words and exclamation points are her own.)

Dear Ryan and Erica,

It is so awesome!!! My name is Zoe! I love Squirrel Girl! I love that she fights crime and it's really cool that she puts her tail in her pants. I would like if Squirrel Girl went to Hawaii and took a break and had a vacation. And then the super heroes can all come to Hawaii where they fight crime, and Squirrel Girl will say "Ahhh! What are you doing? I need a break!"

Please make more books about Squirrel Girl because she is amazing! MORE BOOKS PLEASE!!!!!!!!!!

From
SuperZoe!!!!!!!!!!!!!!!!!!
Age 7

RYAN: Hi Ellie, I love that you've been using our comic as a literacy treat! I think that's the greatest compliment you can give a piece of writing, so thank you so much! The rest of this is from Squirrel Girl to SuperZoe!, so please forward this letter accordingly.

ERICA: HI SUPERZOE! I wish we could take credit for the tail in the pants, but that's from forever ago! All the way back to 1992! I like your vacation idea. We could all use it!

SQUIRREL GIRL: Hi SuperZoe!!

Your letter was awesome and you are awesome. I've got squirrel powers but you've got ALL the powers, so should we team up sometime? I think the answer is: UM, YES PLEASE??

If I went on vacation I wouldn't mind if other super heroes joined me, but if they brought super villains with them then I would totally say "Ahhh! What are you doing? I need a break!" Preferably while sipping a vacation drink out of a coconut. Can it be a vacation without drinking out of a giant nut? I for one prefer not to find out.

Yours in justice,
Squirrel Girl

Next Issue:

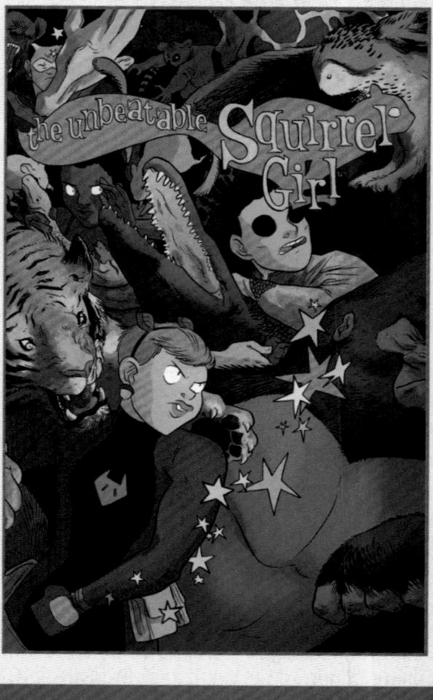
the unbeatable
Squirrel Girl

Attention, Squirrel Scouts! Make sure to check out our production blog, **unbeatablesquirrelgirl.tumblr.com**, where we post behind-the-scenes stuff on how the book gets made, along with all sorts of cool things *you* make: fanart, cosplay, whatever!

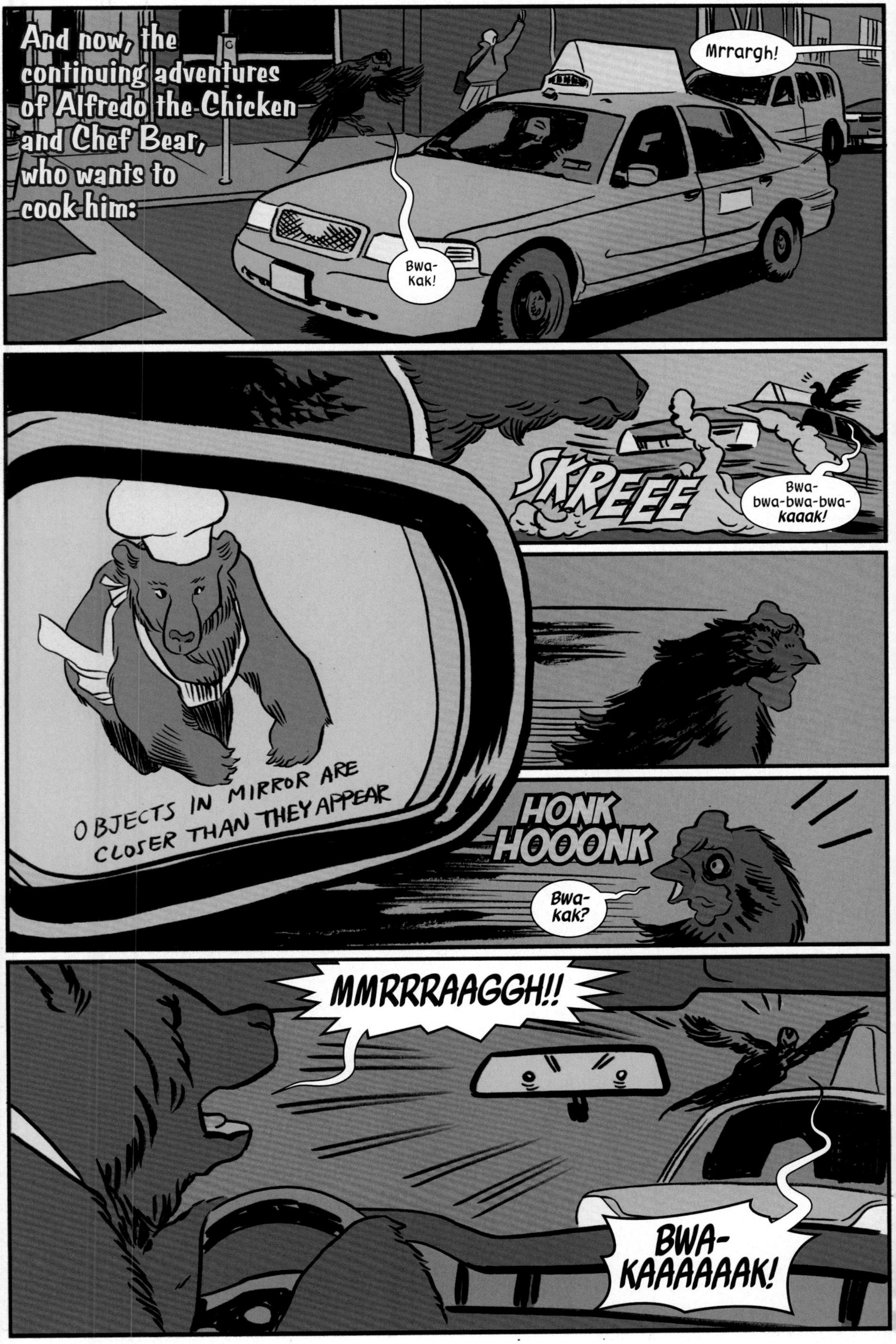
And now, the continuing adventures of Alfredo the Chicken and Chef Bear, who wants to cook him:
Mrrargh!
Bwa-kak!
SKREEE
Bwa-bwa-bwa-bwa-kaaak!
OBJECTS IN MIRROR ARE CLOSER THAN THEY APPEAR
HONK HOOONK
Bwa-kak?
MMRRRAAGGH!!
BWA-KAAAAAAK!

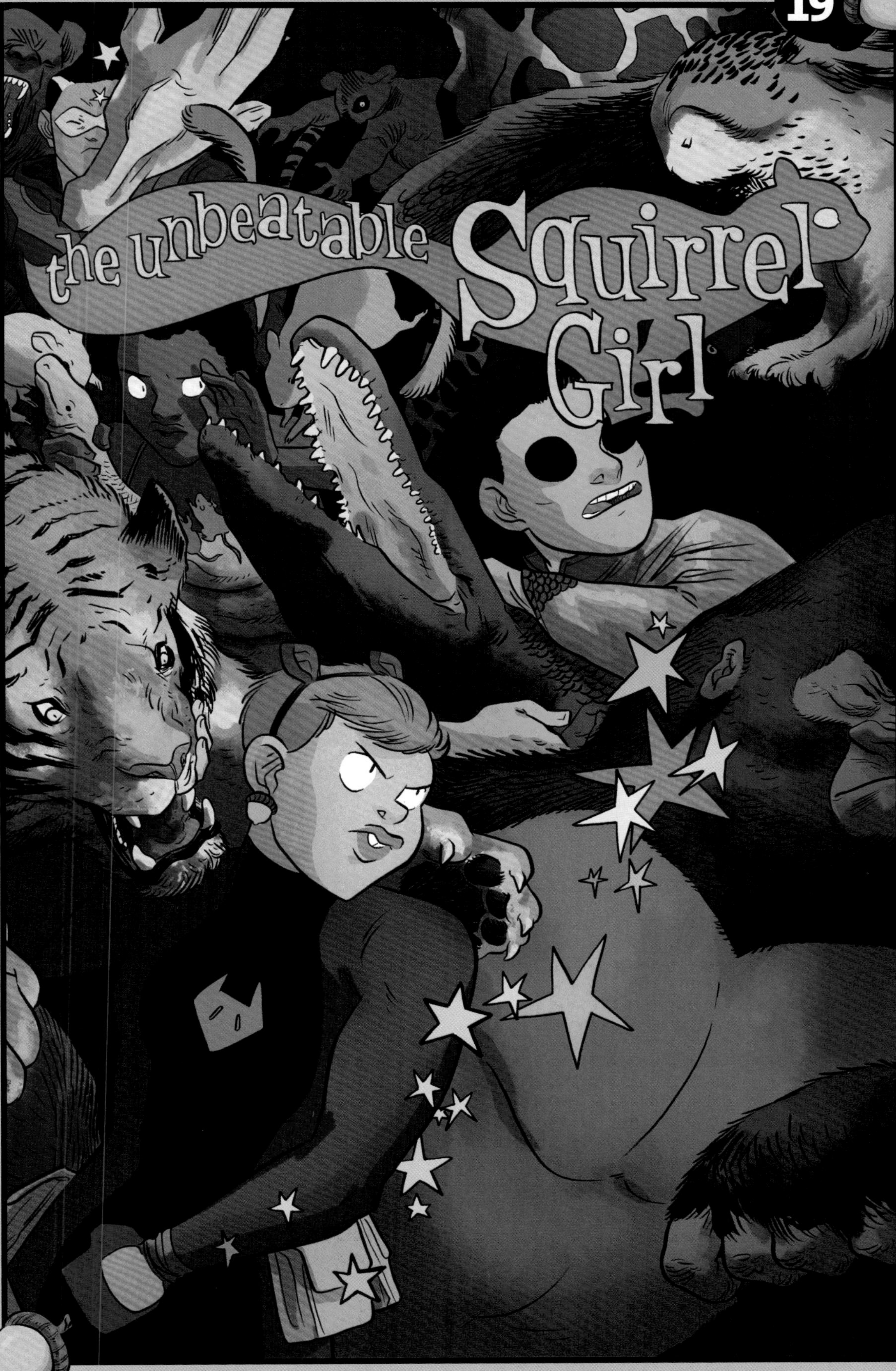
the unbeatable Squirrel Girl

Doreen Green isn't just a second-year computer science student: she secretly also has all the powers of both squirrel and girl! She uses her amazing abilities to fight crime **and** be as awesome as possible. You know her as...The Unbeatable Squirrel Girl! Find out what she's been up to, with...

Squirrel Girl *in a nutshell*

search!

#markII

#ascuteastheyaredeadly

#howardtheduck

#howardthesurlyguyonthestreet

#chefbear

#alfredothechicken

Squirrel Girl @unbeatablesg
Hey so remember how I was kinda bragging about the flying suit a new friend gave me a while back?? Remember how that was a thing?

Squirrel Girl @unbeatablesg
Remember how I was all "fav this if you're a criminal who isn't gonna do crimes anymore now that you know I'MMA FLY NOW"?

Squirrel Girl @unbeatablesg
Remember how I then went on to post how I was definitely gonna KEEP flying forever, b/c my new suit was great and definitely not sabotaged?

Squirrel Girl @unbeatablesg
Remember how all of those were posted in a manner that might, in retrospect, be described as "hubristic"??

Squirrel Girl @unbeatablesg
Well uh

Squirrel Girl @unbeatablesg
Turns out that Greek myth that warned us not to fly too close to the sun was NOT ENTIRELY OFF BASE, IN VERY LIMITED CIRCUMSTANCES??

Tony Stark @starkmantony ✓
@unbeatablesg Icarus, right? Kid and his dad invent wings from wax and feathers, kid flies too close to the sun, wings melt, the end.

Tony Stark @starkmantony ✓
@unbeatablesg Here's the thing about that. So Icarus and his dad invent AMAZING SUITS from SCRATCH while being held PRISONER--

Tony Stark @starkmantony ✓
@unbeatablesg (an idea which, for obvious reasons, really appeals to me on a fundamental level)

Tony Stark @starkmantony ✓
@unbeatablesg --and then one of them dies because he's TOO SUCCESSFUL at FLYING SUIT INVENTION, and that's supposed to teach us something?

Tony Stark @starkmantony ✓
@unbeatablesg I'll tell you what it teaches me. It teaches me that whoever is telling it never studied science.

Tony Stark @starkmantony ✓
@unbeatablesg There's a reason why Everest is snowy at the top instead of being covered in beach towels, sunglasses, and mojitos.

Tony Stark @starkmantony ✓
@unbeatablesg In flight range, air pressure goes down as you go up, and gases under less pressure are slower and colder. Hence, freezing.

Tony Stark @starkmantony ✓
@unbeatablesg In conclusion, it's a ridiculous myth, and in real life Icarus would've a) survived, and b) been lauded as a great engineer.

Tony Stark @starkmantony ✓
@unbeatablesg And I would've hired him.

Tony Stark @starkmantony ✓
@unbeatablesg Anyway. Don't feel bad that you trusted someone. That's what you DO, Squirrel Girl. What are you gonna do, not trust anyone?

Tony Stark @starkmantony ✓
@unbeatablesg That's a horrible way to live your life. And it's not you.

Tony Stark @starkmantony ✓
@unbeatablesg You did nothing wrong. And if there's anything I can do to help, you just let me know.

Tony Stark @starkmantony ✓
@unbeatablesg I may be a disembodied AI in a computer now, but I still know who my friends are.

Squirrel Girl @unbeatablesg
@starkmantony AW TONY <3

Squirrel Girl @unbeatablesg
@starkmantony You're the greatest, holy crap

Squirrel Girl @unbeatablesg
@starkmantony Also it's cute how you keep claiming to be an AI even though that is CLEARLY NOT THE CASE

Squirrel Girl @unbeatablesg
@starkmantony

THANK YOU FOR BEING A FRIEND

Tony Stark @starkmantony ✓
@unbeatablesg Listen, I keep telling you, I can still read those no problem so it's really not a big deal for me.

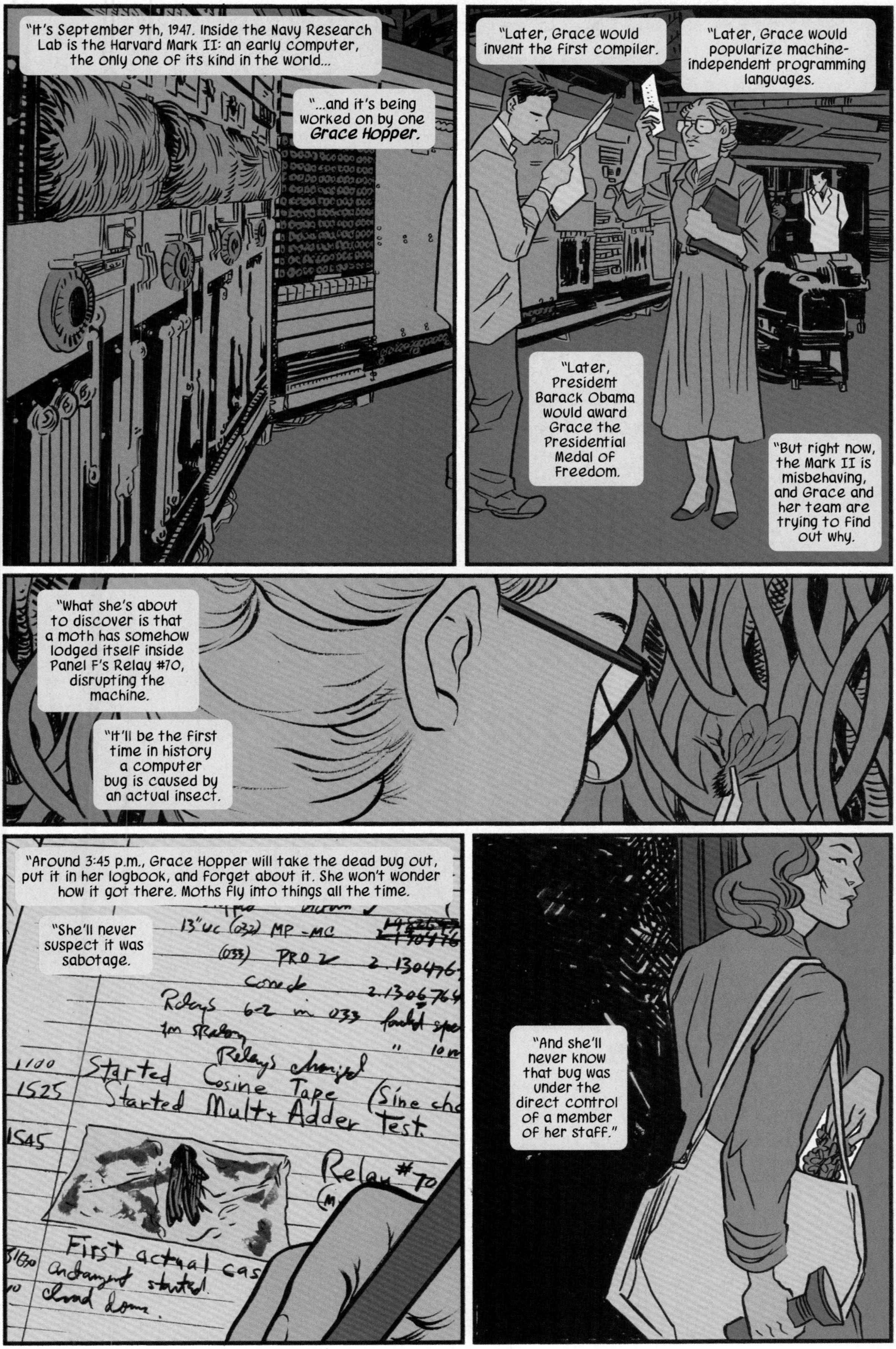

"It's September 9th, 1947. Inside the Navy Research Lab is the Harvard Mark II: an early computer, the only one of its kind in the world...
"...and it's being worked on by one *Grace Hopper.*
"Later, Grace would invent the first compiler.
"Later, Grace would popularize machine-independent programming languages.
"Later, President Barack Obama would award Grace the Presidential Medal of Freedom.
"But right now, the Mark II is misbehaving, and Grace and her team are trying to find out why.
"What she's about to discover is that a moth has somehow lodged itself inside Panel F's Relay #70, disrupting the machine.
"It'll be the first time in history a computer bug is caused by an actual insect.
"Around 3:45 p.m., Grace Hopper will take the dead bug out, put it in her logbook, and forget about it. She won't wonder how it got there. Moths fly into things all the time.
"She'll never suspect it was sabotage.
1100 Started Cosine Tape
1525 Started Mult+ Adder Test.
1545
Relay #70
First actual cas
"And she'll never know that bug was under the direct control of a member of her staff."

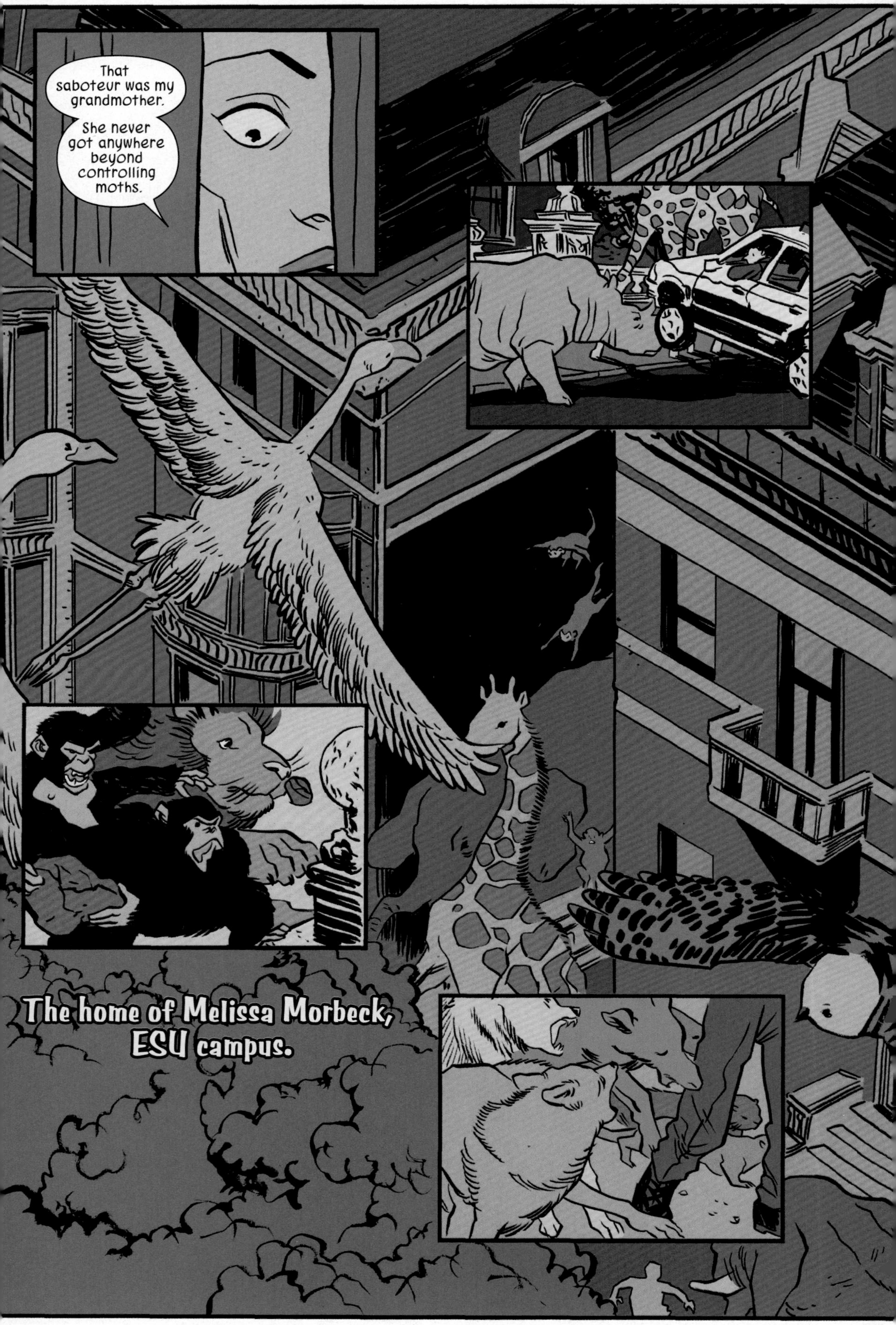

That saboteur was my grandmother.
She never got anywhere beyond controlling moths.
The home of Melissa Morbeck, ESU campus.

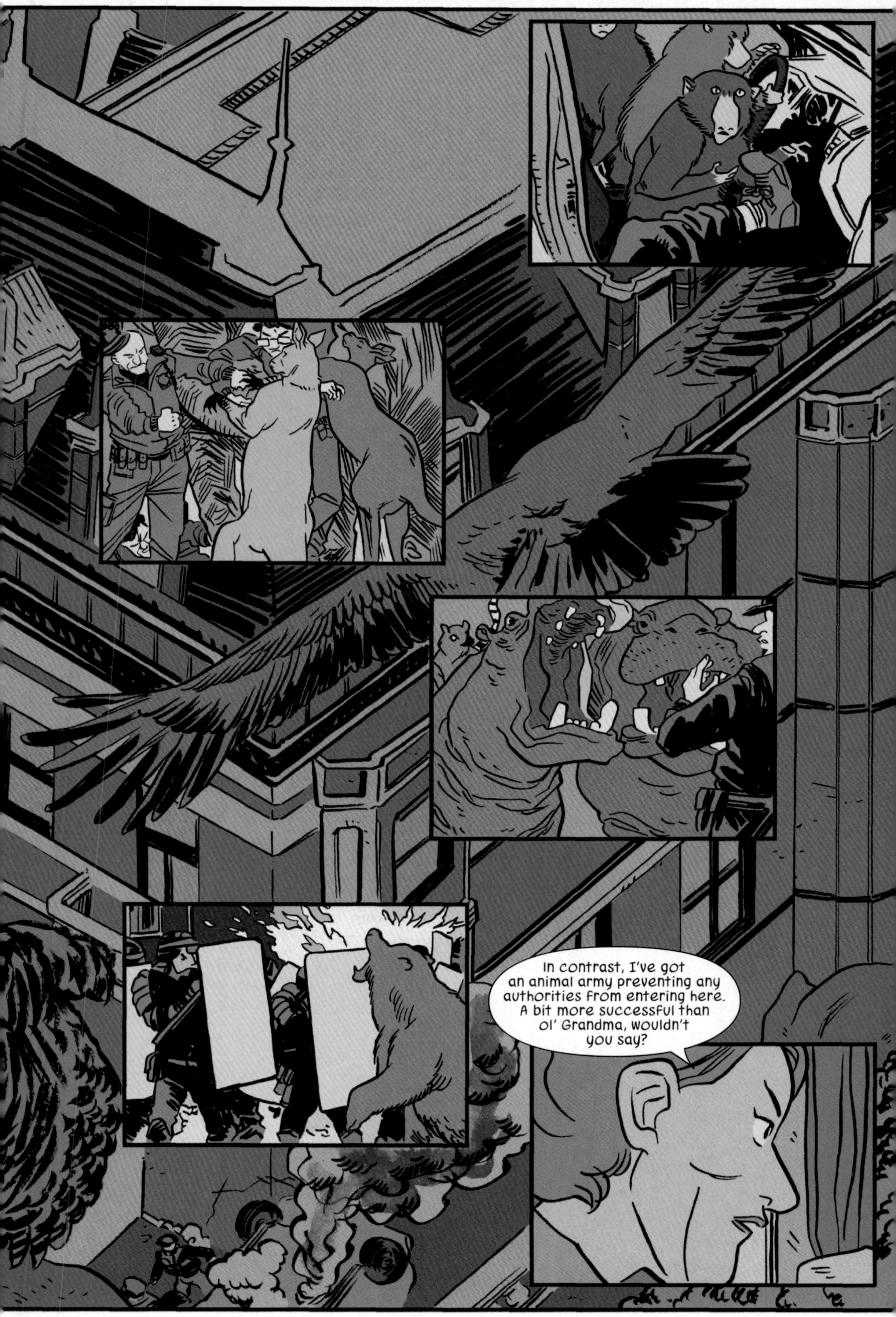
In contrast, I've got an animal army preventing any authorities from entering here. A bit more successful than ol' Grandma, wouldn't you say?

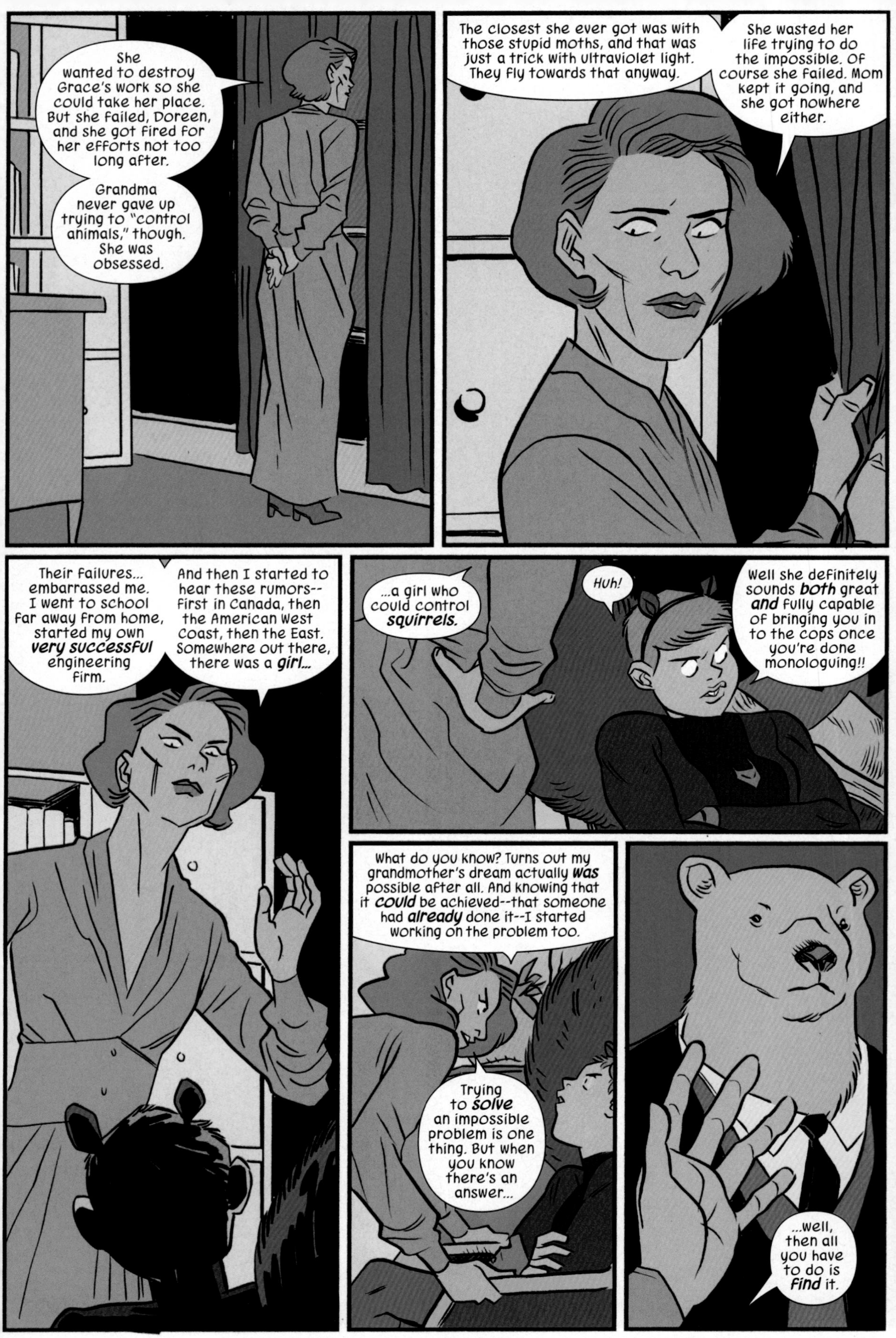
She wanted to destroy Grace's work so she could take her place. But she failed, Doreen, and she got fired for her efforts not too long after.
Grandma never gave up trying to "control animals," though. She was obsessed.
The closest she ever got was with those stupid moths, and that was just a trick with ultraviolet light. They fly towards that anyway.
She wasted her life trying to do the impossible. Of course she failed. Mom kept it going, and she got nowhere either.
Their failures... embarrassed me. I went to school far away from home, started my own **very successful** engineering firm.
And then I started to hear these rumors--first in Canada, then the American West Coast, then the East. Somewhere out there, there was a **girl...**
...a girl who could control **squirrels.**
Huh!
Well she definitely sounds **both** great **and** fully capable of bringing you in to the cops once you're done monologuing!!
What do you know? Turns out my grandmother's dream actually **was** possible after all. And knowing that it **could** be achieved--that someone had **already** done it--I started working on the problem too.
Trying to **solve** an impossible problem is one thing. But when you know there's an answer...
...well, then all you have to do is **find** it.

Melissa is demonstrating some great ***super villain tips*** here: Just ignore someone if they start sassing you when you're monologuing! It breaks your rhythm, plus being rude to them is already kinda villainous anyway. Just ignore the sass!

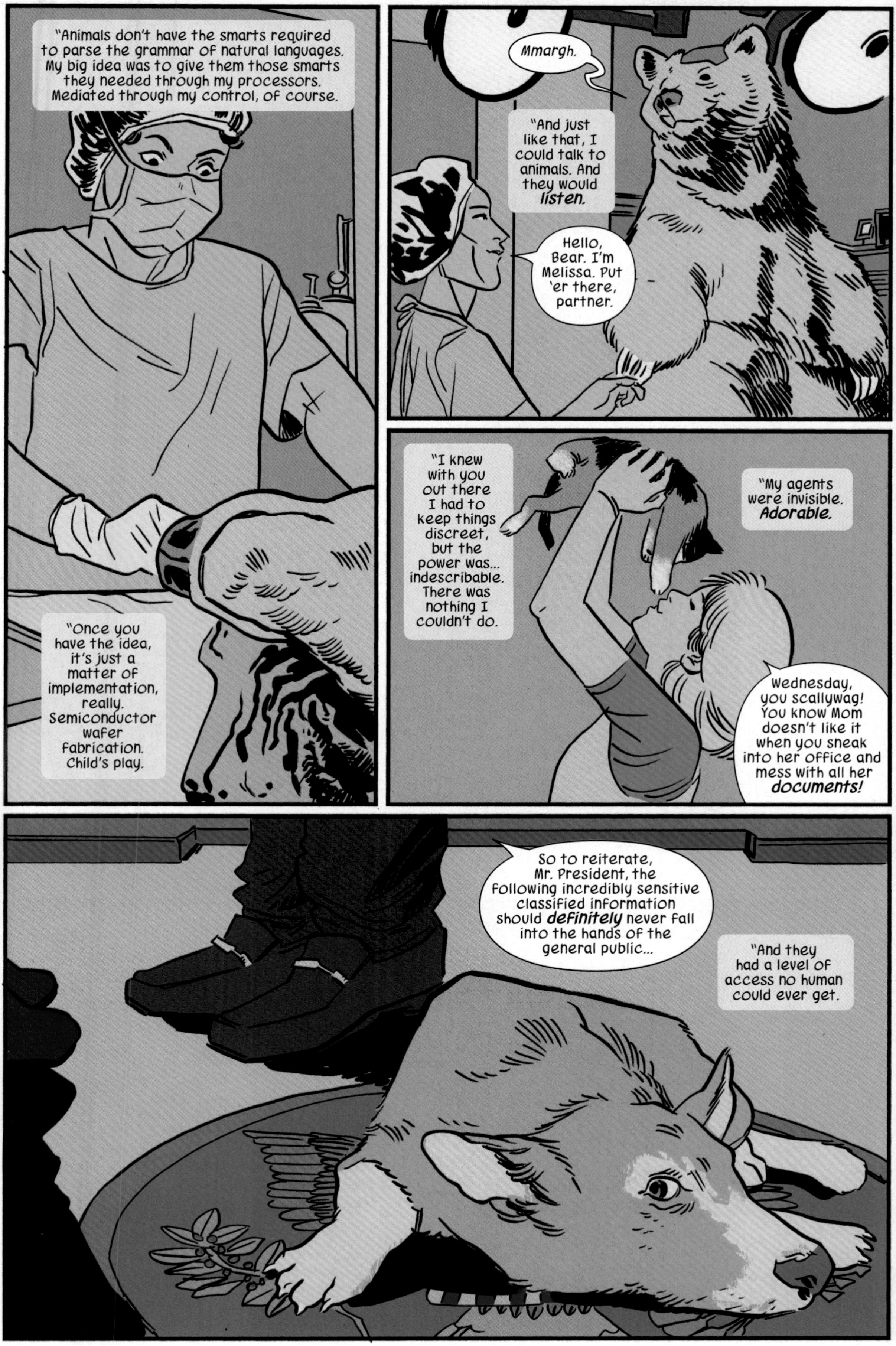

"Animals don't have the smarts required to parse the grammar of natural languages. My big idea was to give them those smarts they needed through my processors. Mediated through my control, of course.
"Once you have the idea, it's just a matter of implementation, really. Semiconductor wafer fabrication. Child's play.
Mmargh.
"And just like that, I could talk to animals. And they would *listen.*
Hello, Bear. I'm Melissa. Put 'er there, partner.
"I knew with you out there I had to keep things discreet, but the power was... indescribable. There was nothing I couldn't do.
"My agents were invisible. *Adorable.*
Wednesday, you scallywag! You know Mom doesn't like it when you sneak into her office and mess with all her *documents!*
So to reiterate, Mr. President, the following incredibly sensitive classified information should *definitely* never fall into the hands of the general public...
"And they had a level of access no human could ever get.

And here's a second *super villain tip*: Always turn the President's dog into a spy. What a great tip! Just don't lend this comic to any real-life super villains because these are some *primo tips!* Also: I'm beginning to think writing super villain tips in our comic *might* not be the brightest idea we've ever had??

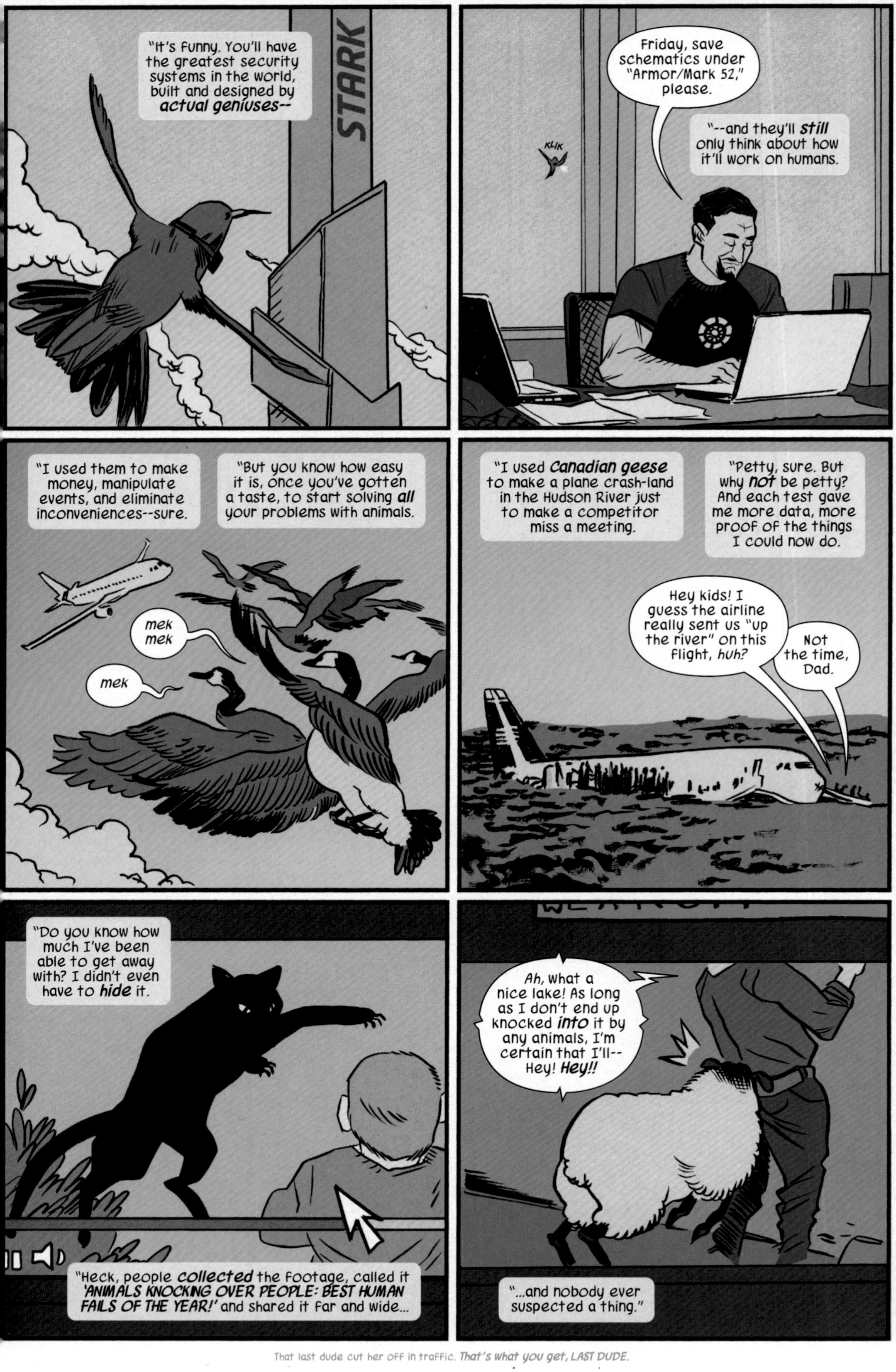
"It's funny. You'll have the greatest security systems in the world, built and designed by actual geniuses--
STARK
Friday, save schematics under "Armor/Mark 52," please.
"--and they'll still only think about how it'll work on humans.
KLIK
"I used them to make money, manipulate events, and eliminate inconveniences--sure.
"But you know how easy it is, once you've gotten a taste, to start solving all your problems with animals.
mek mek
mek
"I used Canadian geese to make a plane crash-land in the Hudson River just to make a competitor miss a meeting.
"Petty, sure. But why not be petty? And each test gave me more data, more proof of the things I could now do.
Hey kids! I guess the airline really sent us "up the river" on this flight, huh?
Not the time, Dad.
"Do you know how much I've been able to get away with? I didn't even have to hide it.
"Heck, people collected the footage, called it 'ANIMALS KNOCKING OVER PEOPLE: BEST HUMAN FAILS OF THE YEAR!' and shared it far and wide...
Ah, what a nice lake! As long as I don't end up knocked into it by any animals, I'm certain that I'll-- Hey! Hey!!
"...and nobody ever suspected a thing."

That last dude cut her off in traffic. *That's what you get, LAST DUDE.*

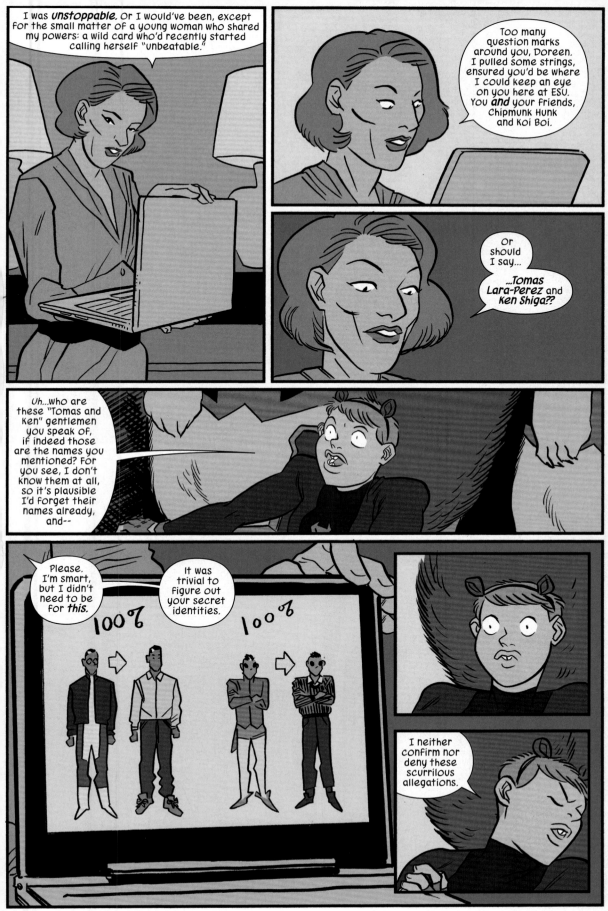

I was **unstoppable.** Or I would've been, except for the small matter of a young woman who shared my powers: a wild card who'd recently started calling herself "unbeatable."

Too many question marks around you, Doreen. I pulled some strings, ensured you'd be where I could keep an eye on you here at ESU. You **and** your friends, Chipmunk Hunk and Koi Boi.

Or should I say... ...Tomas Lara-Perez and Ken Shiga??

Uh...who are these "Tomas and Ken" gentlemen you speak of, if indeed those are the names you mentioned? For you see, I don't know them at all, so it's plausible I'd forget their names already, and--

Please. I'm smart, but I didn't need to be for **this.**

It was trivial to figure out your secret identities.

100% 100%

I neither confirm nor deny these scurrilous allegations.

How hard did I resist the "squirrels are members of the 'Sciuridae' biological family, so instead of 'scurrilous allegations,' Doreen could say 'sciuridious allegations'" pun? *Not hard enough, it **seems**??*

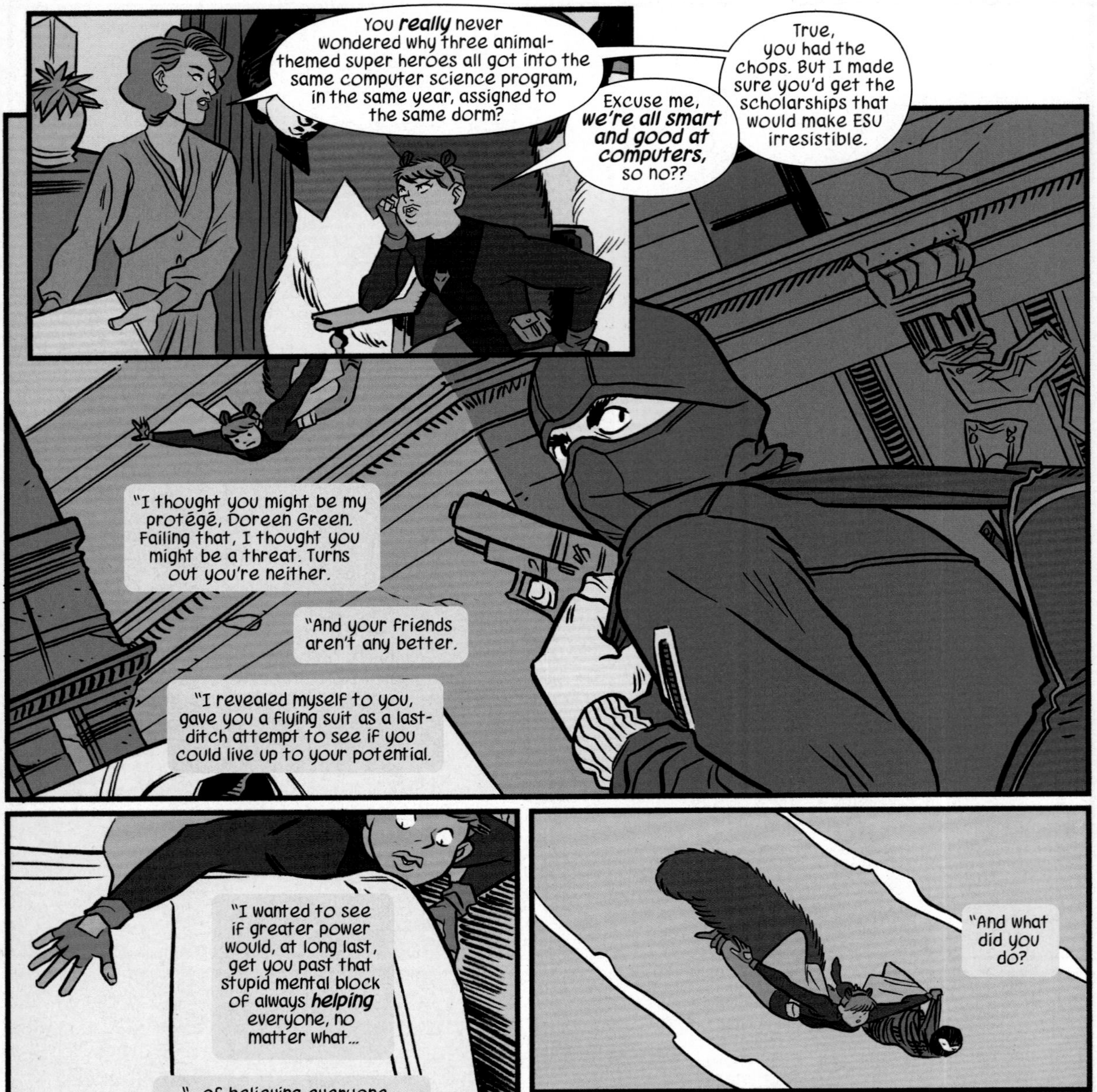
You really never wondered why three animal-themed super heroes all got into the same computer science program, in the same year, assigned to the same dorm?
Excuse me, we're all smart and good at computers, so no??
True, you had the chops. But I made sure you'd get the scholarships that would make ESU irresistible.
"I thought you might be my protégé, Doreen Green. Failing that, I thought you might be a threat. Turns out you're neither.
"And your friends aren't any better.
"I revealed myself to you, gave you a flying suit as a last-ditch attempt to see if you could live up to your potential.
"I wanted to see if greater power would, at long last, get you past that stupid mental block of always helping everyone, no matter what...
"...of believing everyone--even low-life goons--deserved second, third, good grief, even fiftieth chances.
"And what did you do?
"You helped a guy dressed up as a rhino with his self esteem, and you taught a bank robber how to better manage his finances so he wouldn't have to steal.
"SUCH a waste."
SO YOU'VE DISCOVERED SOME SIGNIFICANT DOWNSIDES TO LATE STAGE CAPITALISM
POSITIVE CHANGE
DOLLARS & SENSE

That bank robber's name is "Lewis 'the Chef' Hastings" because of how he robs banks and then hides the stolen money inside cakes. He gives his loved ones cakes with money inside them and they're like, "Lewis, I love your baking but I hate your bank robbing, and especially how you put that gross money that people touched with their dirty hands inside this otherwise delicious cake."

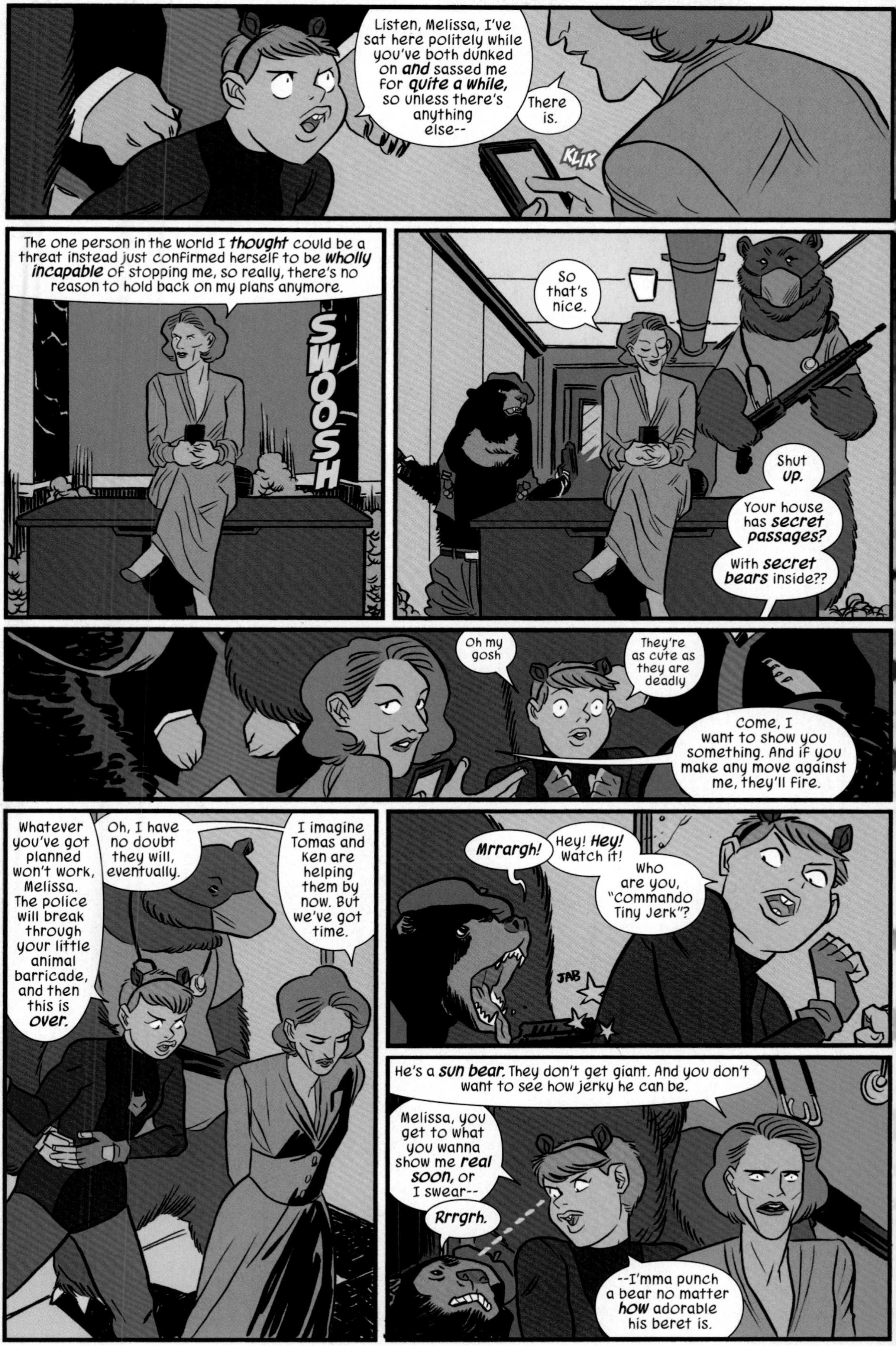
Listen, Melissa, I've sat here politely while you've both dunked on *and* sassed me for *quite a while,* so unless there's anything else--
There is.
KLIK
The one person in the world I *thought* could be a threat instead just confirmed herself to be *wholly incapable* of stopping me, so really, there's no reason to hold back on my plans anymore.
SWOOSH
So that's nice.
Shut *up.*
Your house has *secret passages?*
With *secret bears* inside??
Oh my gosh
They're as cute as they are deadly
Come, I want to show you something. And if you make any move against me, they'll fire.
Whatever you've got planned won't work, Melissa. The police will break through your little animal barricade, and then this is *over.*
Oh, I have no doubt they will, eventually.
I imagine Tomas and Ken are helping them by now. But we've got time.
Mrrargh!
Hey! *Hey!* Watch it!
Who are you, "Commando Tiny Jerk"?
JAB
He's a *sun bear.* They don't get giant. And you don't want to see how jerky he can be.
Melissa, you get to what you wanna show me *real soon,* or I swear--
Rrrgrh.
--I'mma punch a bear no matter *how* adorable his beret is.

They're not just as cute as they are deadly, Doreen: they're also as adorable as they are impatient with your stalling tactics!! And that is *by design.*

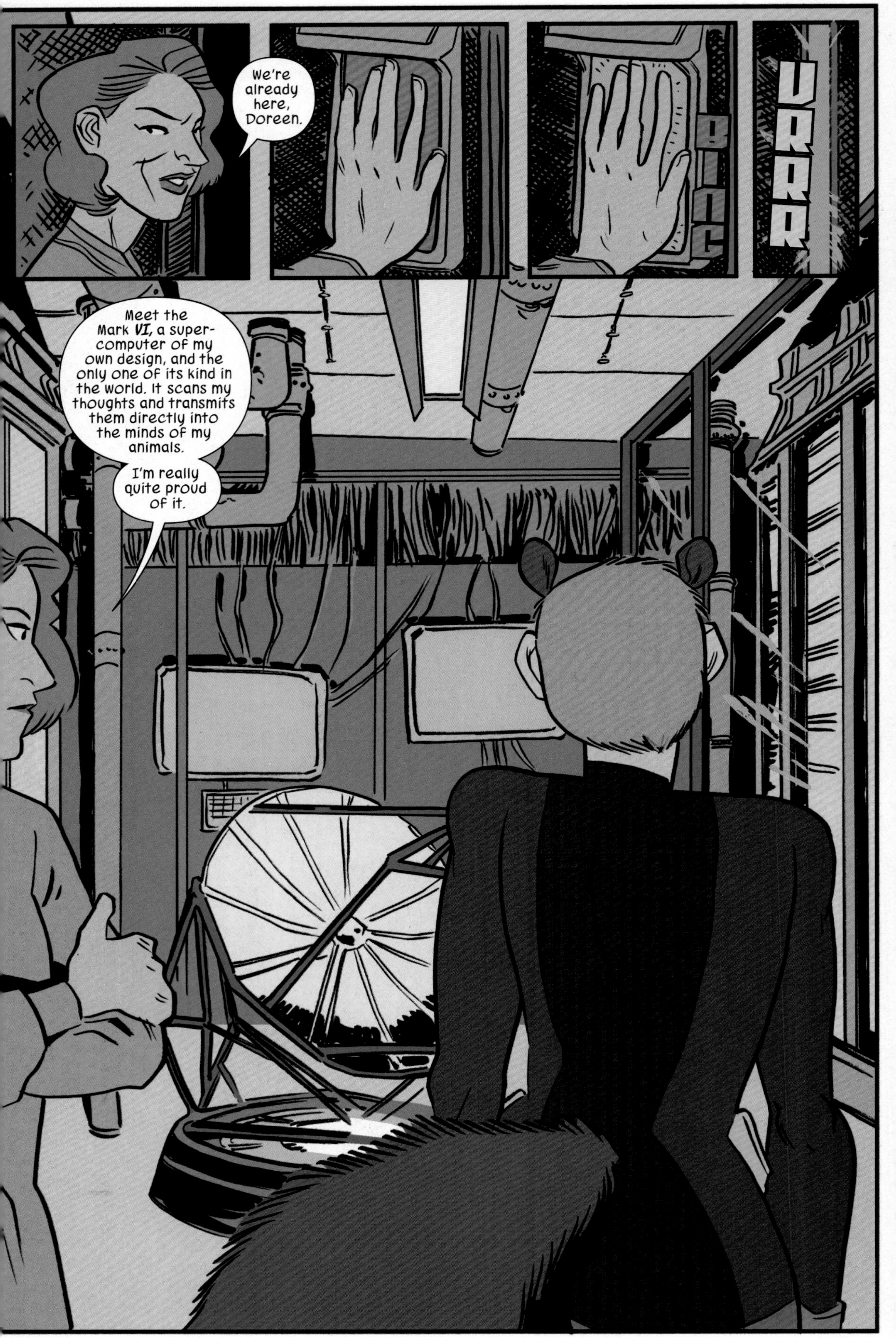
We're already here, Doreen.
BING
URRR
Meet the Mark VI, a super-computer of my own design, and the only one of its kind in the world. It scans my thoughts and transmits them directly into the minds of my animals.
I'm really quite proud of it.

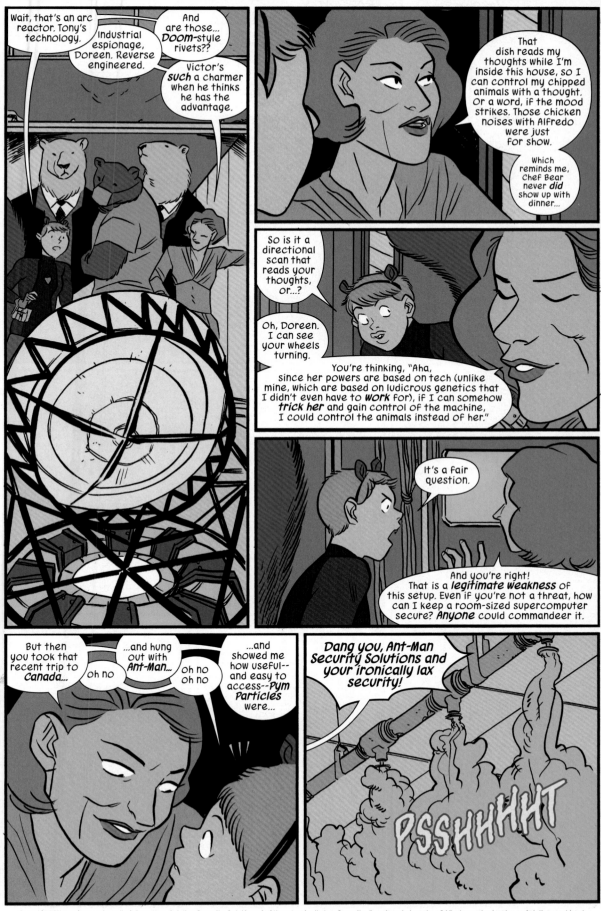

Wait, that's an arc reactor. Tony's technology.

Industrial espionage, Doreen. Reverse engineered.

And are those... DOOM-style rivets??

Victor's SUCH a charmer when he thinks he has the advantage.

That dish reads my thoughts while I'm inside this house, so I can control my chipped animals with a thought. Or a word, if the mood strikes. Those chicken noises with Alfredo were just for show.

Which reminds me, Chef Bear never did show up with dinner...

So is it a directional scan that reads your thoughts, or...?

Oh, Doreen. I can see your wheels turning.

You're thinking, "Aha, since her powers are based on tech (unlike mine, which are based on ludicrous genetics that I didn't even have to WORK for), if I can somehow trick her and gain control of the machine, I could control the animals instead of her."

It's a fair question.

And you're right! That is a legitimate weakness of this setup. Even if you're not a threat, how can I keep a room-sized supercomputer secure? ANYONE could commandeer it.

But then you took that recent trip to Canada...

...and hung out with Ant-Man...

oh no

oh no oh no

...and showed me how useful-- and easy to access--Pym Particles were...

Dang you, Ant-Man Security Solutions and your ironically lax security!

PSSHHHHT

I would 100% read a comic called Dang You, Ant-Man Security Solutions And Your Ironically Lax Security. Imagine what sorts of hilarious misadventures Ant-Man would get up to in that comic! Someone would steal his stuff, he'd shrink down to ant size so he can scream and kick things without causing a scene, then he'd come back up to normal size and try to continue his very important board meeting like nothing happened.

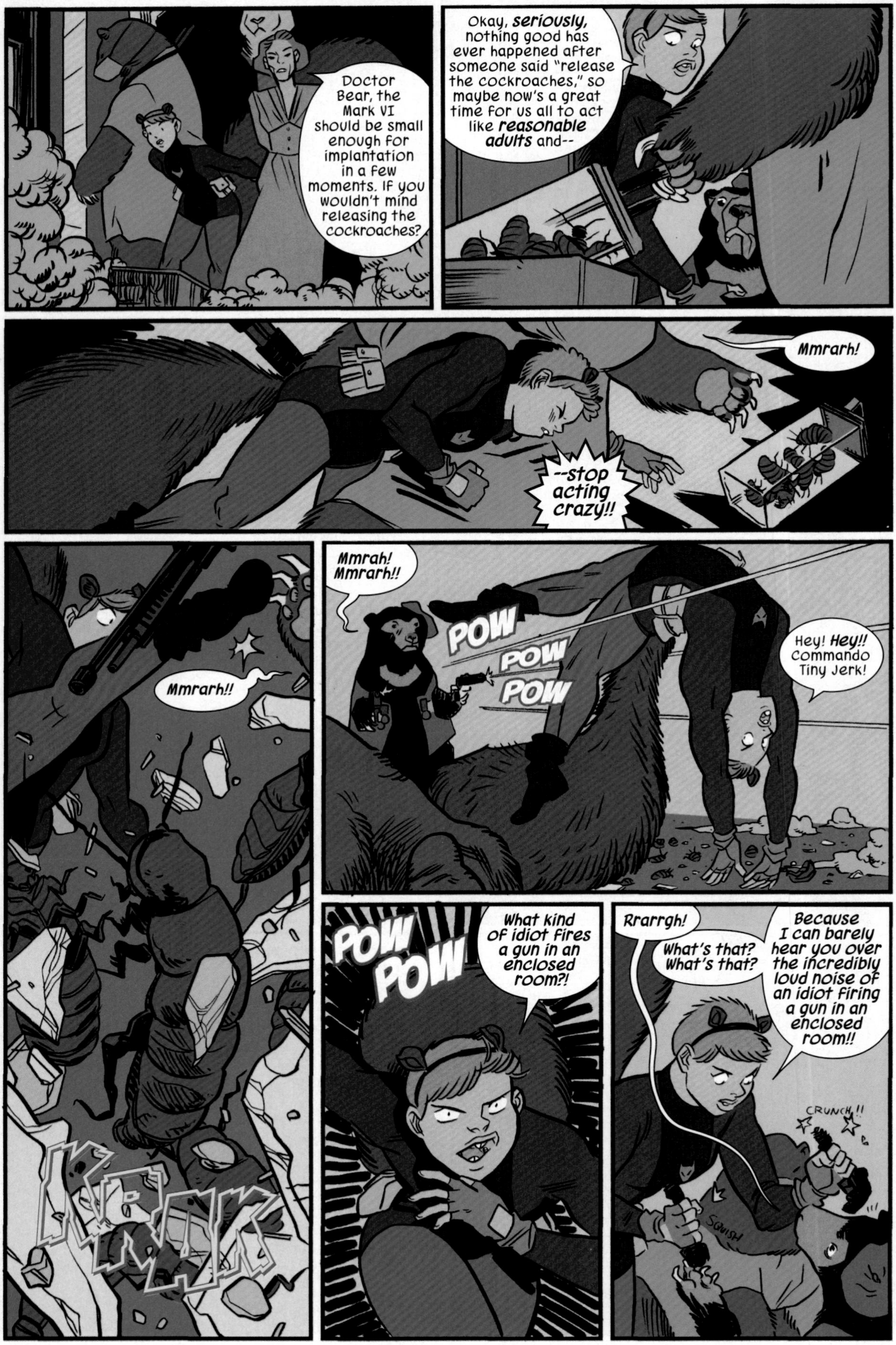
Doctor Bear, the Mark VI should be small enough for implantation in a few moments. If you wouldn't mind releasing the cockroaches?
Okay, seriously, nothing good has ever happened after someone said "release the cockroaches," so maybe now's a great time for us all to act like reasonable adults and--
Mmrarh!
--stop acting crazy!!
Mmrarh!!
KRAK
Mmrah! Mmrarh!!
POW POW POW
Hey! Hey!! Commando Tiny Jerk!
POW POW
What kind of idiot fires a gun in an enclosed room?!
Rrarrgh!
What's that? What's that?
Because I can barely hear you over the incredibly loud noise of an idiot firing a gun in an enclosed room!!
CRUNCH!!
SQUISH

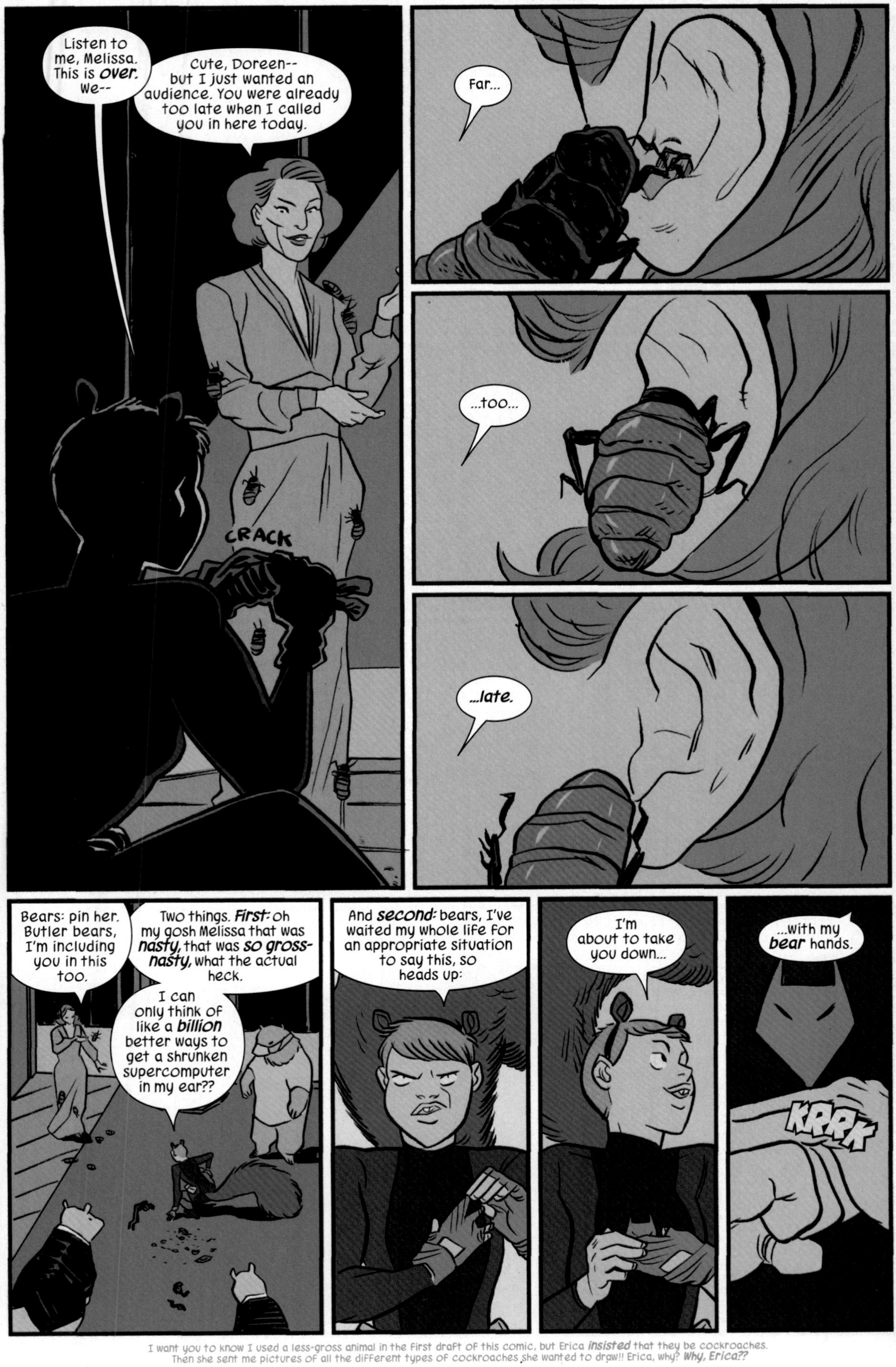
Listen to me, Melissa. This is *over.* We--
Cute, Doreen-- but I just wanted an audience. You were already too late when I called you in here today.
CRACK
Far...
...too...
...late.
Bears: pin her. Butler bears, I'm including you in this too.
Two things. *First:* oh my gosh Melissa that was *nasty,* that was *so gross-nasty,* what the actual heck.
I can only think of like a *billion* better ways to get a shrunken supercomputer in my ear??
And *second:* bears, I've waited my whole life for an appropriate situation to say this, so heads up:
I'm about to take you down...
...with my *bear* hands.
KRRK

I want you to know I used a less-gross animal in the first draft of this comic, but Erica *insisted* that they be cockroaches. Then she sent me pictures of all the different types of cockroaches she wanted to draw!! Erica, why? *Why, Erica??*

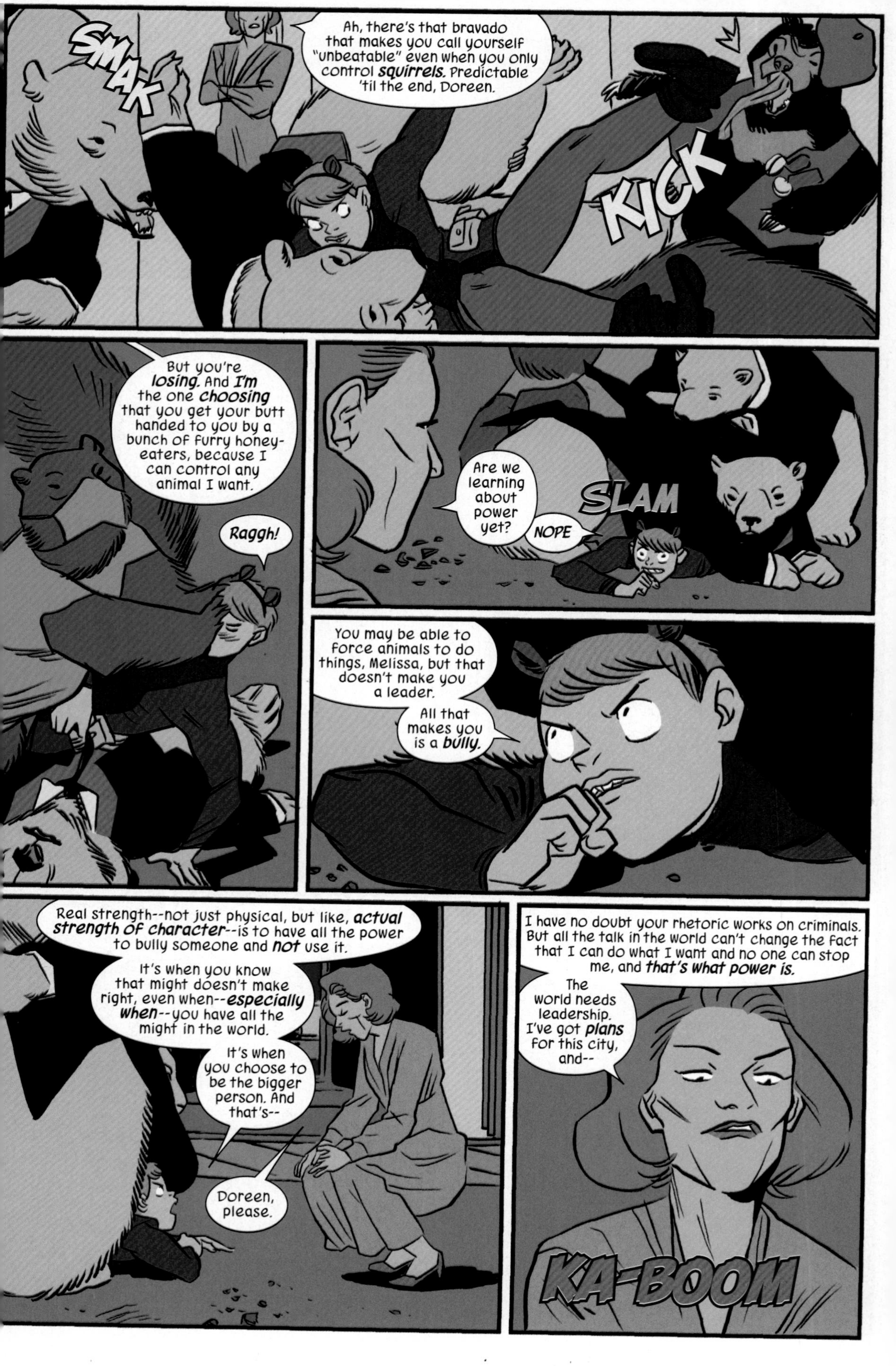
SMAK
Ah, there's that bravado that makes you call yourself "unbeatable" even when you only control squirrels. Predictable 'til the end, Doreen.
KICK
But you're losing. And I'm the one choosing that you get your butt handed to you by a bunch of furry honey-eaters, because I can control any animal I want.
Raggh!
Are we learning about power yet?
SLAM
NOPE
You may be able to force animals to do things, Melissa, but that doesn't make you a leader.
All that makes you is a bully.
Real strength--not just physical, but like, actual strength of character--is to have all the power to bully someone and not use it.
It's when you know that might doesn't make right, even when--especially when--you have all the might in the world.
It's when you choose to be the bigger person. And that's--
Doreen, please.
I have no doubt your rhetoric works on criminals. But all the talk in the world can't change the fact that I can do what I want and no one can stop me, and that's what power is.
The world needs leadership. I've got plans for this city, and--
KA-BOOM

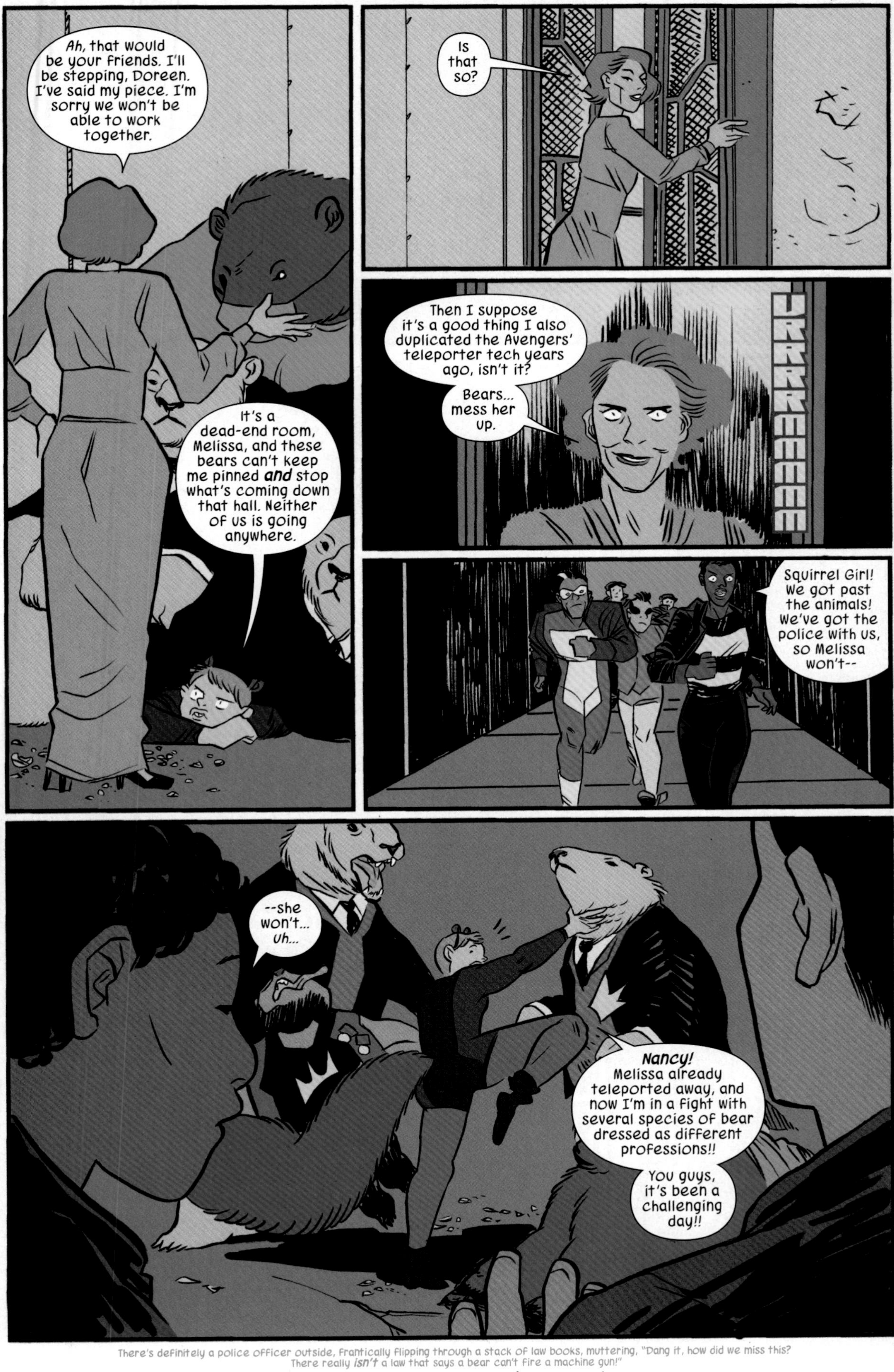
Ah, that would be your friends. I'll be stepping, Doreen. I've said my piece. I'm sorry we won't be able to work together.
It's a dead-end room, Melissa, and these bears can't keep me pinned *and* stop what's coming down that hall. Neither of us is going anywhere.
Is that so?
Then I suppose it's a good thing I also duplicated the Avengers' teleporter tech years ago, isn't it?
Bears... mess her up.
URRRMMMMM
Squirrel Girl! We got past the animals! We've got the police with us, so Melissa won't--
--she won't... uh...
Nancy! Melissa already teleported away, and now I'm in a fight with several species of bear dressed as different professions!!
You guys, it's been a challenging day!!

There's definitely a police officer outside, frantically flipping through a stack of law books, muttering, "Dang it, how did we miss this? There really *isn't* a law that says a bear can't fire a machine gun!"

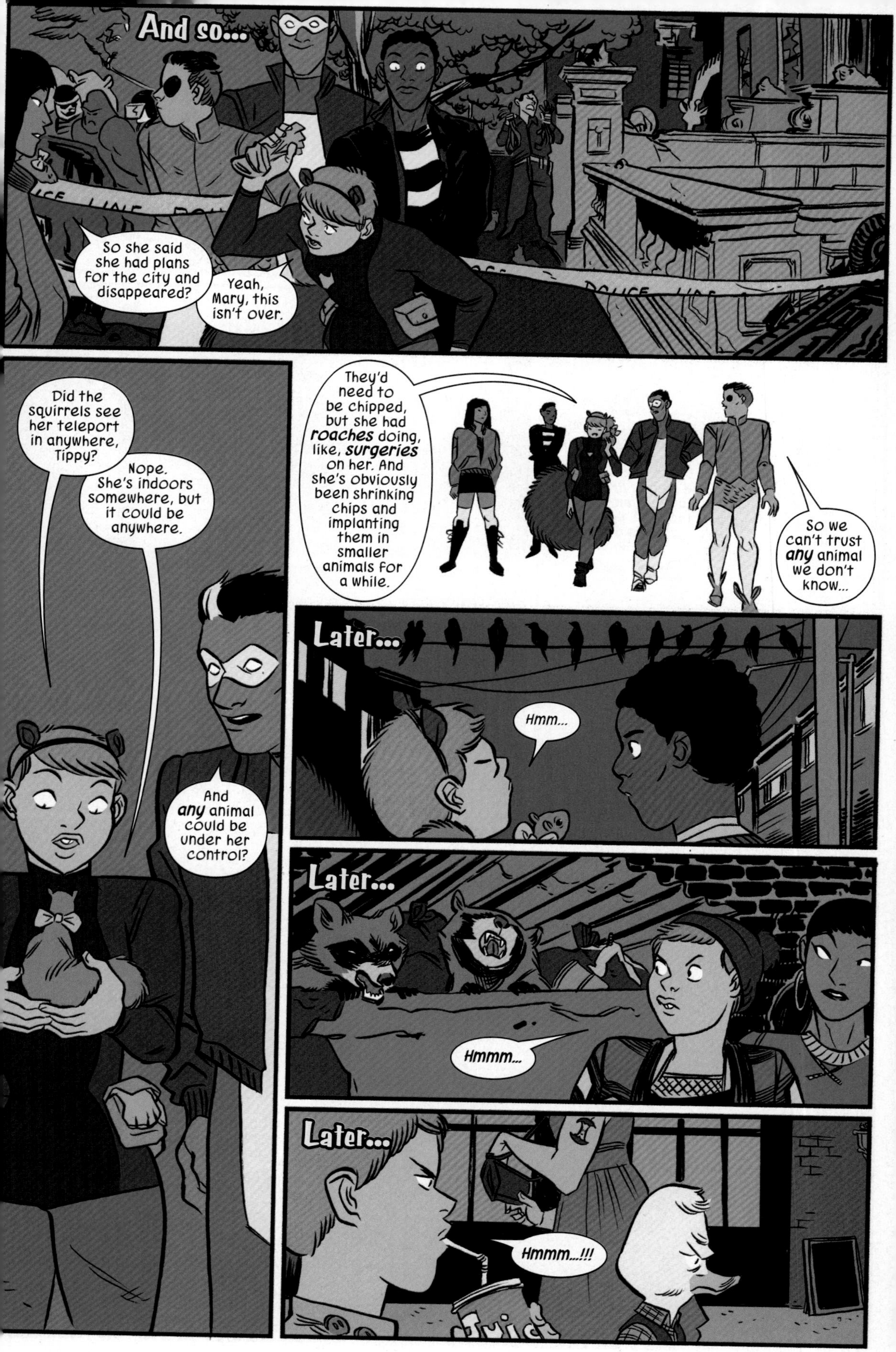
And so...
So she said she had plans for the city and disappeared?
Yeah, Mary, this isn't over.
Did the squirrels see her teleport in anywhere, Tippy?
Nope. She's indoors somewhere, but it could be anywhere.
They'd need to be chipped, but she had roaches doing, like, surgeries on her. And she's obviously been shrinking chips and implanting them in smaller animals for a while.
So we can't trust any animal we don't know...
And any animal could be under her control?
Later...
Hmm...
Later...
Hmmm...
Later...
Hmmm...!!!

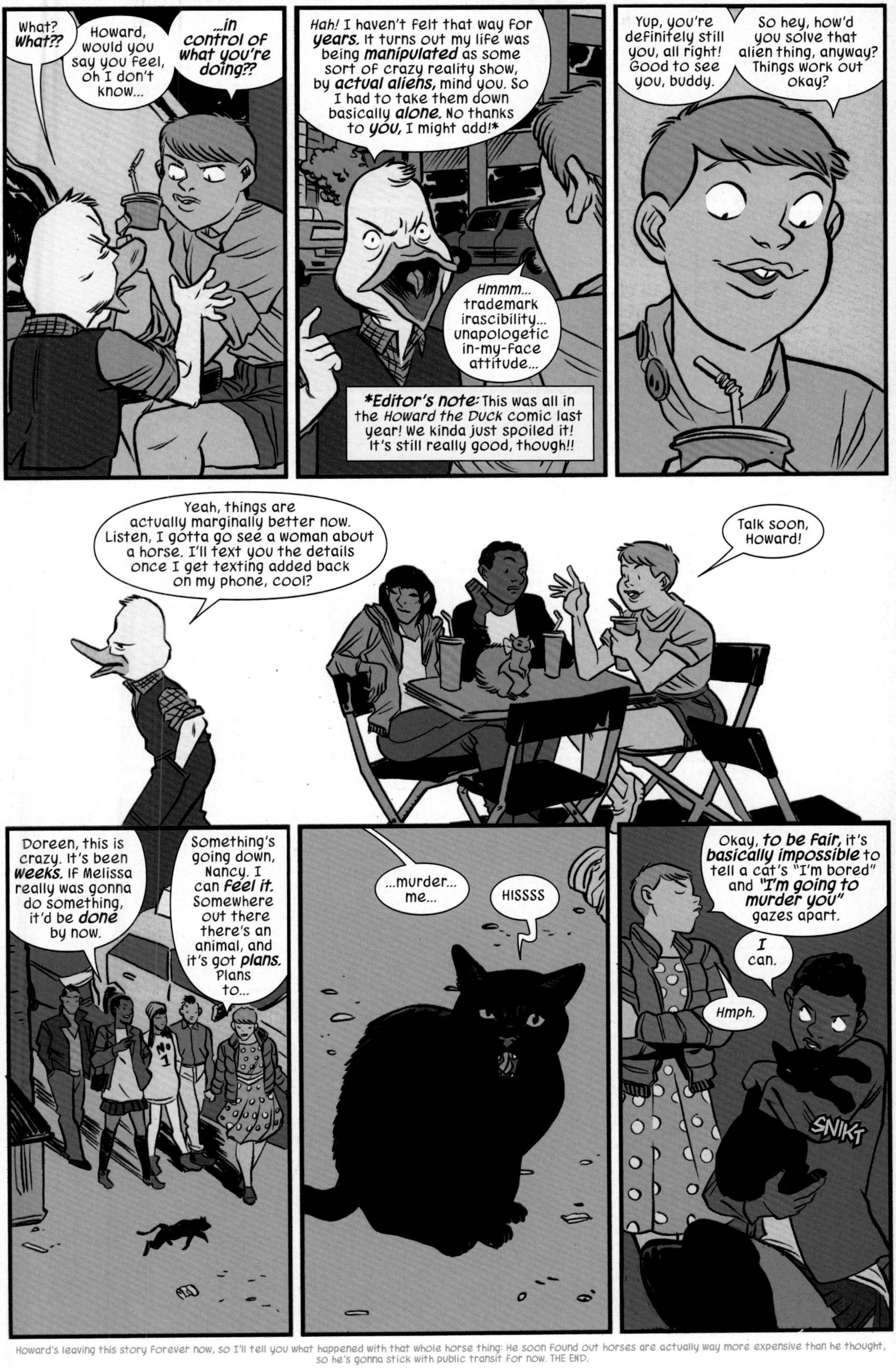
What? What??
Howard, would you say you feel, oh I don't know...
...in control of what you're doing??
Hah! I haven't felt that way for years. It turns out my life was being manipulated as some sort of crazy reality show, by actual aliens, mind you. So I had to take them down basically alone. No thanks to you, I might add!*
Hmmm... trademark irascibility... unapologetic in-my-face attitude...
*Editor's note: This was all in the Howard the Duck comic last year! We kinda just spoiled it! It's still really good, though!!
Yup, you're definitely still you, all right! Good to see you, buddy.
So hey, how'd you solve that alien thing, anyway? Things work out okay?
Yeah, things are actually marginally better now. Listen, I gotta go see a woman about a horse. I'll text you the details once I get texting added back on my phone, cool?
Talk soon, Howard!
Doreen, this is crazy. It's been weeks. If Melissa really was gonna do something, it'd be done by now.
Something's going down, Nancy. I can feel it. Somewhere out there there's an animal, and it's got plans. Plans to...
...murder... me...
HISSSS
Okay, to be fair, it's basically impossible to tell a cat's "I'm bored" and "I'm going to murder you" gazes apart.
I can.
Hmph.
SNIKT

Howard's leaving this story forever now, so I'll tell you what happened with that whole horse thing: He soon found out horses are actually way more expensive than he thought, so he's gonna stick with public transit for now. THE END.

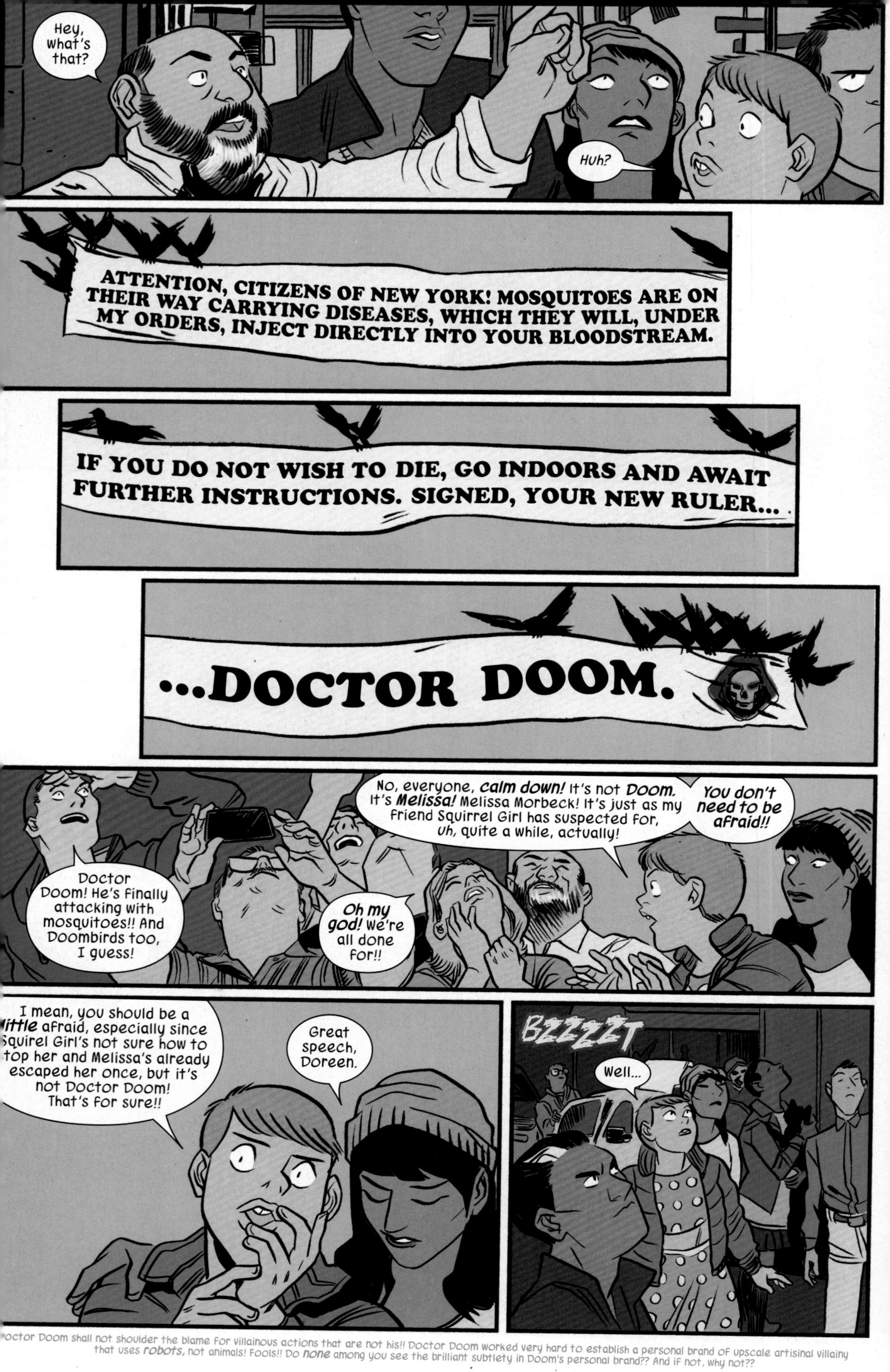
Hey, what's that?
Huh?
ATTENTION, CITIZENS OF NEW YORK! MOSQUITOES ARE ON THEIR WAY CARRYING DISEASES, WHICH THEY WILL, UNDER MY ORDERS, INJECT DIRECTLY INTO YOUR BLOODSTREAM.
IF YOU DO NOT WISH TO DIE, GO INDOORS AND AWAIT FURTHER INSTRUCTIONS. SIGNED, YOUR NEW RULER...
...DOCTOR DOOM.
Doctor Doom! He's finally attacking with mosquitoes!! And Doombirds too, I guess!
Oh my god! We're all done for!!
No, everyone, calm down! It's not Doom. It's Melissa! Melissa Morbeck! It's just as my friend Squirrel Girl has suspected for, uh, quite a while, actually!
You don't need to be afraid!!
I mean, you should be a ittle afraid, especially since quirrel Girl's not sure how to top her and Melissa's already escaped her once, but it's not Doctor Doom! That's for sure!!
Great speech, Doreen.
BZZZZT
Well...

octor Doom shall not shoulder the blame for villainous actions that are not his!! Doctor Doom worked very hard to establish a personal brand of upscale artisinal villainy that uses *robots*, not animals! Fools!! Do *none* among you see the brilliant subtlety in Doom's personal brand?? And if not, why not??

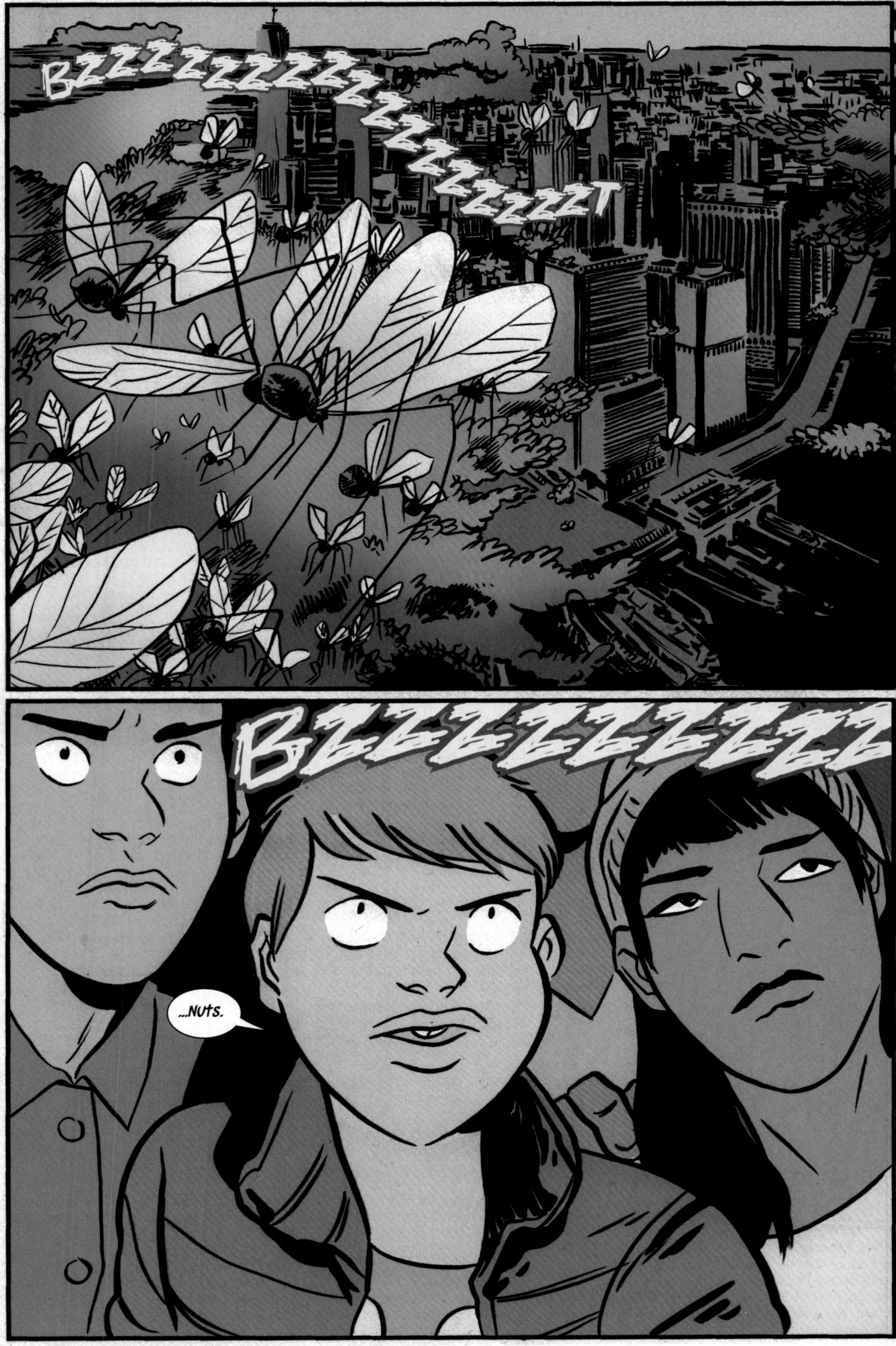
BZZZZZZZZZZZZZZZZZZZZZZZZT
BZZZZZZZZZZZ
...NUTS.

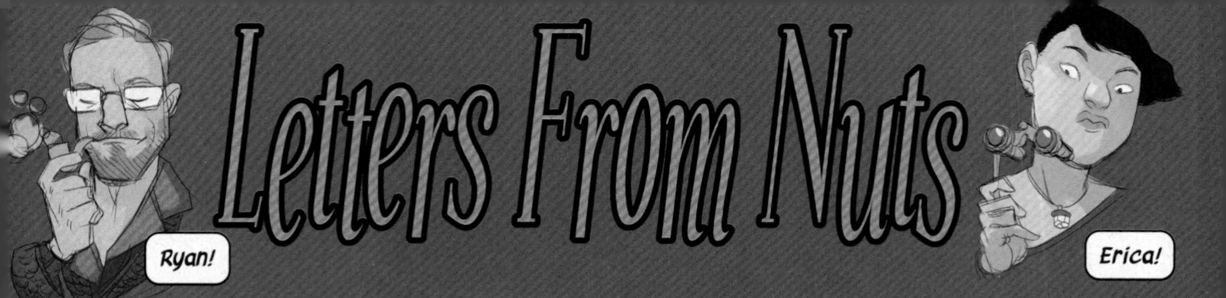
Letters From Nuts
Ryan!
Erica!

Send letters to mheroes@marvel.com or 135 W 50th St, 7th Floor, New York, NY 10020 (Please mark "OKAY TO PRINT")

Dear Erica and Ryan,

This is my daughter Emerson; she's 11--turning 12 next month. She's a super-huge fan of Squirrel Girl and wanted me to share the costume we made her for Literacy Day at school!

Emerson has been reading and re-reading the graphic novels ever since receiving them from her nerd uncle a few months ago. She got the new ones for Christmas and can't put them down. Tippy-Toe is her very favorite character!

Thanks for your time and your stories!

Abby from Canada!

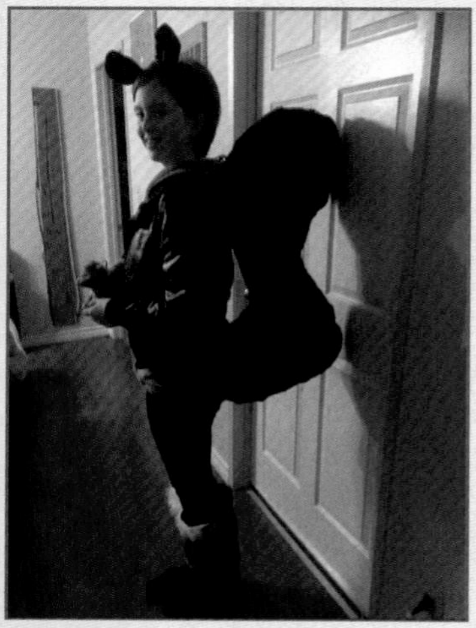

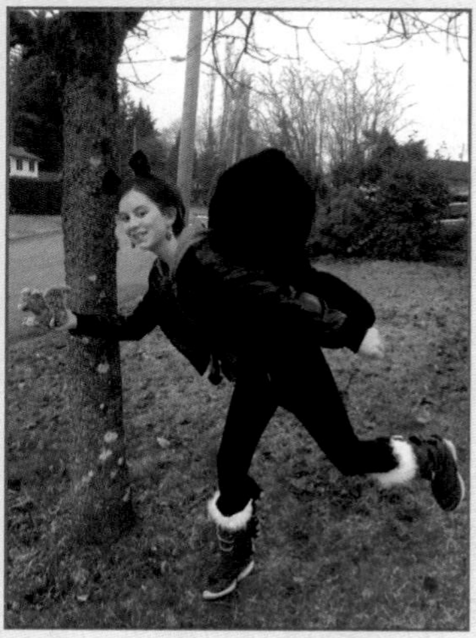

RYAN: Emerson is CLEARLY a woman of taste and skill—that costume is great! We never had Literacy Day when I was in school, but we did have a club at the school library where you could write down what books you'd read, and if you were in the top 2 you'd get a pizza party. I joined late but I read books really quickly and often, so I was one of the winners! The pizza party was MEGA DISAPPOINTING: it was just me and this other kid I didn't know hanging out at lunch hour when we wanted to be outside playing, and ever since then I've tended to read books for pleasure instead of pizza, and have become extremely suspicious of pizza-based bribery.

ERICA: I had neither of these things, or maybe I never noticed because I had zero extracurriculars because I too busy drawing and reading stuff. In my senior year though, the English department let me have the key to the secret other library where they kept the books they didn't teach anymore—JOY LUCK CLUB and A CLOCKWORK ORANGE aplenty! That is a great costume though. I like all the black. NEGA SQUIRREL GIRL.

P.S. Ryan, the next time I'm in town can I use your guest room? I'll bring a pizza.

Dear Ryan and Erica,

THE UNBEATABLE SQUIRREL GIRL is my favorite comic book! You can ask the community over at Destructoid!!! (It's a video game website where I profess my love for Squirrel Girl on a regular basis!) Even my parents know how much I absolutely LOVE Squirrel Girl!!! I just gave a presentation for one of my classes three days ago, where I explained that Squirrel Girl is 100% the biggest thing that influenced me to go back to school and pursue a degree in Computer Science! I'm a 29-year-old, large, bald, bearded man, and I am a huge fan of your work! Please, keep being amazing forever.

Sincerely,
Kevin
Richmond, VA

P.S. One of my friends at Destructoid even drew Squirrel Girl (and three of my other favorite characters of all time) on this lovely picture that they made for me as a Secret Santa gift!!!!

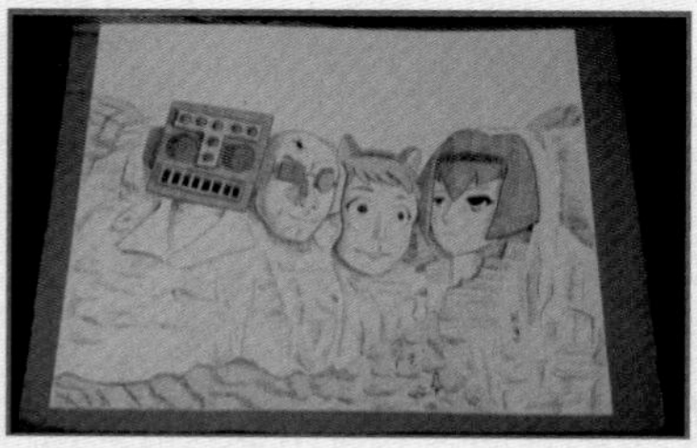

Pictured (from left to right): The Destructoid Robot (the site mascot), Spider Jerusalem (TRANSMETROPOLITAN), Squirrel Girl (!!!), and Dorothy (from the anime BIG O)

RYAN: Ahhh, this is great! I know 3/4s of those characters. Also: I am not a bald man, but I'm really considering shaving my head. HERE'S THE PITCH: I keep my beard, but I shave it just at the glasses line, so the glasses form a dividing space between hairy face and bald head. I think it'd look super awesome, but I haven't taken the plunge yet. This is all to say: as a bald, bearded man, you are kinda living my (most recent) dream?? Also: congrats on going back to school as an adult! I have a friend who recently did that too, and she doesn't regret it at all now that she's graduated. Hooray for education!

ERICA: Ryan, I do not care how much hair you plan on having but please do not create tangents. Don't do it. Kevin, I'm glad you like the book! Fun fact: my first few jobs out of school were in video games. I was at Harmonix for the insanity that was THE BEATLES: ROCK BAND.

Hi Erica and Ryan,

I was so shocked when you told me that nice young woman Melissa was evil that I went into denial. However, after some reflection, I've accepted that a trans-reality crush is unlikely to redeem her, so I'm ready to move on to the remaining stages of grief. Oh comics, why do you hurt me when I love you SO much?!

I also want to tell you that you have upset the routine I have for reading comics. When I bought comics I'd sort them so I'd read any new series or one-offs first, and then least-anticipated (still pretty good; I'm a fussy reader) to most-anticipated new issue. I've been doing this for decades. My friends and family make jokes about how much I like routine. You've broken my system. For the last three months I have been unable to defer gratification in regards to reading SQUIRREL GIRL. Your comic's changed my life, guys.

Finally, and this is awkward because it's in a letter, so it looks manipulative, but I want to say it anyway, your letter pages are wonderful—a must-read part of your comic.

Best wishes,
David Morris

RYAN: Haha, I'm sorry, David! I've never been a combo breaker before, especially a decades-long streak. Doreen "The Exception" Green for the win! Also thanks for the props on our letters page: it's one of my favorite things (you all send in such nice words and great pictures), so I'm always happy when Marvel sends us the (virtual) mailbag for Letter Column Day.

ERICA: I don't know why letter columns ever went away! Anyway, I understand the need for routine. My routine is very important to me. I do my work in the back of the same cafe every day, and the baristas know my name and drink to the point where if I change my order, they'll call me over to make sure someone didn't write down the wrong thing. Also, since you brought up Melissa's reveal—while I was working on that issue I made Chicken Alfredo and Ryan was rightfully horrified at me.

Hi Squirrel People,

My cat, Moogle, would like to audition for the part of Cat-Thor in the movie that will inevitably get made once Nancy's genius is recognized. She's not quite worthy enough to lift the hammer yet, but has promised to get in moral shape in time for filming.

Thanks for your consideration. Stay awesome,

Matt

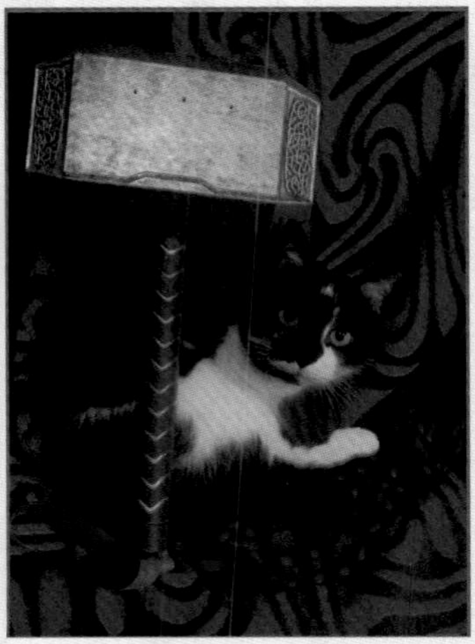

RYAN: I hereby greenlight this motion picture on the strength of this image alone. Make it happen, whoever is in charge of movies! Just because I don't know your name doesn't mean you shouldn't immediately do what I say!

ERICA: She doesn't have to lift it. She could be the Bill Bixby to a Maine Coon's Lou Ferigno, assuming that Cat-Thor works with traditional Thor rules and we work in a Donald Blake situation.

Dear Erica and Ryan,

I just want to say that Squirrel Girl has made my life so much better. Your secret formula mixes the right amount of humor, butt-kicking, computer science, puns, and awesome. While I don't know the whole formula, I know how much awesome there is: all of the awesome. Yep. 100% of the awesome is crammed into every panel. Now some people would be panicking at this thought, worried that there is no awesome left for anything else. But I know that one simply needs to think about Doreen, and then everything gets to bask in her reflected awesome. This allows me to shine awesome over everything in my life.

Please keep doing everything that you do,

Miguel Valdespino

RYAN: Miguel, thank you! Putting as many awesome things as we can into each panel is our secret goal, so it's super great that you noticed!

ERICA: Doreen is pretty awesome, which makes it easy to figure out the rest.

Hello,

I have just finished reading the first paperback of THE UNBEATABLE SQUIRREL GIRL, collecting the first four issues of the series. WOW, this comic book has given me hope for the future of comics! I thought they were all dark and violent nowadays, but I found SQUIRREL GIRL to be funny, creative, and exciting like old-school comics used to be!

Also, I love that you are printing the letters columns. They are fun and make me feel part of your community!

Keep up the good work!

Aaron
Santa Monica, CA

RYAN: More love for the letters page this month! AND IT'S THE ONE PAGE WE CAN'T FULLY TAKE THE CREDIT FOR.

ERICA: It's the most writing I ever have to do in one month though--unless someone on the internet is saying that ROBOCOP is not very good.

I am so excited to be writing to you guys. So excited, that I might pull a Doreen and ramble a bit.

First off, I would like to recount how I had found and eventually fell in love with everyone's favorite hero. It all started the way most things tend to in today's world. I was scrolling aimlessly on the internet, when I found a website that had all the Marvel characters and a power grid for comparison. Well, I found Onslaught, who had a full power grid, and decided to find all the characters with a full grid. Well, the next character I found was, of course, Squirrel Girl. I was dumbfounded. At first I thought "surely this is a mistake," and I decided to read what it said about her. In my defense, the article I read said nothing of Doctor Doom, Thanos, or any of that. All it said was that the other kids made fun of her "deformities" (there was no picture so I had no idea what she looked like; I wasn't smart enough to realize it meant her teeth and tail) and that she tried to kill a guy named Bug-Eyed Voice (literally the lamest sounding villain ever) in an effort to impress Iron Man. That was it. Nothing of her unbeatableness, none of the extensive list of vanquished foes, nada.

Many moons later, I found out who Thanos was. Then I discovered Squirrel Girl beat him. That's all it took for me. I went to a local comic-book store and found issue #2 (vol. 2, I later found out. That was very confusing). I read it, then thought of nothing but it until I could go back and get issues #3-5. I then checked out #1-5 of vol. 1 at the library (those places DO rock!). Then came issue #8 (back at vol. 2), and for Christmas, #9-15 (parents rock!). I starved myself until I could get issue #6 and #7, but since it never happened (got #6 of vol. 1 though; that's how I figured out there was two volumes), I just delved into #8 and on. Which is funny, it's like that one recap page on issue #9 you questioned printing was precisely put in for me because it filled exactly what I needed to bridge the gap. So thank you, and rest at ease, it was the right choice.

A few more random things: I noticed no one mentioned this, but the intro thing in issue #9 lists "Brotastic Brad" but shows a picture of Nancy (or someone—definitely not Brad). I don't mean to be tedious, but kept wondering if it was an honest mistake, an effort to get Brad to denounce his blogging, or (what I personally hope is going on) a secret sweepstakes contest thing where one special person gets a slightly edited copy of an issue and they have to spot it and mail it to you to claim their prize. And none of the rules or even the contest was announced, so you must wait and see if anyone noticed and wins. I really hope that's the case.

No matter what happens with that last point, I love your comic book. Keep it up guys! I'm glad we can have a high-spirited, clean-humored comic book to read. Plus, it is super educational! Tree lobsters are awesome!

From one Ryan to another (and to you too, Erica),

Your pal,
Ryan Lewis

P.S. I can't help but ask, who on this vast expanse of dirt we call Earth is Claude?! The guy on the cover of issue #8? I kept expecting him to show up. Thought he was Brad at first. I just don't understand. Who is that guy caressing Squirrel Girl? Why is he mentioned by name on the cover? And caressing? On the cover?!

RYAN: The Brad thing was a coloring error: he switches skin tones in that one page only because it turns out that we CAN make mistakes sometimes, just to mix things up! But I have been assured it'll be fixed for the trade. Hopefully–hopefully we remembered to fix it for the trade?? Claude is a made-up person who appeared because we tried to make the most romance-novel cover in the world, and needed the most romance-novel name in the world. Attention, all real-life Claudes who are reading this right now: feel confident! You got this, man!!

ERICA: Didn't we have a long e-mail thread going trying to figure out what his name should be? All the text on the (second) issue 8 cover was the result of four people going back and forth for what seemed like a day. Claude is low-rent Fabio. Since the theme of this letters page seems to be me sharing weird details that are only tangentially related: The first Fabio book cover I ever saw was the copy of THE TWO TOWERS I got from the library where he seemed to be Legolas.

Next Issue:

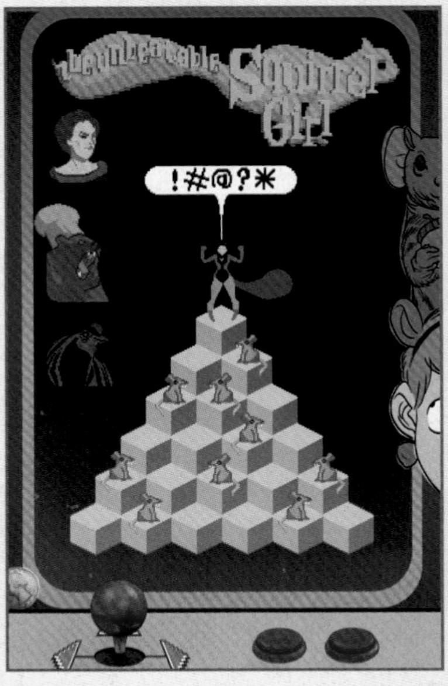
!#@?*

Attention, Squirrel Scouts! Make sure to check out our production blog, **unbeatablesquirrelgirl.tumblr.com**, where we post behind-the-scenes stuff on how the book gets made, along with all sorts of cool things *you* make: fanart, cosplay, whatever!

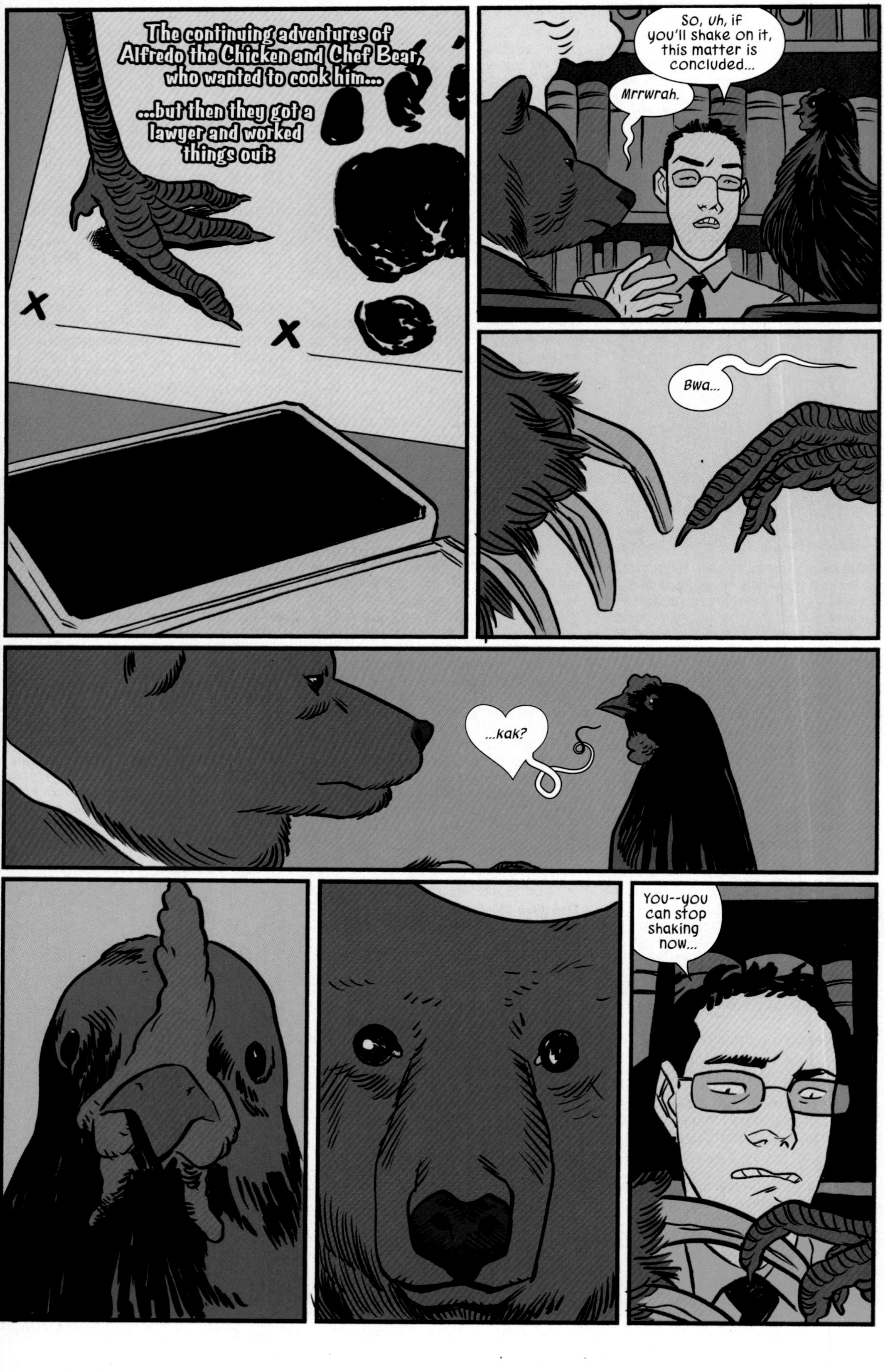
The continuing adventures of Alfredo the Chicken and Chef Bear, who wanted to cook him...
...but then they got a lawyer and worked things out:
X
X
So, uh, if you'll shake on it, this matter is concluded...
Mrrwrah.
Bwa...
...kak?
You--you can stop shaking now...

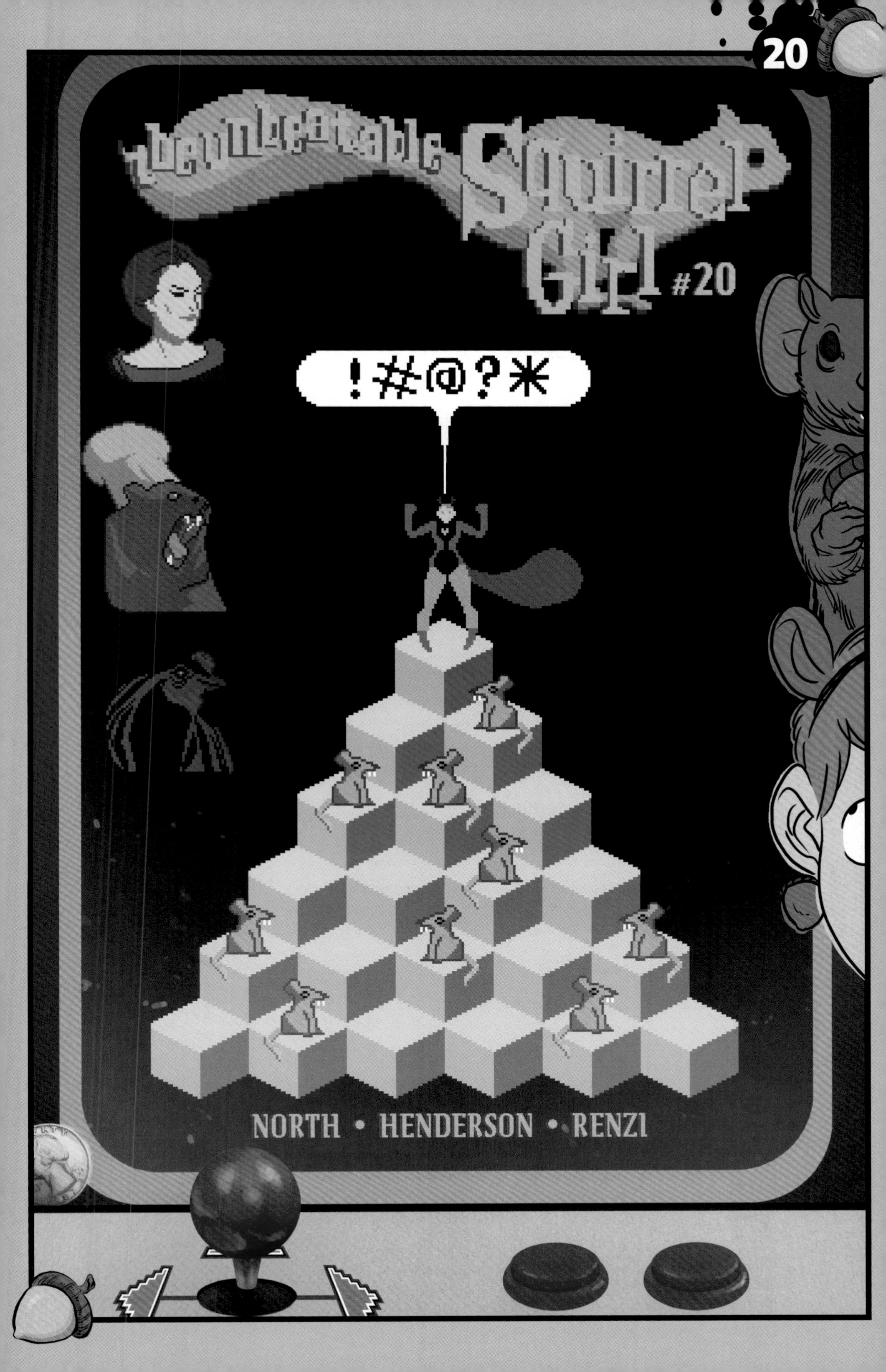
20
The Unbeatable Squirrel Girl #20
!#@?*
NORTH • HENDERSON • RENZI

Doreen Green isn't just a second-year computer science student: she secretly also has all the powers of both squirrel and girl! She uses her amazing abilities to fight crime ***and*** *be as awesome as possible. You know her as...* ***The Unbeatable Squirrel Girl!*** *Find out what she's been up to, with...*

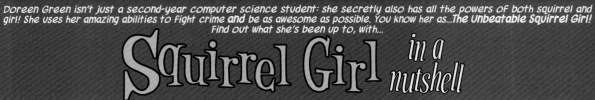

Squirrel Girl in a nutshell

Squirrel Girl @unbeatablesg
MELISSA MORBECK CALL-OUT POST

Squirrel Girl @unbeatablesg
She publicly acts like she's this kind tech billionaire lady with awesome teas, but it's not true! SHE'S AMASSING AN ANIMAL ARMY!!

Squirrel Girl @unbeatablesg
She controls them through microchips in their brains! It's gross! She made cockroaches put a shrunken computer in her EAR!!

Squirrel Girl @unbeatablesg
(Fun fact: when I got up this morning, I did not want to see cockroaches put a shrunken ANYTHING in ANYONE'S ear, but here we are)

Squirrel Girl @unbeatablesg
Anyway, that banner pulled by birds that says Doctor Doom is behind this? Don't believe it! It's her! IT'S ALWAYS HER.

Squirrel Girl @unbeatablesg
SHE'S the one who makes animals act like jerks! She's the one threatening the city with disease-carrying mosquitoes!!

Mosquito Man @skeetyman
Well met, @unbeatablesg! Sounds like you need the pest-repelling power... of MOSQUITO MAN!

Squirrel Girl @unbeatablesg
@skeetyman wait, for real?

Squirrel Girl @unbeatablesg
@skeetyman Okay this is awesome, I am always happy to meet another hero!

Squirrel Girl @unbeatablesg
@skeetyman Mosquito Man, I too fight for justice. If you can break the mosquitoes from Melissa's control, WE CAN SAVE THE DAY.

Squirrel Girl @unbeatablesg
@skeetyman Follow me so I can DM coordinates to meet up!

Mosquito Man @skeetyman
@unbeatablesg Our coordinates are your local Mosquito Man retailer! Say "bye" to bugs with over FOUR power-packed citronella scents!

Squirrel Girl @unbeatablesg
@skeetyman oh my god i thought you were a super hero but you're a brand of bugspray

Squirrel Girl @unbeatablesg
@skeetyman i can't believe we're in the middle of a city-wide crisis and you're selling bugspray and citronella candles on social media

Squirrel Girl @unbeatablesg
@skeetyman look up "disappointment" on Wikipedia and the entire article is just a screengrab of this convo

Mosquito Man @skeetyman
@unbeatablesg Don't forget to tell your followers we're the Bugspray That Bites Back™ for 10% off your next purchase!

Squirrel Girl @unbeatablesg
@skeetyman NO

Squirrel Girl @unbeatablesg
@skeetyman i will NOT

Tippy-Toe @yoitstippytoe
@unbeatablesg chtt cchttk ktttc

Squirrel Girl @unbeatablesg
@yoitstippytoe true enough Tippy, I should get back to saving the day instead of sassing #brands online

Tippy-Toe @yoitstippytoe
@unbeatablesg churrkt chrtt

Squirrel Girl @unbeatablesg
@yoitstippytoe also yes, I should change into my super-hero outfit real quick

Tippy-Toe @yoitstippytoe
@unbeatablesg cktt chutt!

Squirrel Girl @unbeatablesg
@yoitstippytoe i've never used phone booths?? every restaurant ever has a bathroom i can duck into no problem??

Mosquito Man @skeetyman
@unbeatablesg @yoitstippytoe Speaking of restaurants, are you a restaurateur with a patio? Mosquito Man can help keep the bugs at bay!

Squirrel Girl @unbeatablesg
@skeetyman OH MY GOD HAS THIS EVER WORKED

search!

#tippyshaircareregimen

#doomsgiantthirstymouth

#alfredothechicken

#chefbear

#lilbusta

#jjj

The DEADLIEST Animal in the World

What is the most dangerous game? (In the "animal" sense, not in the "board game" sense, though I believe the most dangerous board game is Jenga because it could fall on you?) Is it snakes? Sharks? Humans themselves? Hah hah no, it's none of those--it's **MOSQUITOES**. Check it out:

APPROX NUMBER OF HUMANS KILLED BY ANIMALS PER YEAR:

(according to the World Health Organization, who would know this sort of thing)

	SHARKS
10	WOLVES
10	LIONS
100	ELEPHANTS
100	HIPPOS
500	CROCS
1,000	FRESHWATER SNAILS
10,000	RABID DOGS
25,000	SNAKES
50,000	
475,000	HUMAN-ON-HUMAN VIOLENCE, HEY, HUMANS, MAYBE CALM DOWN A BIT
	MOSQUITOES
725,000	

So yeah, mosquitoes can carry disease, and they're on every continent except Antarctica, so if you find yourself surrounded by unfamiliar mosquitoes, maybe don't offer up some bare arms to these flying blood parasites right away, huh??

Well, Melissa wasn't lying. Mosquitoes really *are* the most dangerous animal on the planet.

Great. Just great.

Snails: *Surprisingly* high up on that list, yeah? Turns out it's not the snails themselves that are a threat (*phew*), but parasites they carry that can mess with humans too. Nice try, snails! You want everyone to think you're tough but now we all know you're just surprisingly unwell!!

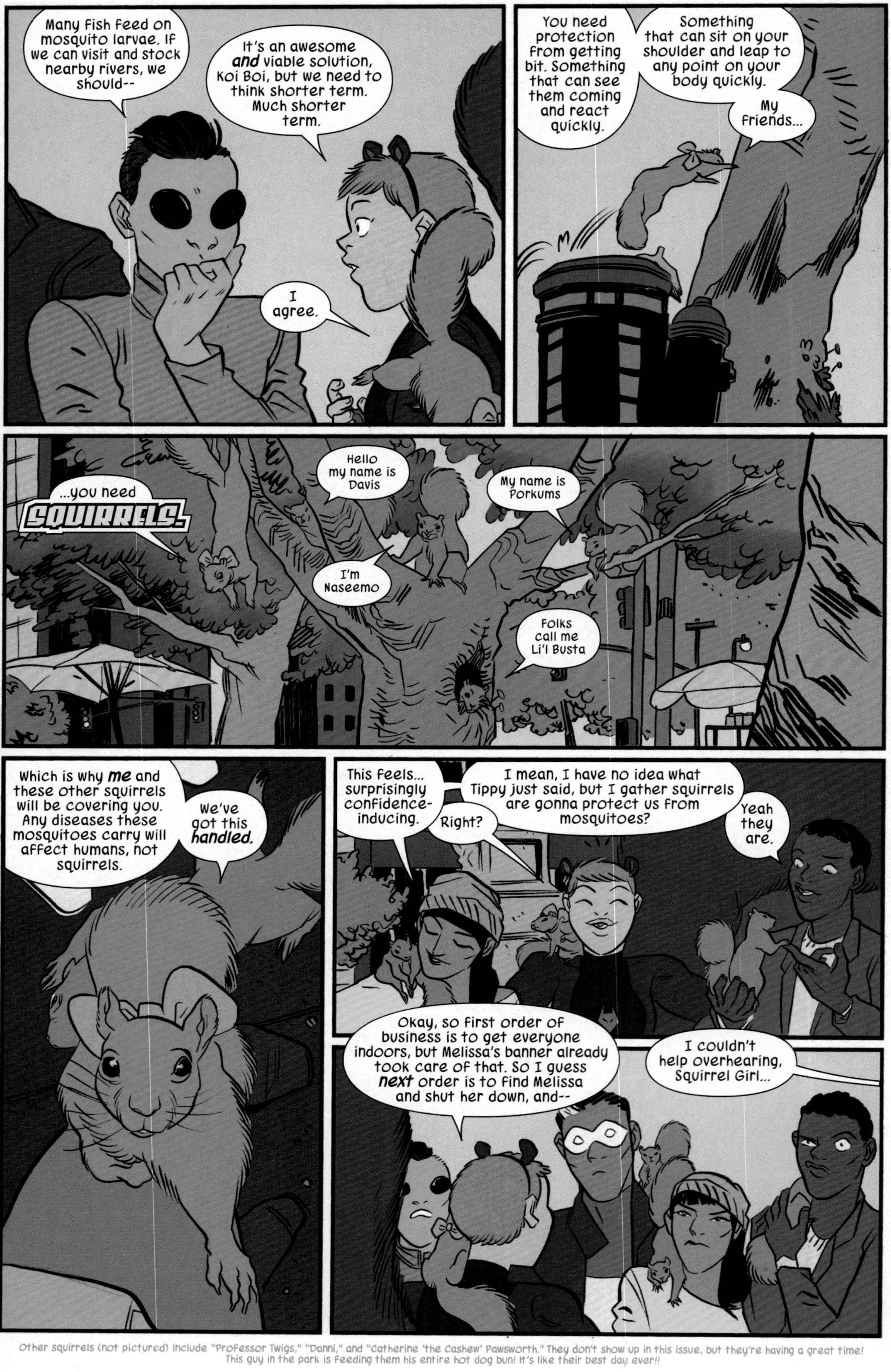
Many fish feed on mosquito larvae. If we can visit and stock nearby rivers, we should--
It's an awesome *and* viable solution, Koi Boi, but we need to think shorter term. Much shorter term.
I agree.
You need protection from getting bit. Something that can see them coming and react quickly.
Something that can sit on your shoulder and leap to any point on your body quickly.
My friends...
...you need
SQUIRRELS.
Hello my name is Davis
My name is Porkums
I'm Naseemo
Folks call me Li'l Busta
Which is why *me* and these other squirrels will be covering you. Any diseases these mosquitoes carry will affect humans, not squirrels.
We've got this *handled.*
This feels... surprisingly confidence-inducing.
I mean, I have no idea what Tippy just said, but I gather squirrels are gonna protect us from mosquitoes?
Right?
Yeah they are.
Okay, so first order of business is to get everyone indoors, but Melissa's banner already took care of that. So I guess *next* order is to find Melissa and shut her down, and--
I couldn't help overhearing, Squirrel Girl...

Other squirrels (not pictured) include "Professor Twigs," "Danni," and "Catherine 'the Cashew' Pawsworth." They don't show up in this issue, but they're having a great time! This guy in the park is feeding them his entire hot dog bun! It's like their best day ever!!

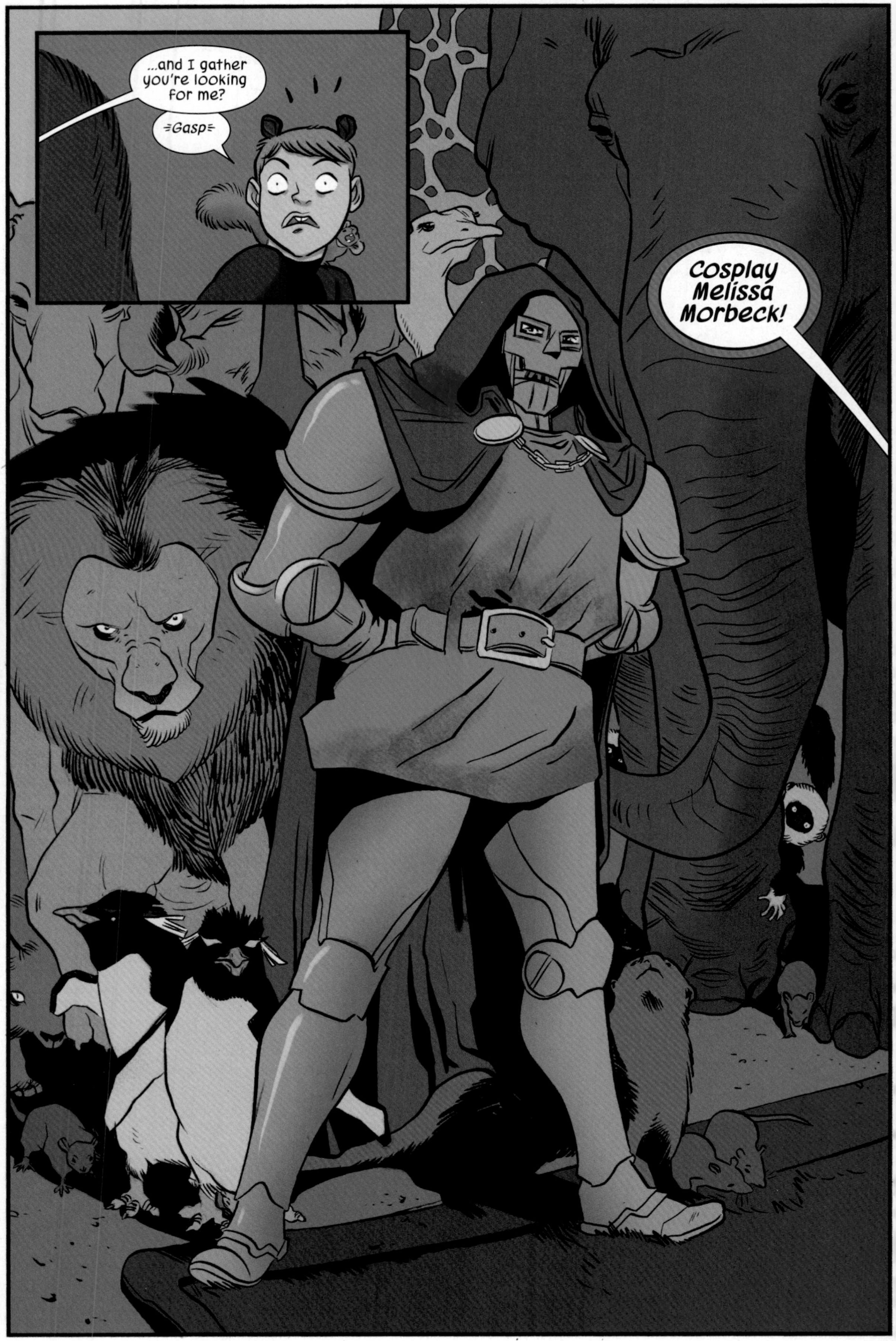
...and I gather you're looking for me?
=Gasp=
Cosplay Melissa Morbeck!

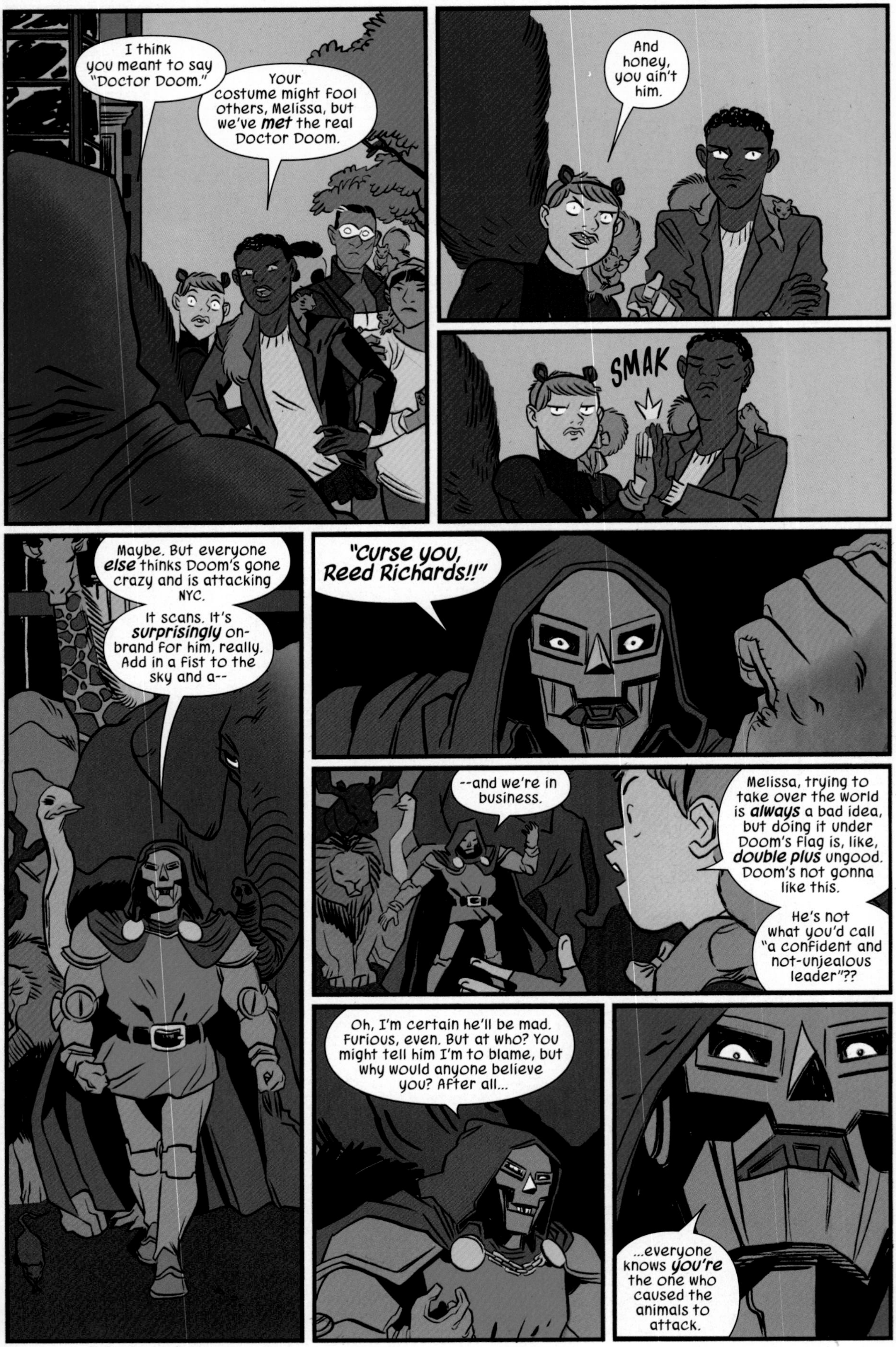

I think you meant to say "Doctor Doom."
Your costume might fool others, Melissa, but we've **met** the real Doctor Doom.
And honey, you ain't him.
SMAK
Maybe. But everyone **else** thinks Doom's gone crazy and is attacking NYC.
It scans. It's **surprisingly** on-brand for him, really. Add in a fist to the sky and a--
"Curse you, Reed Richards!!"
--and we're in business.
Melissa, trying to take over the world is **always** a bad idea, but doing it under Doom's flag is, like, **double plus** ungood. Doom's not gonna like this.
He's not what you'd call "a confident and not-unjealous leader"??
Oh, I'm certain he'll be mad. Furious, even. But at who? You might tell him I'm to blame, but why would anyone believe you? After all...
...everyone knows **you're** the one who caused the animals to attack.

Doom is not what you'd call "a confident, not-unjealous, calm, just, and non-egotistical leader who is open to compromise," but he ***is*** what you'd call "a leader who will ***definitely*** invest in public work projects, so long as they all involve attaching giant versions of his head to every national landmark."

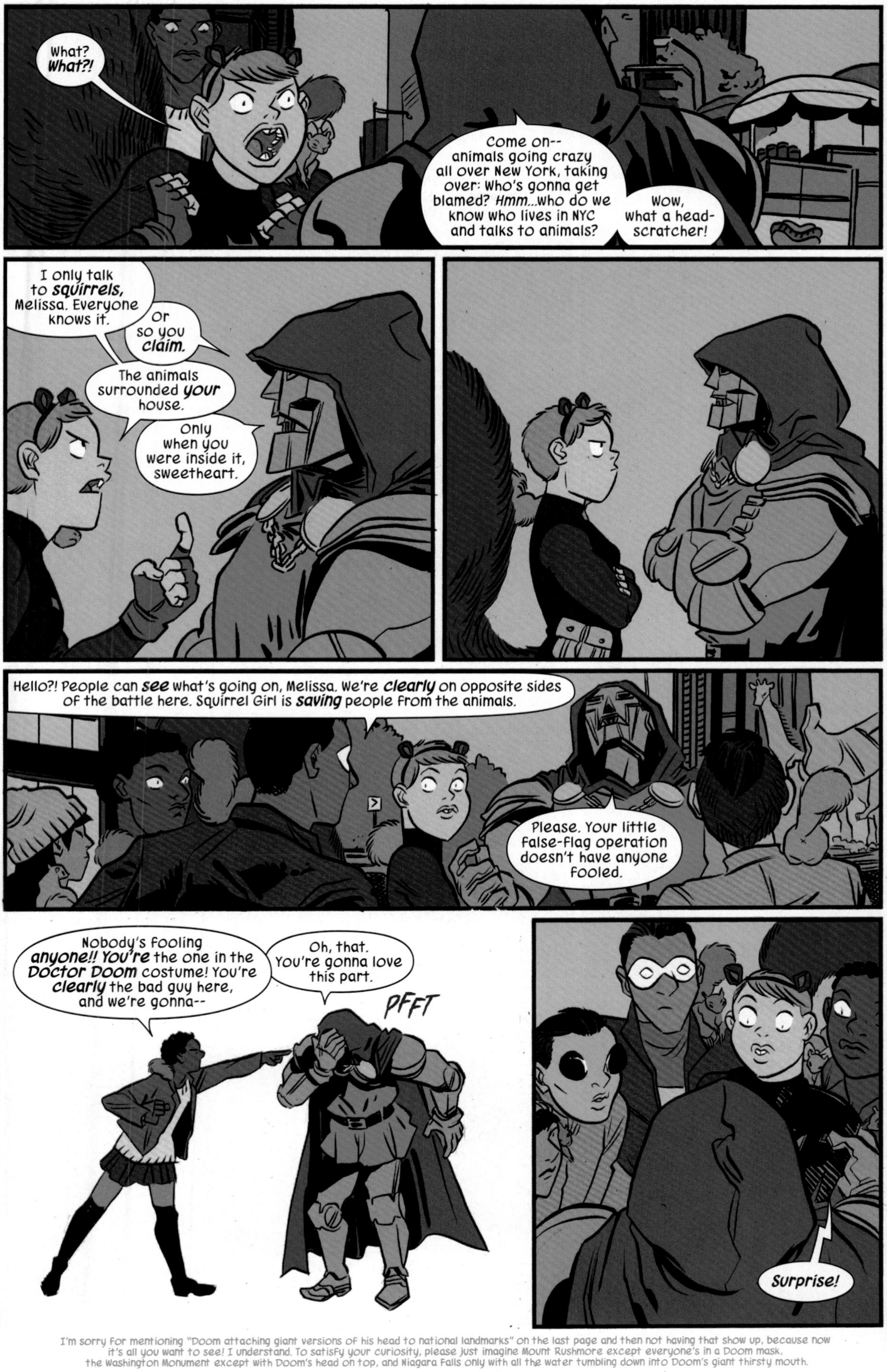
What? What?!
Come on-- animals going crazy all over New York, taking over: Who's gonna get blamed? Hmm...who do we know who lives in NYC and talks to animals?
Wow, what a head-scratcher!
I only talk to squirrels, Melissa. Everyone knows it.
Or so you claim.
The animals surrounded your house.
Only when you were inside it, sweetheart.
Hello?! People can see what's going on, Melissa. We're clearly on opposite sides of the battle here. Squirrel Girl is saving people from the animals.
Please. Your little false-flag operation doesn't have anyone fooled.
Nobody's fooling anyone!! You're the one in the Doctor Doom costume! You're clearly the bad guy here, and we're gonna--
Oh, that. You're gonna love this part.
PFFT
Surprise!

I'm sorry for mentioning "Doom attaching giant versions of his head to national landmarks" on the last page and then not having that show up, because now it's all you want to see! I understand. To satisfy your curiosity, please just imagine Mount Rushmore except everyone's in a Doom mask, the Washington Monument except with Doom's head on top, and Niagara Falls only with all the water tumbling down into Doom's giant thirsty mouth.

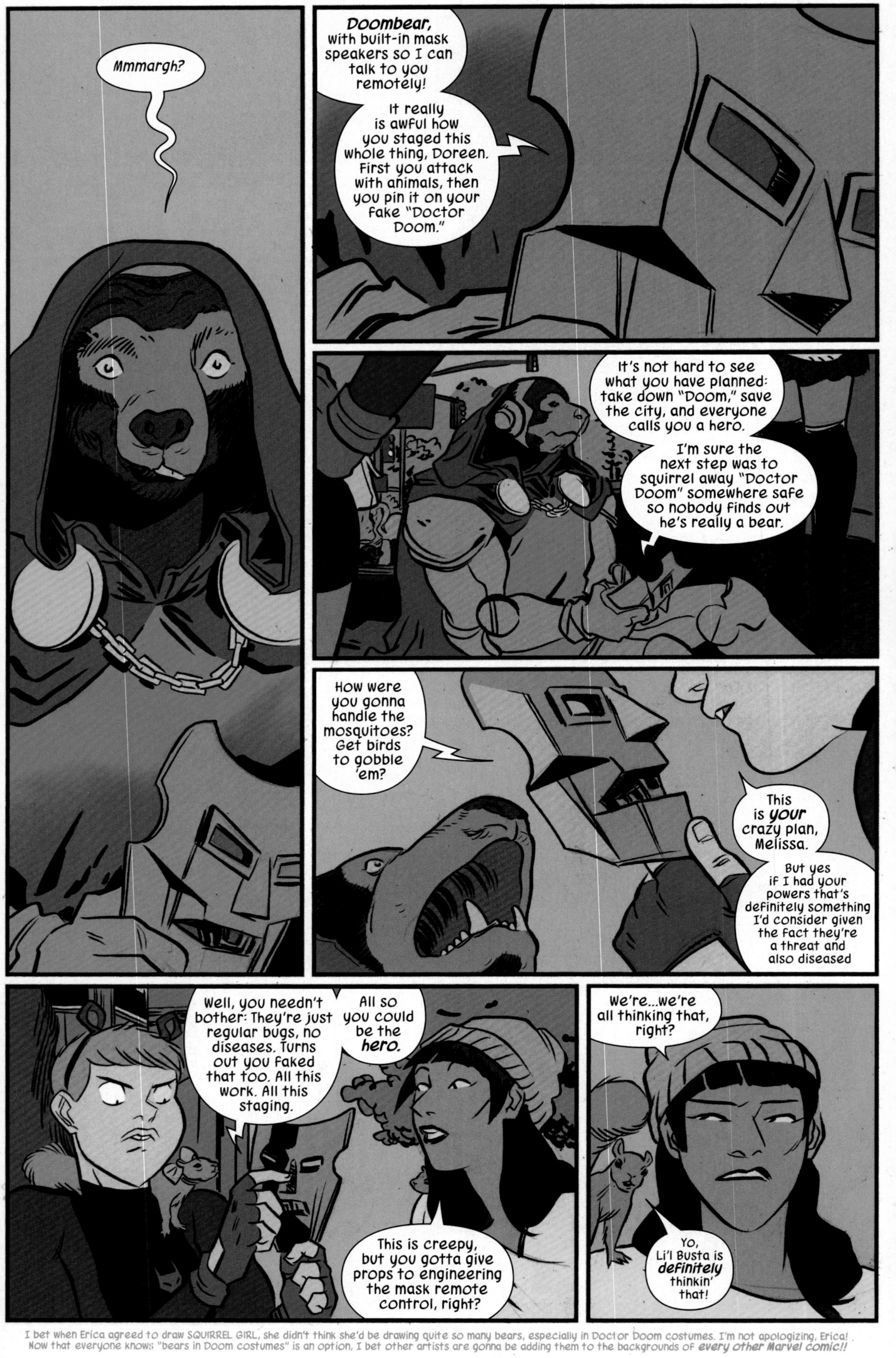
Mmmargh?
Doombear, with built-in mask speakers so I can talk to you remotely!
It really is awful how you staged this whole thing, Doreen. First you attack with animals, then you pin it on your fake "Doctor Doom."
It's not hard to see what you have planned: take down "Doom," save the city, and everyone calls you a hero.
I'm sure the next step was to squirrel away "Doctor Doom" somewhere safe so nobody finds out he's really a bear.
How were you gonna handle the mosquitoes? Get birds to gobble 'em?
This is *your* crazy plan, Melissa.
But yes if I had your powers that's definitely something I'd consider given the fact they're a threat and also diseased
Well, you needn't bother: They're just regular bugs, no diseases. Turns out you faked that too. All this work. All this staging.
All so you could be the *hero.*
This is creepy, but you gotta give props to engineering the mask remote control, right?
We're...we're all thinking that, right?
Yo, Li'l Busta is *definitely* thinkin' that!

I bet when Erica agreed to draw SQUIRREL GIRL, she didn't think she'd be drawing quite so many bears, especially in Doctor Doom costumes. I'm not apologizing, Erica! Now that everyone knows "bears in Doom costumes" is an option, I bet other artists are gonna be adding them to the backgrounds of ***every other Marvel comic!!***

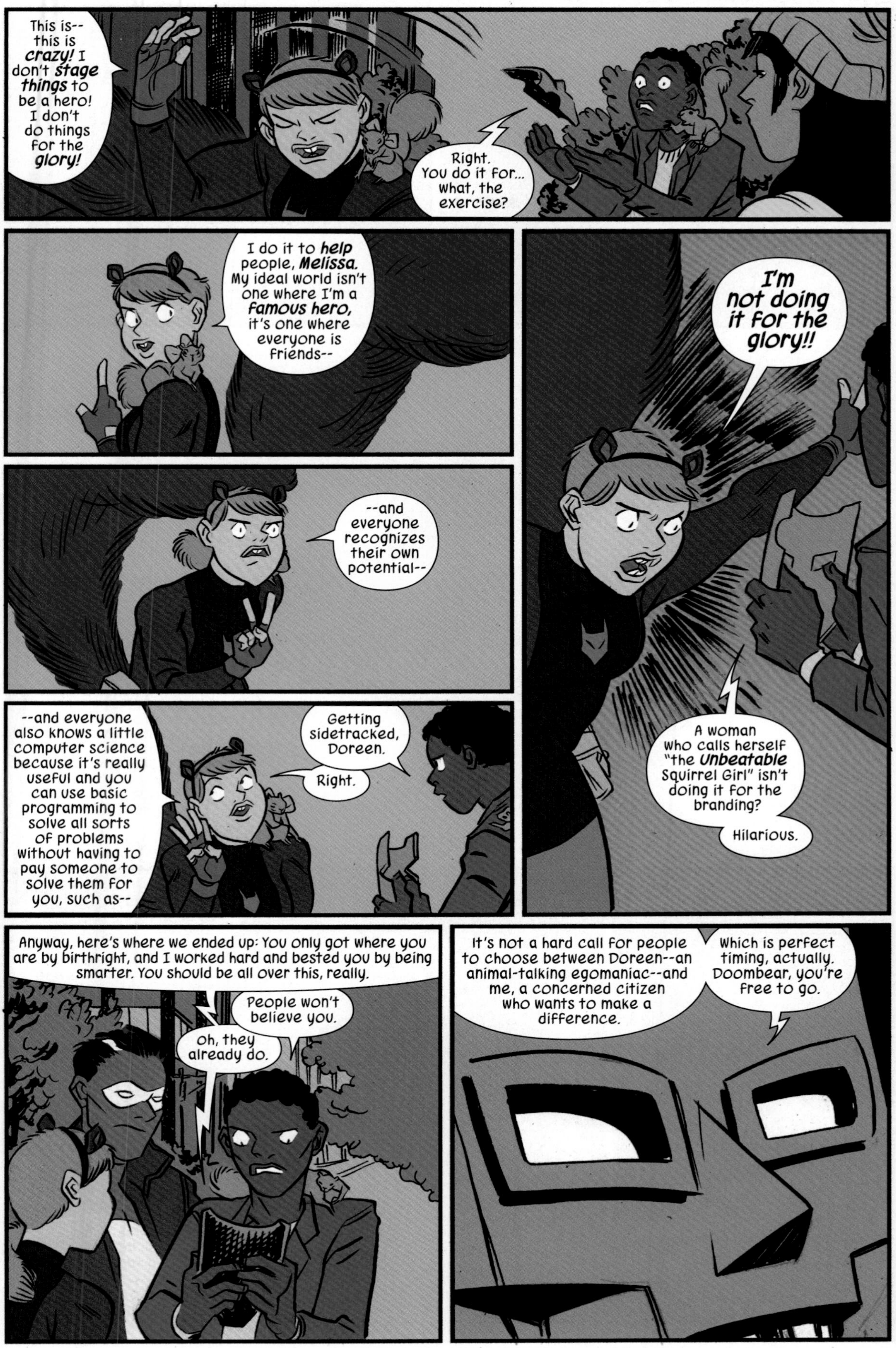
This is-- this is crazy! I don't stage things to be a hero! I don't do things for the glory!
Right. You do it for... what, the exercise?
I do it to help people, Melissa. My ideal world isn't one where I'm a famous hero, it's one where everyone is friends--
--and everyone recognizes their own potential--
--and everyone also knows a little computer science because it's really useful and you can use basic programming to solve all sorts of problems without having to pay someone to solve them for you, such as--
Getting sidetracked, Doreen.
Right.
I'm not doing it for the glory!!
A woman who calls herself "the Unbeatable Squirrel Girl" isn't doing it for the branding?
Hilarious.
Anyway, here's where we ended up: You only got where you are by birthright, and I worked hard and bested you by being smarter. You should be all over this, really.
People won't believe you.
Oh, they already do.
It's not a hard call for people to choose between Doreen--an animal-talking egomaniac--and me, a concerned citizen who wants to make a difference.
Which is perfect timing, actually. Doombear, you're free to go.

It's actually really lucky for Doombear that he found work that ties in to both his name *and* his interests so perfectly.

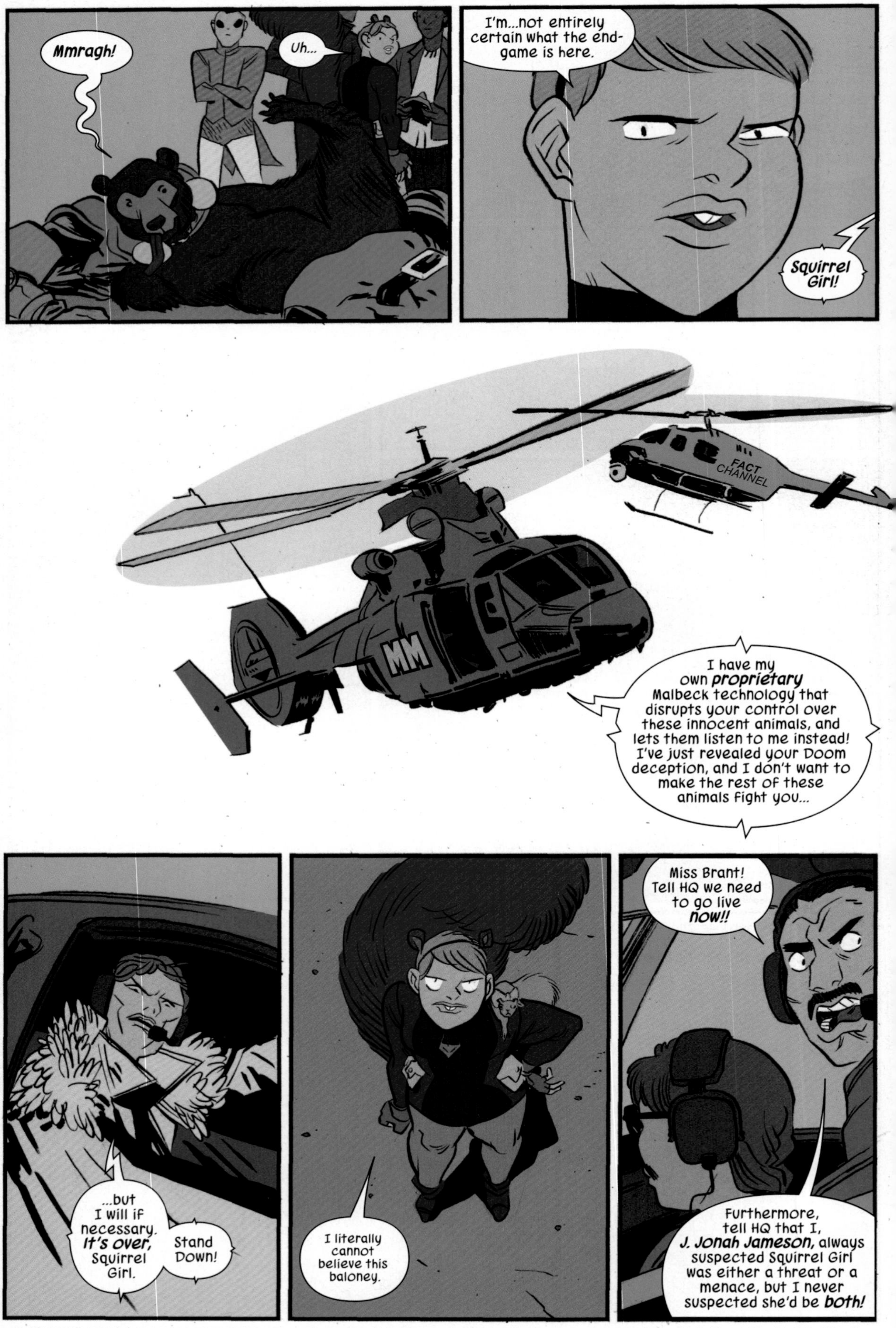
Mmragh!
Uh...
I'm...not entirely certain what the end-game is here.
Squirrel Girl!
I have my own **proprietary** Malbeck technology that disrupts your control over these innocent animals, and lets them listen to me instead! I've just revealed your Doom deception, and I don't want to make the rest of these animals fight you...
FACT CHANNEL
MM
...but I will if necessary. ***It's over,*** Squirrel Girl.
Stand Down!
I literally cannot believe this baloney.
Miss Brant! Tell HQ we need to go live ***now!!***
Furthermore, tell HQ that I, ***J. Jonah Jameson,*** always suspected Squirrel Girl was either a threat or a menace, but I never suspected she'd be ***both!***

Miss Brant! It's very kind of you to begin working for me again even though I've never actually taken the time to learn your first name! Wait...it's not "Miss," is it? Is it "Miss"? I'm just gonna assume it's "Miss," Miss Brant!

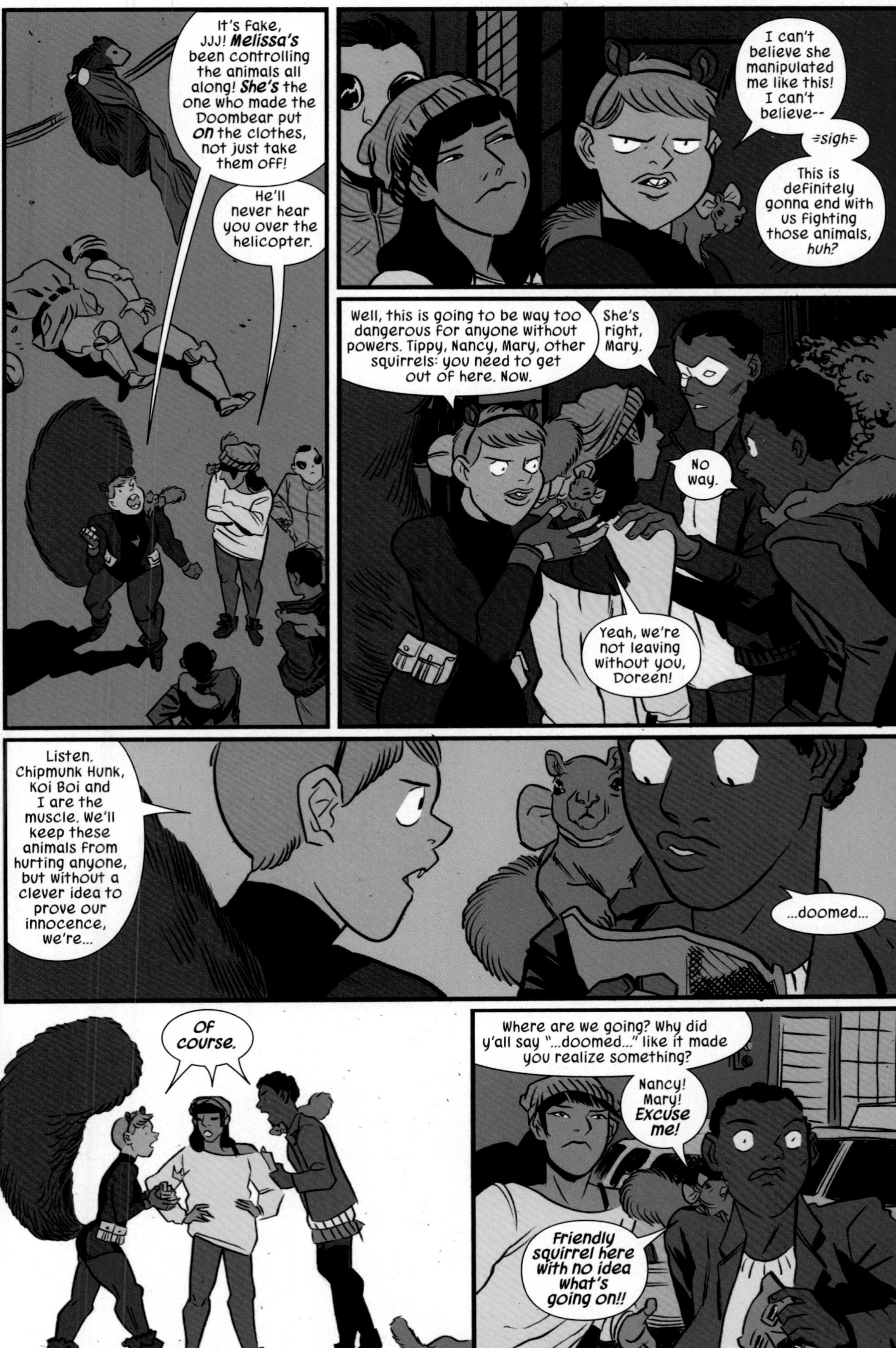
It's fake, JJJ! *Melissa's* been controlling the animals all along! *She's* the one who made the Doombear put *on* the clothes, not just take them off!
He'll never hear you over the helicopter.
I can't believe she manipulated me like this! I can't believe--
=sigh=
This is definitely gonna end with us fighting those animals, *huh?*
Well, this is going to be way too dangerous for anyone without powers. Tippy, Nancy, Mary, other squirrels: you need to get out of here. Now.
She's right, Mary.
No way.
Yeah, we're not leaving without you, Doreen!
Listen. Chipmunk Hunk, Koi Boi and I are the muscle. We'll keep these animals from hurting anyone, but without a clever idea to prove our innocence, we're...
...doomed...
Of course.
Where are we going? Why did y'all say "...doomed..." like it made you realize something?
Nancy! Mary! *Excuse me!*
Friendly squirrel here with no idea what's going on!!

Helicopters are extremely loud, especially for the people on them! We didn't add them here, but just imagine large ***"whump whump whump," "bzzzrrrrrtttt,"*** and ***"[HOLY SMOKES, EVEN MORE LOUD HELICOPTER NOISES??]"*** sound effects drawn all over the appropriate panels.

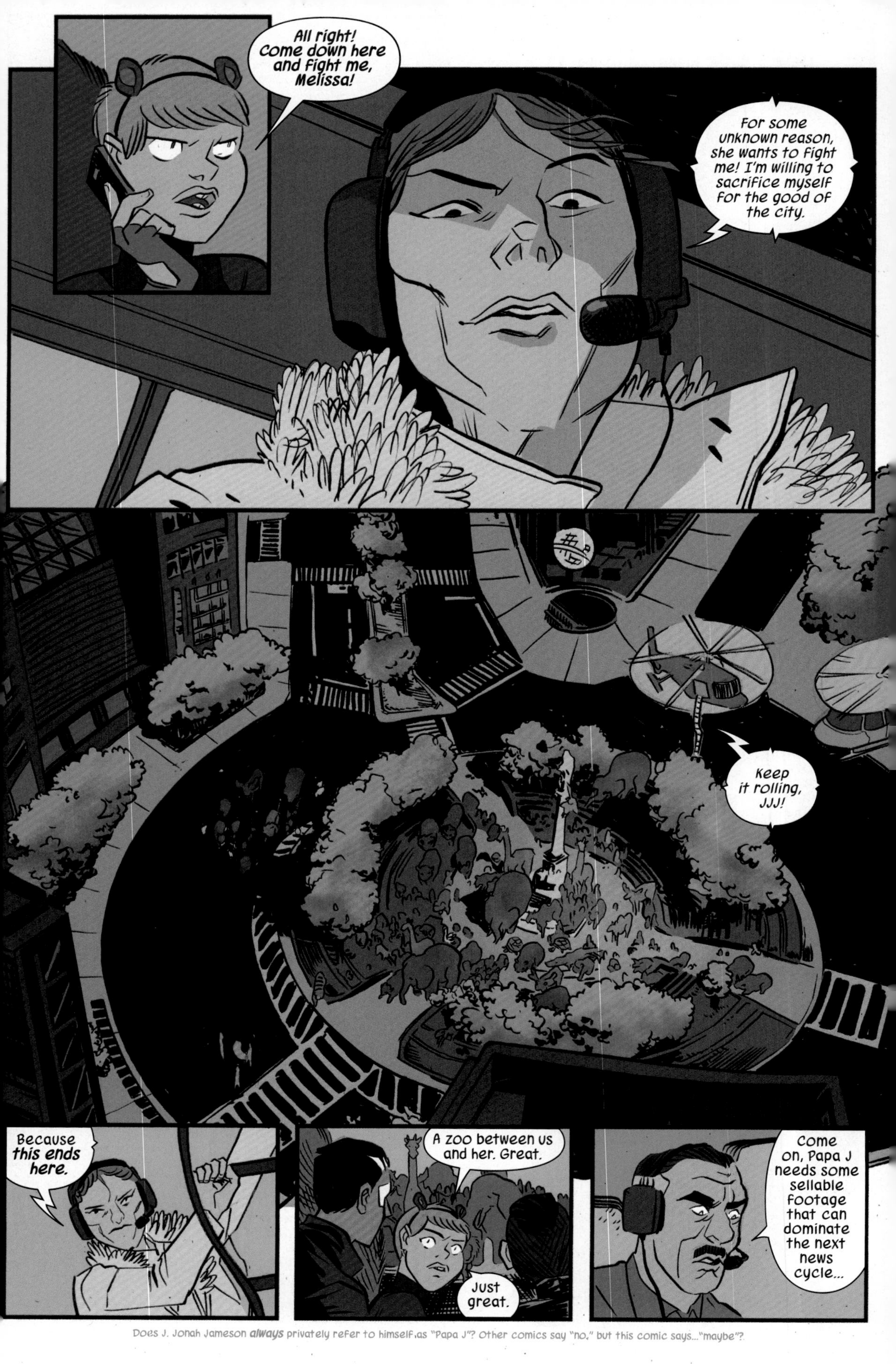
All right! Come down here and fight me, Melissa!
For some unknown reason, she wants to fight me! I'm willing to sacrifice myself for the good of the city.
Keep it rolling, JJJ!
Because this ends here.
A zoo between us and her. Great.
Just great.
Come on, Papa J needs some sellable footage that can dominate the next news cycle...

Does J. Jonah Jameson ***always*** privately refer to himself as "Papa J"? Other comics say "no," but this comic says..."maybe"?

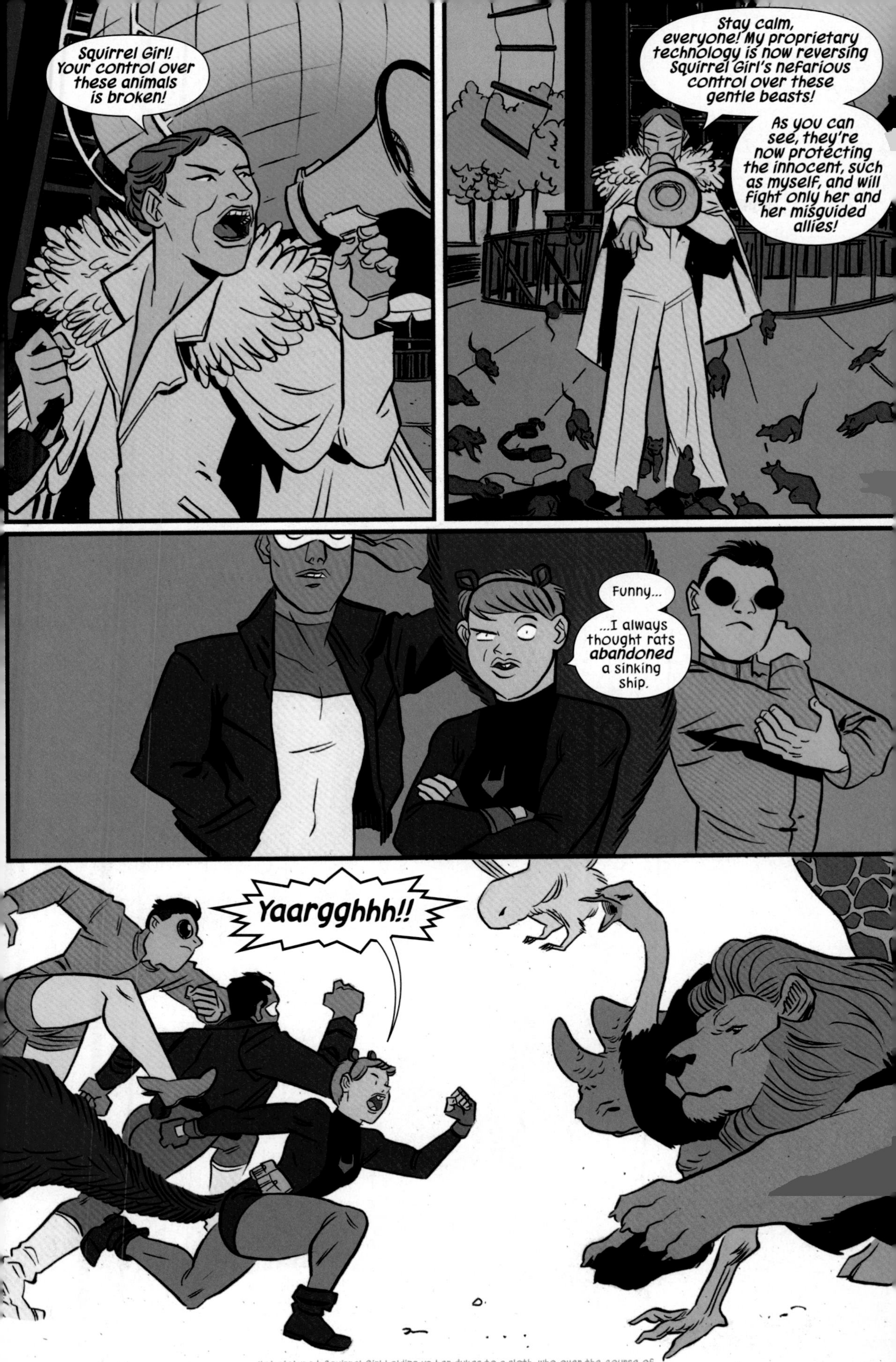
Squirrel Girl! Your control over these animals is broken!
Stay calm, everyone! My proprietary technology is now reversing Squirrel Girl's nefarious control over these gentle beasts!
As you can see, they're now protecting the innocent, such as myself, and will fight only her and her misguided allies!
Funny...
...I always thought rats *abandoned* a sinking ship.
Yaargghhh!!

Not pictured: Squirrel Girl holding up her dukes to a sloth, who over the course of a few panels very slowly extends a punch towards her, and when he finally finishes, the entire fight scene is over and Squirrel Girl says, "Okay nevermind we're good here."

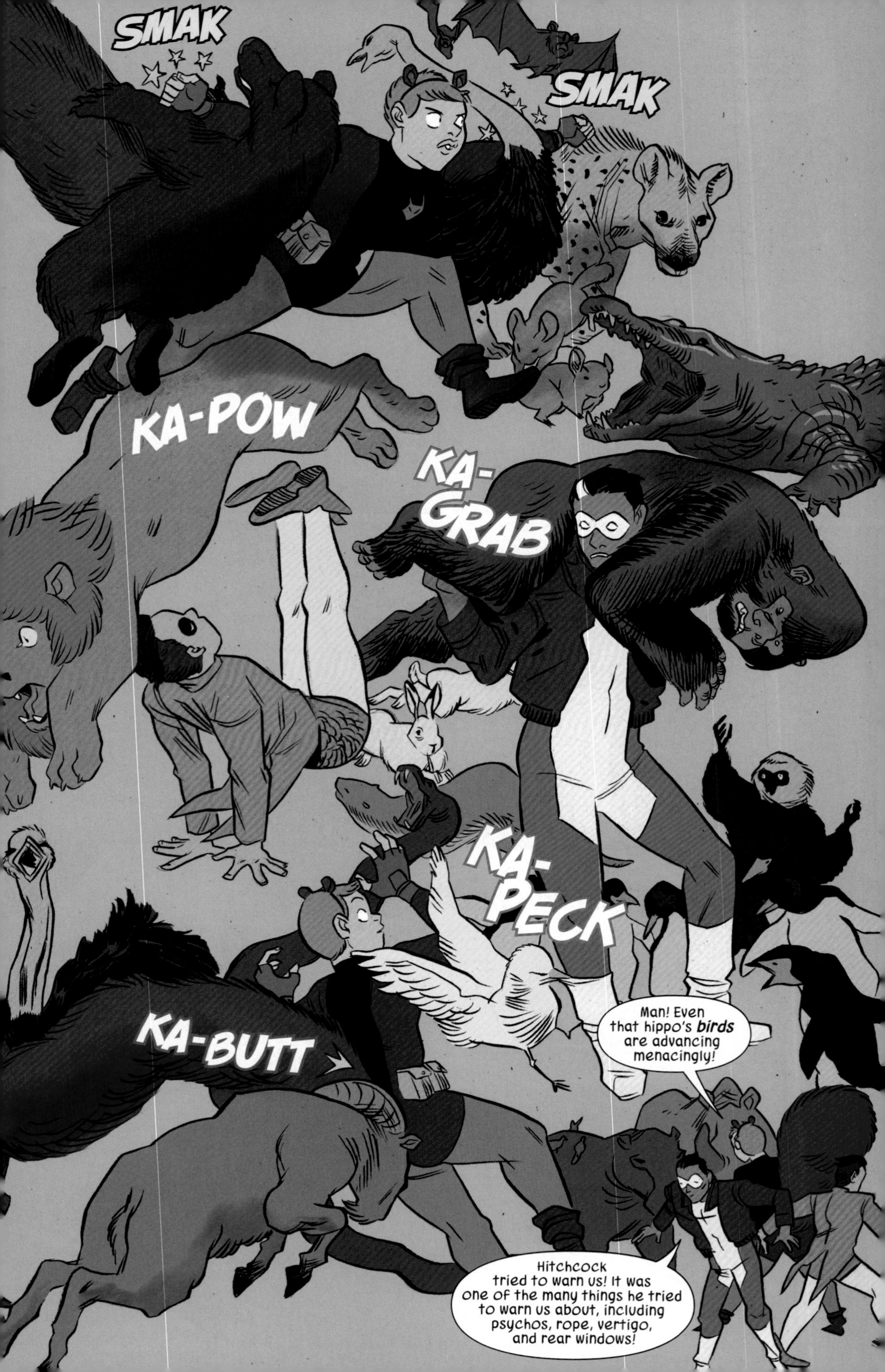
SMAK
SMAK
KA-POW
KA-GRAB
KA-PECK
KA-BUTT
Man! Even that hippo's *birds* are advancing menacingly!
Hitchcock tried to warn us! It was one of the many things he tried to warn us about, including psychos, rope, vertigo, and rear windows!

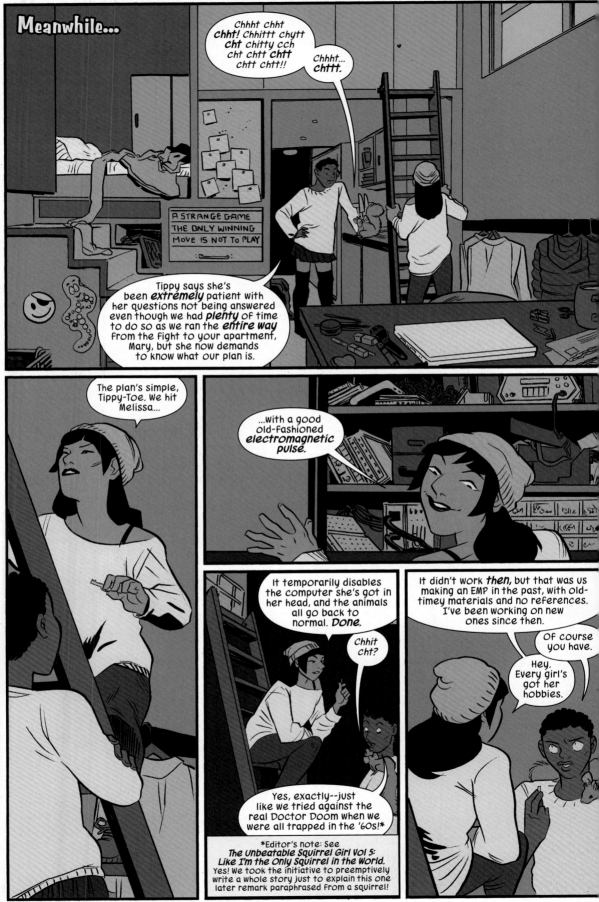

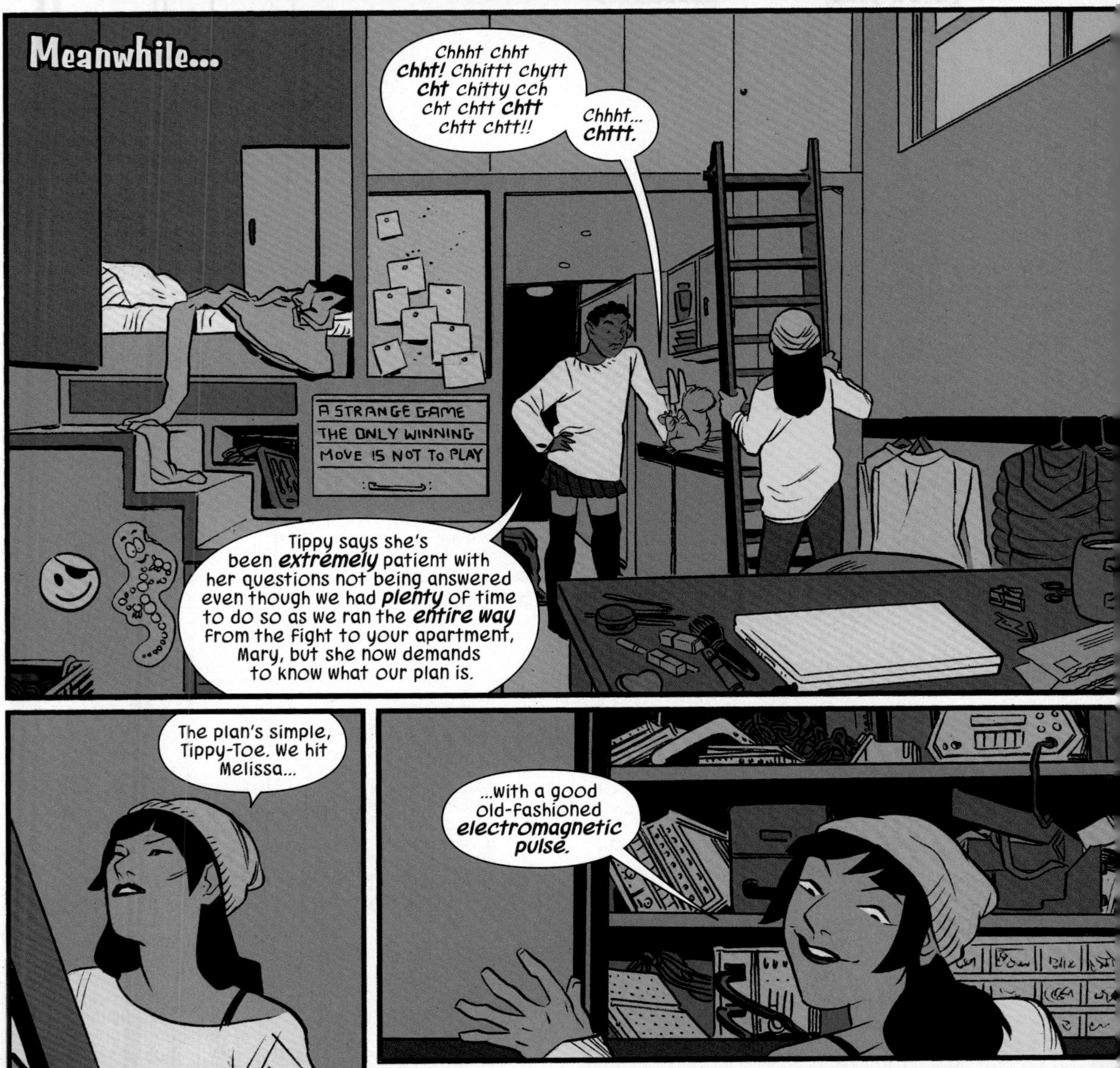
Meanwhile...
Chhht chht chht! Chhittt chytt cht chitty cch cht chtt chtt chtt chtt!!
Chhht... chttt.
A STRANGE GAME
THE ONLY WINNING
MOVE IS NOT TO PLAY
Tippy says she's been extremely patient with her questions not being answered even though we had plenty of time to do so as we ran the entire way from the fight to your apartment, Mary, but she now demands to know what our plan is.
The plan's simple, Tippy-Toe. We hit Melissa...
...with a good old-fashioned electromagnetic pulse.
It temporarily disables the computer she's got in her head, and the animals all go back to normal. Done.
Chhit cht?
Yes, exactly--just like we tried against the real Doctor Doom when we were all trapped in the '60s!*
*Editor's note: See The Unbeatable Squirrel Girl Vol 5: Like I'm the Only Squirrel in the World. Yes! We took the initiative to preemptively write a whole story just to explain this one later remark paraphrased from a squirrel!
It didn't work then, but that was us making an EMP in the past, with old-timey materials and no references. I've been working on new ones since then.
Hey. Every girl's got her hobbies.
Of course you have.

Doreen taught her friends how to talk to squirrels back in (our first) issue #8! It was a very kind thing to do, not just for Tippy, and not just for her friends, but also for me, the writer, so I don't have to spend 100% of the comic with Doreen saying, "What's that, Tippy? Nathan 'Cable' Summers fell down a well? *Again??*"

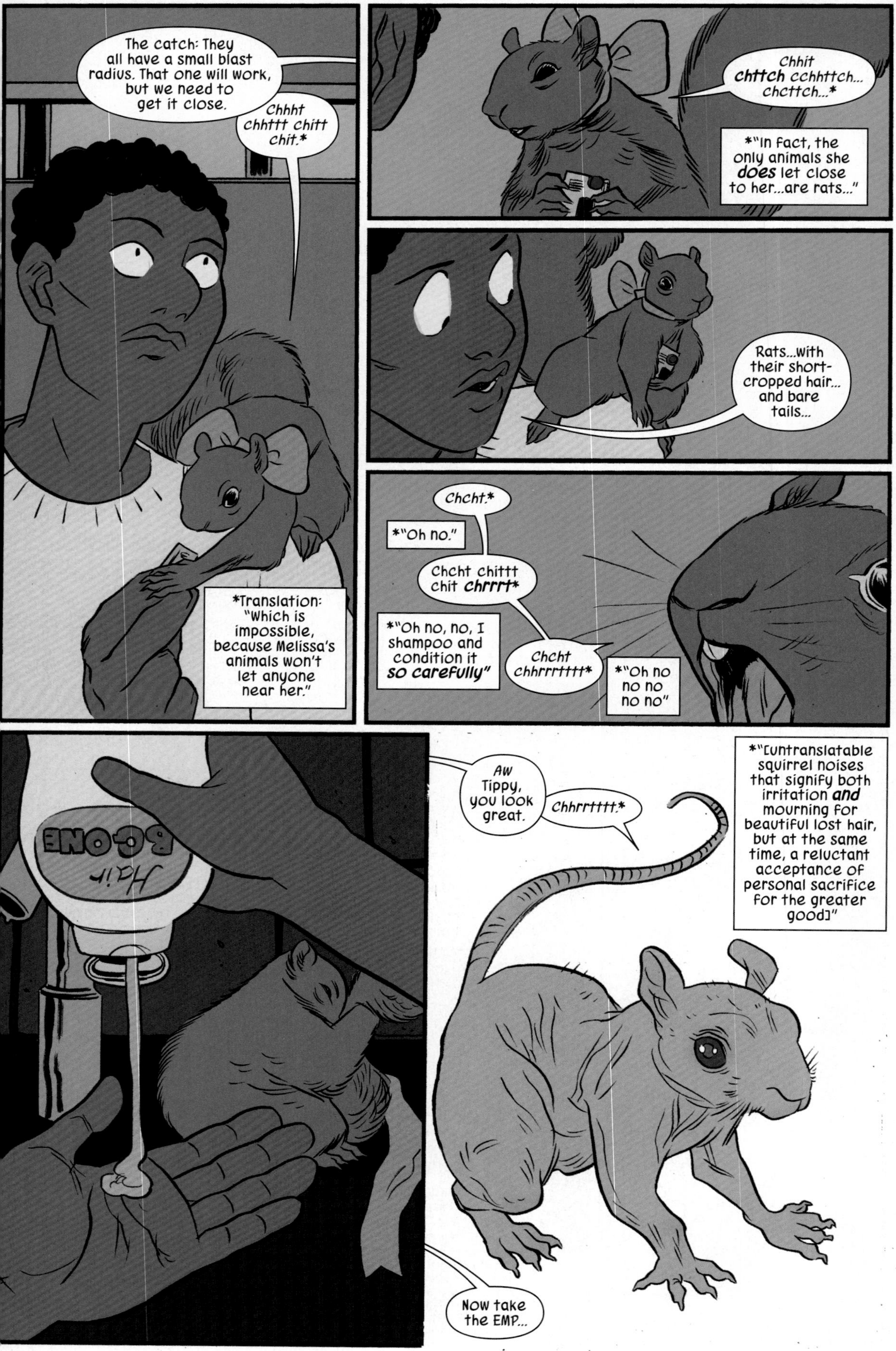
The catch: They all have a small blast radius. That one will work, but we need to get it close.
Chhht chhttt chitt chit.*
*Translation: "Which is impossible, because Melissa's animals won't let anyone near her."
Chhit chttch cchhttch... chcttch...*
*"In fact, the only animals she does let close to her...are rats..."
Rats...with their short-cropped hair... and bare tails...
Chcht.*
*"Oh no."
Chcht chittt chit chrrrt*
*"Oh no, no, I shampoo and condition it so carefully"
Chcht chhrrrtttt*
*"Oh no no no no no"
Hair B-GONE
Aw Tippy, you look great.
Chhrrtttt.*
*"[untranslatable squirrel noises that signify both irritation and mourning for beautiful lost hair, but at the same time, a reluctant acceptance of personal sacrifice for the greater good]"
Now take the EMP...

P.S., In case you're wondering, Nathan "Cable" Summers got out of that well. He's actually in a new well now. It's, *uh,* for unrelated reasons.

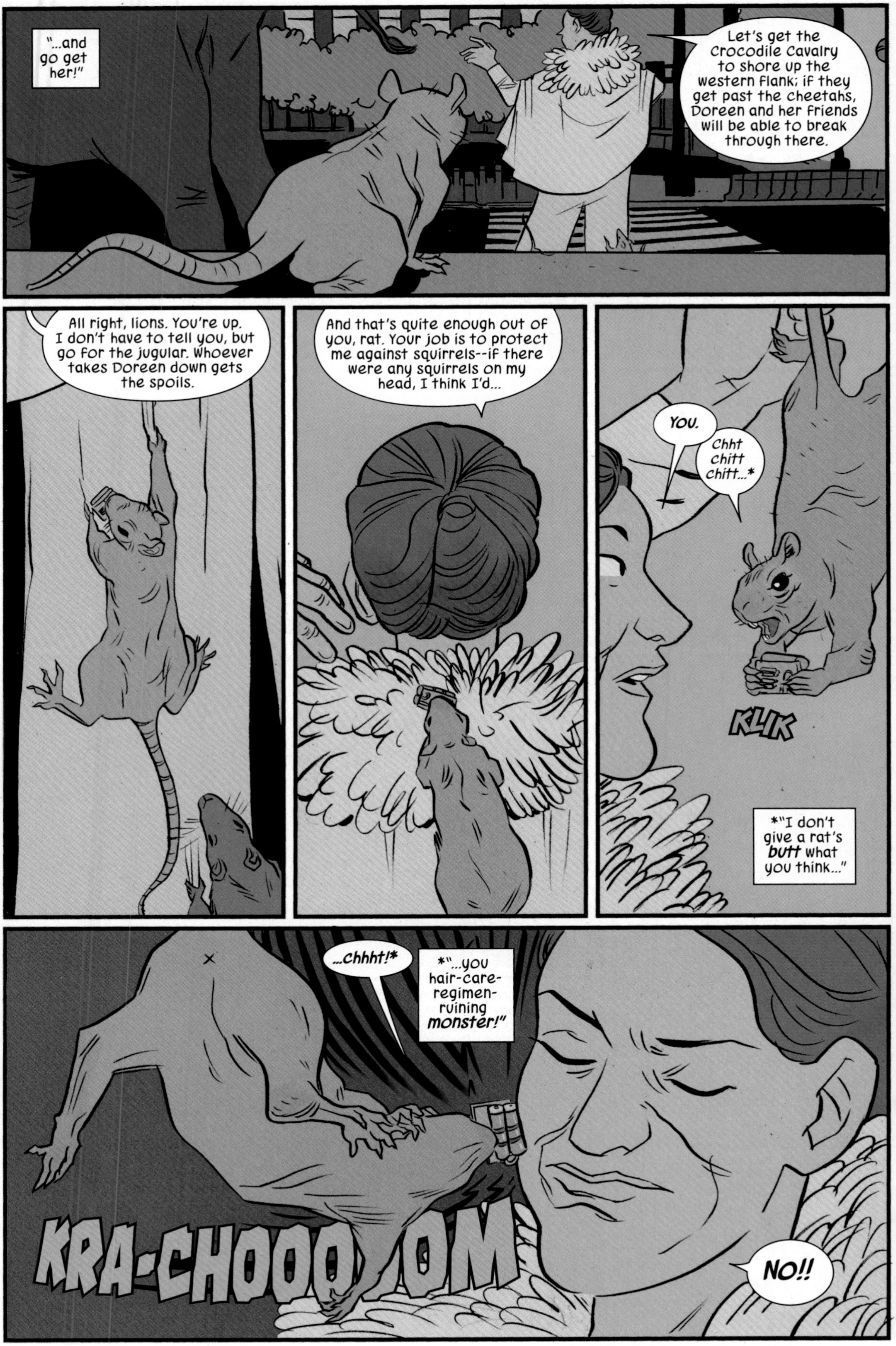
"...and go get her!"
Let's get the Crocodile Cavalry to shore up the western flank; if they get past the cheetahs, Doreen and her friends will be able to break through there.
All right, lions. You're up. I don't have to tell you, but go for the jugular. Whoever takes Doreen down gets the spoils.
And that's quite enough out of you, rat. Your job is to protect me against squirrels--if there were any squirrels on my head, I think I'd...
YOU.
Chht chitt chitt...*
KLIK
*"I don't give a rat's **butt** what you think..."
...chhht!*
*"...you hair-care-regimen-ruining **monster!**"
KRA-CHOOOOOM
NO!!

Normally EMPs are silent and invisible, but not in the Marvel Universe! The Marvel Universe is the world outside your window except for two changes: a) super powers, and b) visible EMP radiation that makes a *"kra-chooooom!"* sound in certain circumstances. Otherwise: *largely identical?*

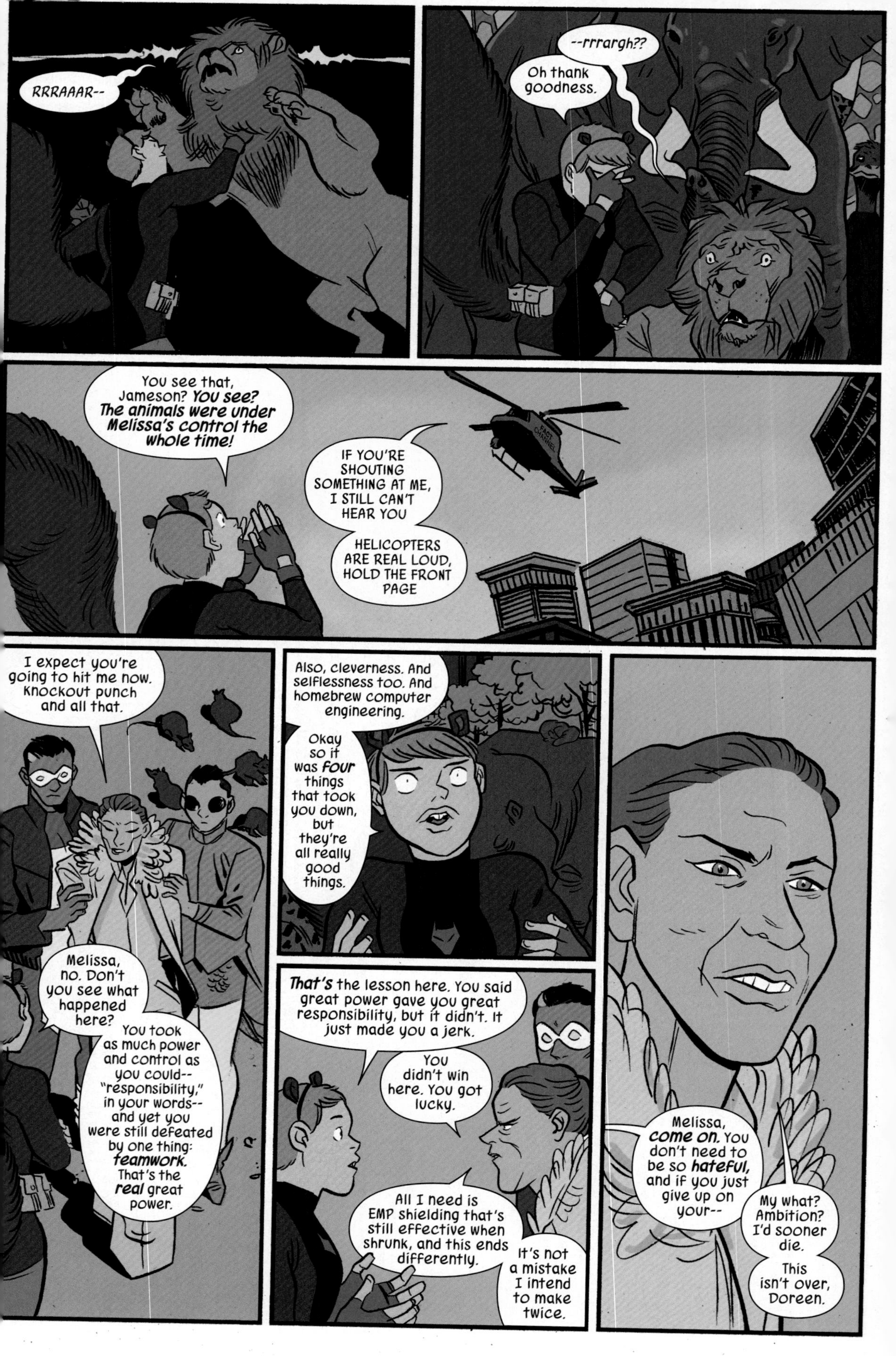
RRRAAAR--
--rrrargh??
Oh thank goodness.
You see that, Jameson? *You see? The animals were under Melissa's control the whole time!*
IF YOU'RE SHOUTING SOMETHING AT ME, I STILL CAN'T HEAR YOU
HELICOPTERS ARE REAL LOUD, HOLD THE FRONT PAGE
FACT CHANNEL
I expect you're going to hit me now. Knockout punch and all that.
Melissa, no. Don't you see what happened here?
You took as much power and control as you could-- "responsibility," in your words-- and yet you were still defeated by one thing: *teamwork.* That's the *real* great power.
Also, cleverness. And selflessness too. And homebrew computer engineering.
Okay so it was *four* things that took you down, but they're all really good things.
That's the lesson here. You said great power gave you great responsibility, but it didn't. It just made you a jerk.
You didn't win here. You got lucky.
All I need is EMP shielding that's still effective when shrunk, and this ends differently.
It's not a mistake I intend to make twice.
Melissa, *come on.* You don't need to be so *hateful,* and if you just give up on your--
My what? Ambition? I'd sooner die.
This isn't over, Doreen.

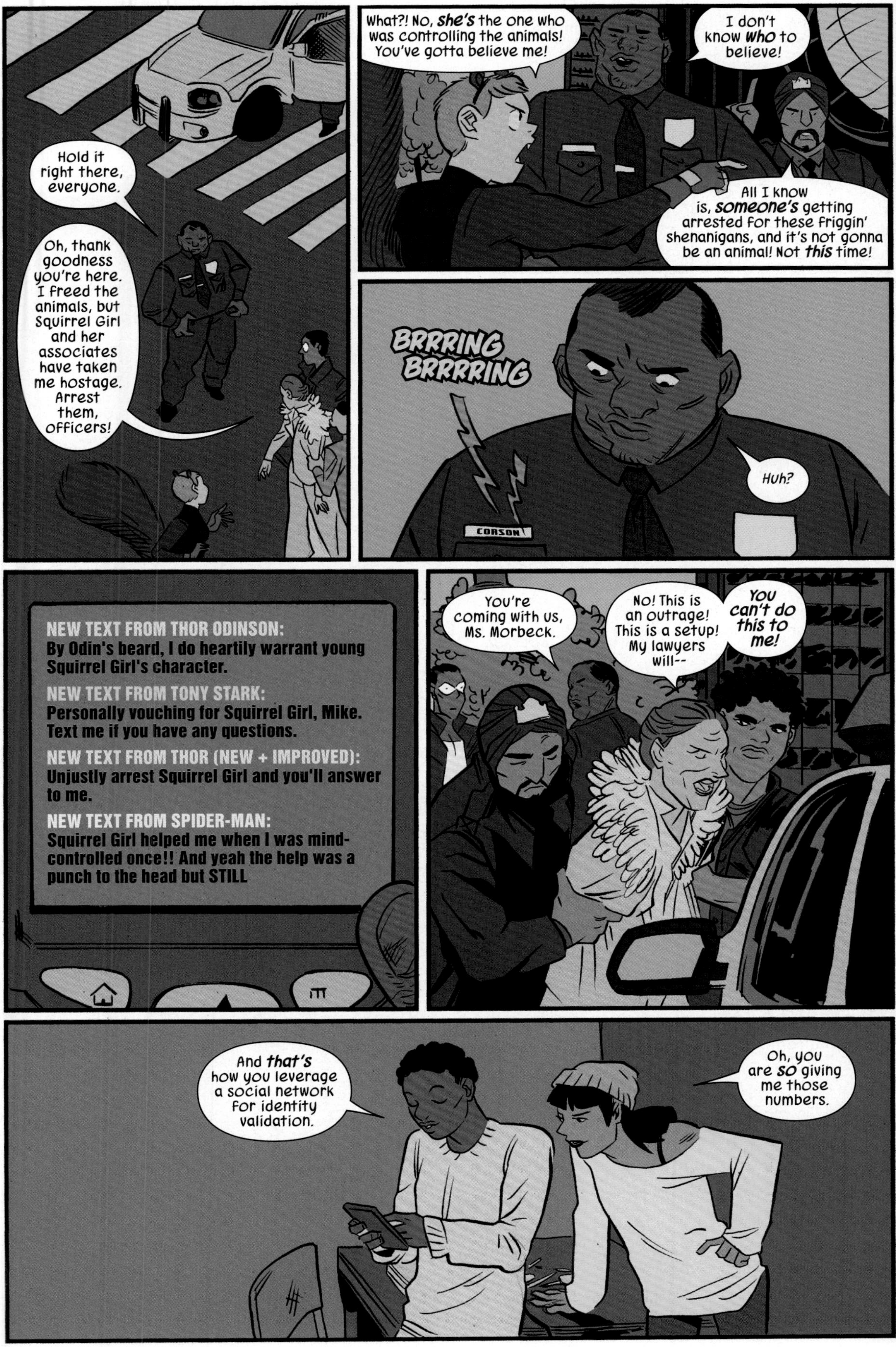
Hold it right there, everyone.
Oh, thank goodness you're here. I freed the animals, but Squirrel Girl and her associates have taken me hostage. Arrest them, officers!
What?! No, she's the one who was controlling the animals! You've gotta believe me!
I don't know who to believe!
All I know is, someone's getting arrested for these friggin' shenanigans, and it's not gonna be an animal! Not this time!
BRRRING BRRRRING
CORSON
Huh?
NEW TEXT FROM THOR ODINSON:
By Odin's beard, I do heartily warrant young Squirrel Girl's character.
NEW TEXT FROM TONY STARK:
Personally vouching for Squirrel Girl, Mike. Text me if you have any questions.
NEW TEXT FROM THOR (NEW + IMPROVED):
Unjustly arrest Squirrel Girl and you'll answer to me.
NEW TEXT FROM SPIDER-MAN:
Squirrel Girl helped me when I was mind-controlled once!! And yeah the help was a punch to the head but STILL
You're coming with us, Ms. Morbeck.
No! This is an outrage! This is a setup! My lawyers will--
You can't do this to me!
And that's how you leverage a social network for identity validation.
Oh, you are SO giving me those numbers.

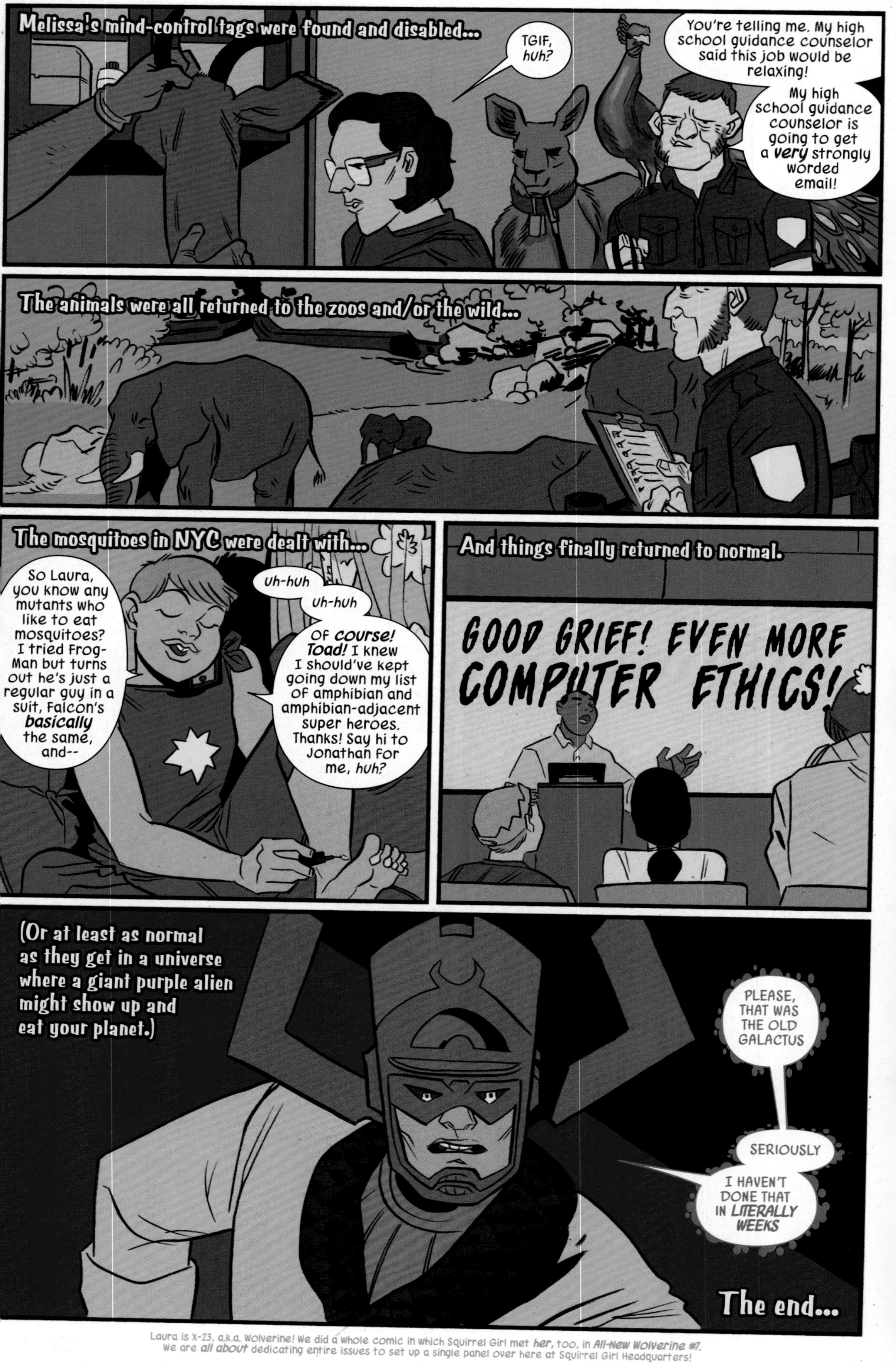
Melissa's mind-control tags were found and disabled...
TGIF, huh?
You're telling me. My high school guidance counselor said this job would be relaxing!
My high school guidance counselor is going to get a very strongly worded email!
The animals were all returned to the zoos and/or the wild...
The mosquitoes in NYC were dealt with...
So Laura, you know any mutants who like to eat mosquitoes? I tried Frog-Man but turns out he's just a regular guy in a suit, Falcon's basically the same, and--
Uh-huh
Uh-huh
Of course! Toad! I knew I should've kept going down my list of amphibian and amphibian-adjacent super heroes. Thanks! Say hi to Jonathan for me, huh?
And things finally returned to normal.
GOOD GRIEF! EVEN MORE COMPUTER ETHICS!
(Or at least as normal as they get in a universe where a giant purple alien might show up and eat your planet.)
PLEASE, THAT WAS THE OLD GALACTUS
SERIOUSLY
I HAVEN'T DONE THAT IN LITERALLY WEEKS
The end...

Laura is X-23, a.k.a. Wolverine! We did a whole comic in which Squirrel Girl met *her*, too, in *All-New Wolverine #7*. We are *all about* dedicating entire issues to set up a single panel over here at Squirrel Girl Headquarters!

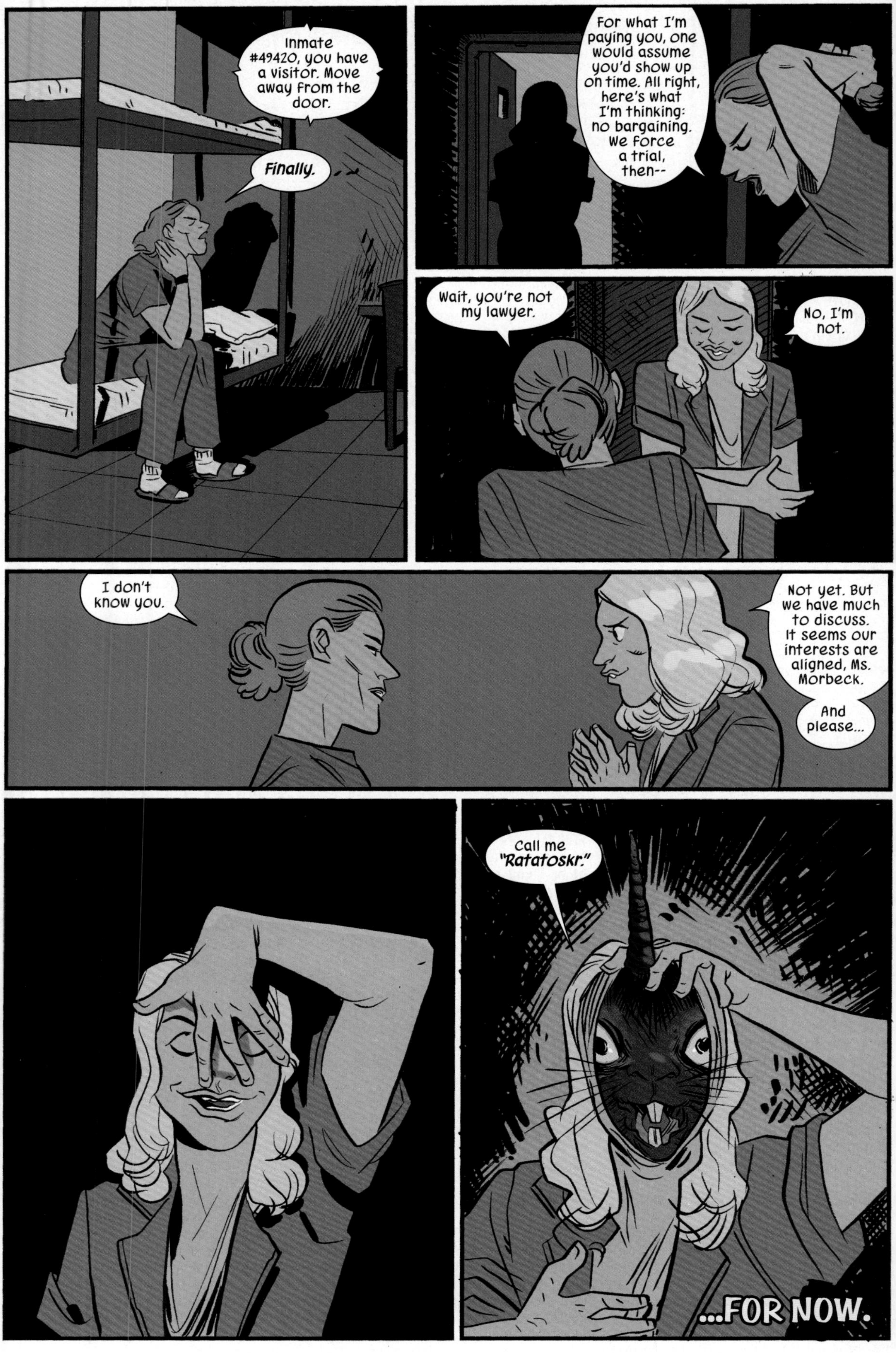
Inmate #49420, you have a visitor. Move away from the door.
Finally.
For what I'm paying you, one would assume you'd show up on time. All right, here's what I'm thinking: no bargaining. We force a trial, then--
Wait, you're not my lawyer.
No, I'm not.
I don't know you.
Not yet. But we have much to discuss. It seems our interests are aligned, Ms. Morbeck.
And please...
Call me "Ratatoskr."
...FOR NOW.

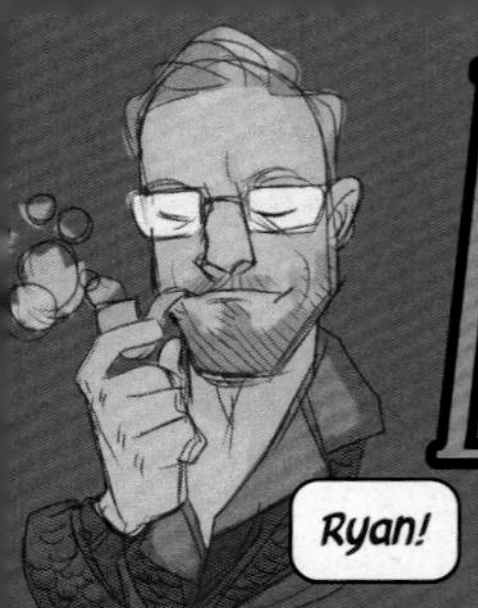
Ryan!

Letters From Nuts

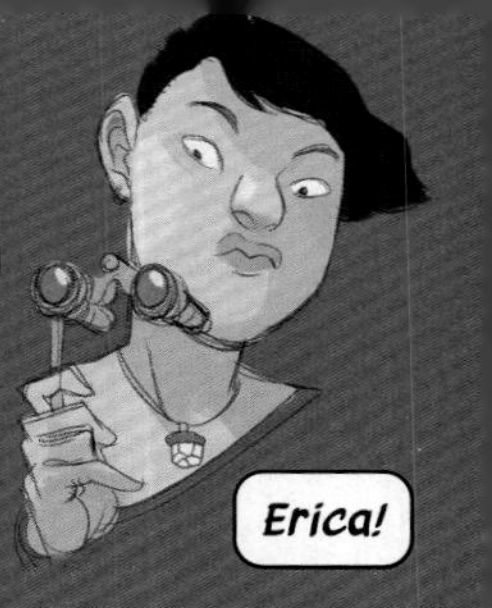
Erica!

Send letters to mheroes@marvel.com or 135 W 50th St, 7th Floor, New York, NY 10020 (Please mark "OKAY TO PRINT")

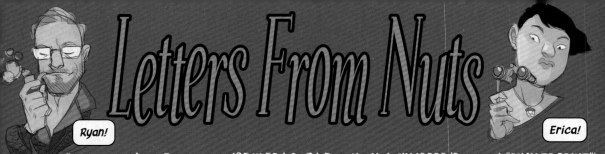

Ryan and Erica,

YOU GUYS ARE SO UNBELIEVABLY FABULOUS. I used to be an occasional comics reader, and then I discovered the SQUIRREL GIRL trades at my local library…and now I'm literally a RABID DEVOURER OF COMICS. In the reading sense, not the food sense. That'd be gross and most definitely not nutritious.

Anyway, I've got a question, and I'm hoping I won't get in trouble with Marvel for including a DC character in this, but…what's the deal with Mole Man wearing Captain Cold's glasses? (Totally not complaining. Snart is my heart).

Thank you thank you thank you for the amazing work you do. If I had half the talent and wit you have in your left pinkies, I'd be very fortunate indeed. :)

Amy Levenson
South Florida

P.S. My friends are planning on kidnapping me for my first convention in a few months, so of course I'm already planning my Nancy cosplay (also a first!). I'll send pictures if I manage to pull it off.

RYAN: I was going to say, "Mole Man first appeared in 1961 while Captain Cold first appeared afterwards," but I did a search and it turned out that Captain Cold first appeared in 1957! So what the heck, Mole Man? YOU ARE BITING THE STYLE OF ANOTHER PERSON FROM ANOTHER UNIVERSE.

But the real answer is, Mole Man lives underground and so can't see in bright light, so he uses those glasses to minimize the amount of light reaching his eyes. They're also used for snow blindness for the same reasons, so it makes sense that Captain Cold would wear them while he's, you know, in the Arctic colds he's apparently captaining, but I dunno why he wears them on the regular.

I think we are all on-record here in the SQUIRREL GIRL letters pages as being extremely pro-cosplay pictures, so send 'em in when they happen!!

ERICA: I need to see more Nancy cosplay! I know she's a tough one because she's a regular person without a uniform, which is why you don't see her a lot, but I want it!

Also, I didn't design Mole Man! I am all for his adult onesie with a structured cape look, though.

I've been enjoying your comics for the past few months, ever since I first managed to get my hands on them. Last night, I decided to introduce my littlest sister to them, and since I wanted to read them at the same time, we ended up both sitting on my bed looking at them while I read them out loud. I've never been much of a fan of reading comics out loud before, because they're so visual, but it worked surprisingly well with yours. I did voices, and it was a lot of fun. (I forgot that Kraven is Russian until after coming up with his voice, and so didn't give him a Russian accent, whoops.) In fact, it was so awesome that when I was done, my other little sister, who was in the room while we were reading, later asked to be able to read the comics too. Therefore, I have gotten both of my little sisters hooked on your comics. Thank you for bringing them into existence!

Also, I dressed up as Squirrel Girl for Halloween last year, and it was really fun. I even made a utility belt, in which I carried my phone and a bunch of almonds for snacking.

Sincerely, your fan,
Hannah Lerum

RYAN: THIS IS THE CUTEST STORY (AND THE GREATEST ASIDE MINI-STORY IN THE SECOND PARAGRAPH). Here is a secret: I do the voices too when I write, so every one of Kraven's lines gets read out loud in a horrible Canadian/Russian accent. This is also one of the reasons why I write only when nobody else is around.

ERICA: I work in cafes all the time, because at a certain point you just need to have other humans near you (also they make better coffee than I do), and I'm just picturing Ryan muttering to himself in bad Russian in that scenario.

To Ryan and Erica,

Hello from England! I just wanted to say that SG is my absolute favorite Marvel hero at the moment, and every second Wednesday of the month is brightened by her appearance in our local comic store. You guys are awesome, she's awesome—she has given me and my fellow comic fans, Sam Molly, Benji and Edgar plenty of awesome things to talk about! Like her, I'm a second-year university student (journalism posse!), so seeing her managing butt-kicking and essay writing is a great source of hype!

All the best,
Thomas L.

RYAN: Thanks, Thomas! This is super great to hear. As a Canadian, we share the same beautiful Queen, but also the same love of (correctly) putting the (absolutely necessary) letter "u" in places that Americans don't. I'm afraid they're going to edit them out of your letter, so I've restored them here: uuuuuuuuu. You're welcoume.

ERICA: English is a complicated enough language with rules that don't work across the board. There's no need to add letters to words that clearly don't need them.

Dear Erica and Ryan,

We want to thank you for your treatment of a population that is often victimized by prejudice: rats. We are pet rats, but write in solidarity with our wild brothers and sisters. Being controlled by super villains is a drag, but at least your magazine depicts rats with accuracy and respect.
We always thought of squirrels as annoying show-offs—with their *big eyes* and *bushy tails* that humans think are *so* cute—but now we are reassessing those fellow rodents. This is all thanks to Squirrel Girl and your wonderful magazine.

Is a redoubtable Rat Brat too much to hope for in the future?

Sincerely,

Floyd, Elmer, Martin, Jabberwocky, Stan, Ed, Mama Grace, Tillie, and Dora—via our human amanuensis, Bernadette Bosky

RYAN: Oh uh we kinda used some squirrel-positive and rat-negative imagery in this issue I'M SORRY ABOUT THAT!!! In my defense: I had a friend with a pet rat in high school, and it was the first rat I ever met, and she was great (the rat) (the friend was pretty great too, honestly) (just a great time all around at her house). Rat Brat was actually one of the things I considered way before our first issue (when Chipmunk Hunk was but a gleam in my eye), so in an alternate universe this is very close to your perfect comic magazine!

ERICA: Fun Erica trivia: I picked up a pet rat while he was fairly young because I really wanted a rat and told my boyfriend at the time that he was a mouse because he really DID NOT want a rat around. By the time he was full-sized it was too late! MWAHAHA.

Marvel staff,

I have been getting back into comic books after quite a long lapse. I was broke for a while, then I joined the military and couldn't keep print comics around for very long. I would pick them up here and there, but didn't have somewhere to put them. I'm still in the military, but I'm in a more stable situation. I got the Marvel Unlimited app and I started a pull list at my FLCS. It started with a couple of books I was interested in because of the creators' webcomics. (Wolverine was always my favorite, along with Punisher. And you killed them both! Where else was I going to turn?) Ryan North and Christopher Hastings are hilarious. So I picked up THE UNBEATABLE SQUIRREL GIRL and GWENPOOL. Man oh man, those are some of the best books out there. I love that Marvel has really encouraged these offbeat style books. I like the direction Marvel is going. Well, I did. I heard today that some of my favorite books are being canceled, and that my two current favorites, TUSG and GWENPOOL, might be on the chopping block. Well, if that happens, I might just put the comic hobby down again. I sincerely hope you don't cancel good books. I'm sorry if they're not making you the money you feel you need from them, but maybe think about the fact they don't have movies or TV shows to bump their fan base. Please keep making such good books!

Sincerely,
SGT Marc Muehling
G Co 113th FSC

RYAN: Chris Hastings and I have a history together (of really good friendship! He's great! I love that guy!), so I was stoked to hear that he was writing GWENPOOL. And, as YOU know because you read it, but as others might not, he even picked up on the adventures of Old Lady Squirrel Girl in the past in a GWENPOOL story! So I am the #1 fan of Chris Hastings over here. I don't get to decide which books get canceled (EXCEPT SQUIRREL GIRL, NOBODY CANCEL THAT BOOK), but if you haven't heard the news, let me tell you: a SQUIRREL GIRL and NEW WARRIORS TV show has just been announced for 2018! It'll be on Freeform, and it'll star the same Doreen Green we know and love. SQUIRREL GIRL IS COMING TO TV, AHHHHHHHHH.

ERICA: People have been saying we're canceled since issue #1—the first volume's #1—and if you're reading this you're holding the (ohmygod) 28th issue of SQUIRREL GIRL and there are five more outlined/almost finished so I'm not too worried??

P.S. I know it says issue 20, but remember how we had eight issues and then it rebooted eight months later? It was like two years ago.

Dear Erica, Ryan and the rest of the team,

This is what your comic has done to my brain:

I finally get around to going to the cinema to see *Logan*, and, as I sit there, watching the blood-soaked, R-rated carnage, this thought suddenly comes to me: "Truly, Wolverine was the best at what he did: He could count to 255 on one hand in binary.*"

May your wonderful talking squirrel comic—or talking human comic, as it is surely marketed in squirrel territories—long continue to skew my mind. And while I'm here, a big thanks to the—unfortunately now rather embattled—Sheffield Public Libraries for introducing me to it in the first place (I'm a university librarian myself; it never hurts to give other librarians a fillip for all the great stuff they do).

Yours Sincerely,
Sandy Buchanan,
Sheffield,
UK

*It might be a good idea for someone who doesn't have an arts background to check this fact.

RYAN: Sandy, your math is correct, well done! And that is an amazing thing to think during *Logan*. I am so happy and proud. And I am always happy to give a shout-out to libraries! I gave a talk at my local library (the Toronto Public Library) and I showed that scene during the Enigmos arc in which we gave librarians a shout-out in the text. I had to insist that it was real and not something I made up just to butter up the audience! Thank you to the Sheffield Public Library for reppin' our talking squirrel/talking human comic!

ERICA: I still haven't read issue #11. Always moving forward, never back! Although that means that people will keep referencing it and I will have to nod politely, so maybe I should, but every time I think I should I really just take a much-needed rest.

P.S. HOW GOOD WAS *LOGAN???* SO GOOD.

The wardrobes in our house just got so much cooler! I surprised my six-year-old twin daughters with THE UNBEATABLE SQUIRREL GIRL T-shirts, and they love them. We're super stoked to have official Erica Henderson gear that we can wear to show support for our favorite Marvel series. The girls have a bit of growing left before they fully fit in their shirts, but that'll just be something for them to look forward to.

Hopefully there are plans for more Squirrel Girl clothing in the near future!

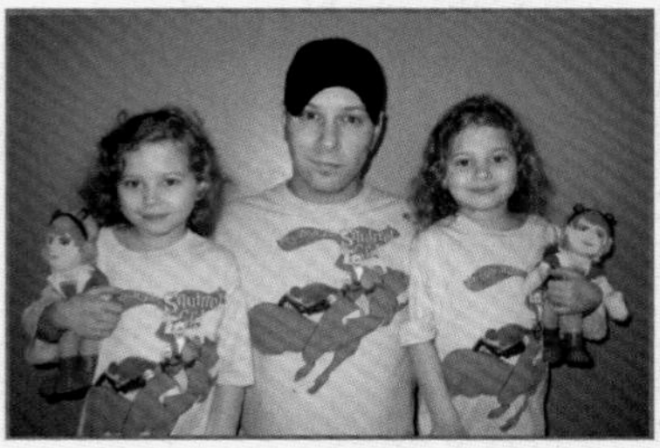

Darrick Patrick
Dayton, Ohio

P.S. I'm including a photograph of Logann, Nola, and I sporting our new attire.

RYAN: AHHHH I LOVE THIS, I LOVE THOSE SQUIRREL GIRL DOLLS, ABSOLUTELY EVERYTHING ABOUT THIS PHOTO IS A+++

ERICA: Unfortunately the shirts are all licensed out, but I'd keep checking that WeLoveFine site!

Dear Unbeatable Squirrel Warriors,

I have been reading for about half a year, and I absolutely LOVE this comic. I just recently discovered that Squirrel Girl will be on FREEFORM. I can't wait! Where was I going with this? Oh, right. Well, earlier today, I was sitting on my porch eating a peanut butter sandwich, in memory of Monkey Joe. I have corn hanging on my tree, so that squirrels will eat it. A squirrel was on a branch, near the corn, and it ripped the corn right out of the tree and stole it! Probably the weirdest thing I've seen this week. Now, I have a question. Could you come to my hometown of Kokomo, Indiana, possibly, for Kokomo-Con?

Bye for now, Unbeatable Squirrel Warriors!
Sarah King

RYAN: Sarah, around this time last year, some cartoonist friends and I were camping in the beautiful woods of Alaska with no cell phone signals or Internet, and we spent a long time—over an hour—arguing about whether "Kokomo" in the Beach Boys song was a real place. It's the kind of debate that could be settled today in two seconds, but with that option not available to us, all we could do was scour our memories for whatever Kokomo facts we had, and then rely on our skills in rhetoric to try to convince others. It was so much fun! My friend Jon recalled that the song mentioned Kokomo was "off the Florida Keys," which I thought was very convincing on the "it's real" side—why would the Boys of the Beach specify such an exact location for a fake place? I mention this because the first thing we ALL did when we got back was look up all the Kokomo information we could, and now I know all the Kokomo facts, which means I am more familiar with Kokomo, Indiana, than you might expect! And if Erica and I ever go down to Kokomo—we'll get there fast and then we'll take it slow—I'd be more than happy to share them.

ERICA: There is a strange old lady who lives in the strange house at the end of my street who leaves what appears to be an entire loaf of bread out every day for the birds (please don't do this as bread does not contain all the nutrition that animals need), and if I'm walking by right as she's just put it out, I can usually catch a squirrel or two stealing several slices from the birds and running off. They're pretty opportunistic and feisty.

P.S. Oh my god that song is in my head now—but the Muppets version.

P.P.S. Why would you hold a cartoonist retreat in a place with no internet? I don't understand. You did this on purpose, Ryan?

Next Issue:

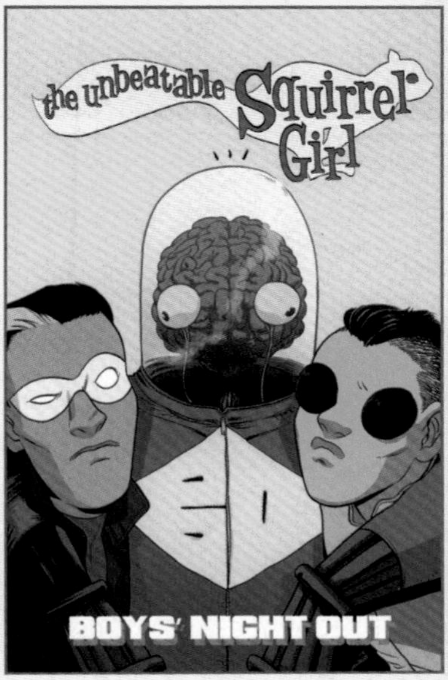
the unbeatable Squirrel Girl
BOYS' NIGHT OUT

Attention, Squirrel Scouts! Make sure to check out our production blog, **unbeatablesquirrelgirl.tumblr.com**, where we post behind-the-scenes stuff on how the book gets made, along with all sorts of cool things *you* make: fanart, cosplay, whatever!

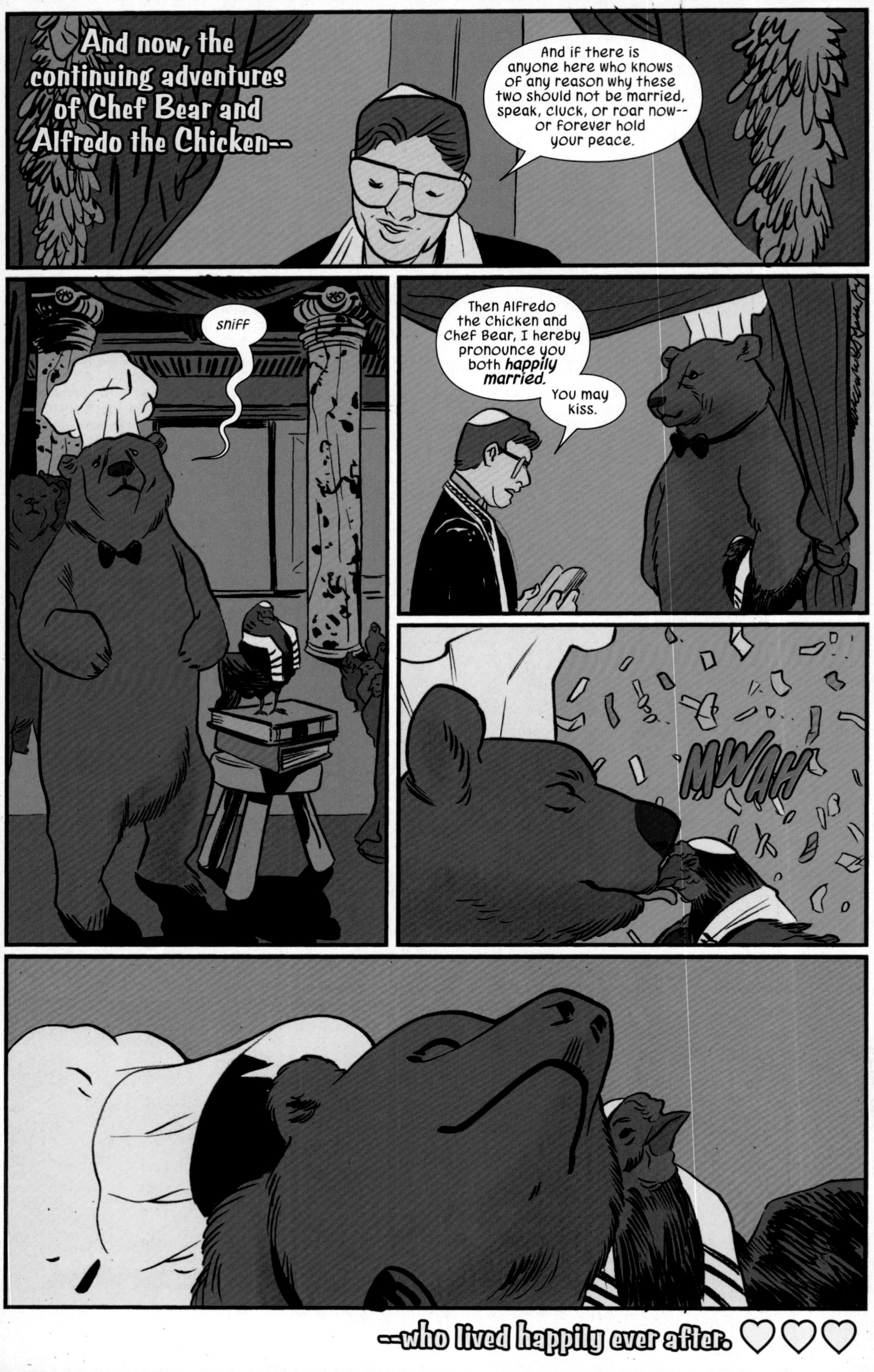
And now, the continuing adventures of Chef Bear and Alfredo the Chicken--
And if there is anyone here who knows of any reason why these two should not be married, speak, cluck, or roar now--or forever hold your peace.
sniff
Then Alfredo the Chicken and Chef Bear, I hereby pronounce you both *happily married.*
You may kiss.
MWAH
--who lived happily ever after. ♡♡♡

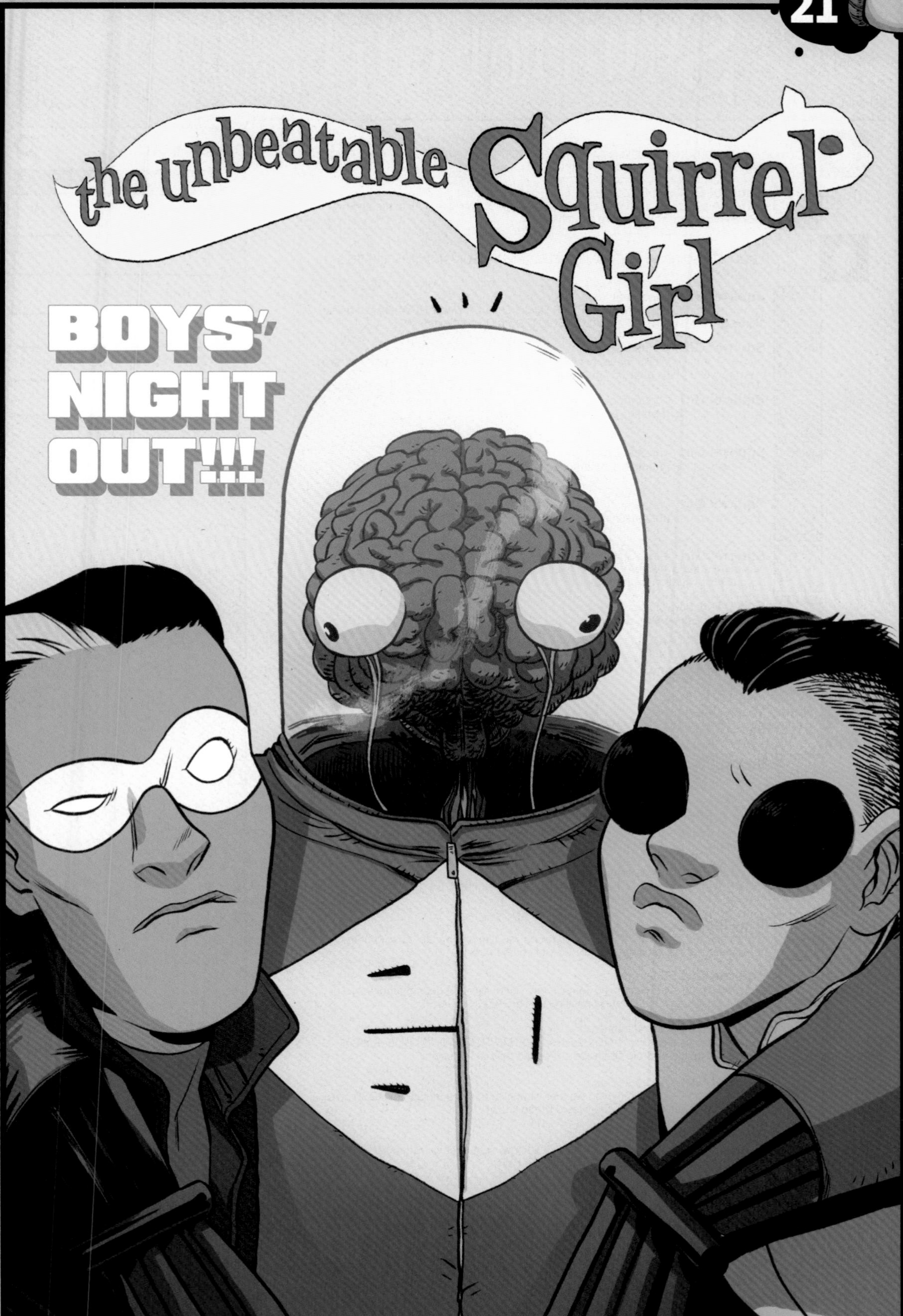
the unbeatable Squirrel Girl
BOYS' NIGHT OUT!!!

Doreen Green isn't just a second-year computer science student: she secretly also has all the powers of both squirrel and girl! She uses her amazing abilities to fight crime **and** be as awesome as possible. You know her as...**The Unbeatable Squirrel Girl!**

Find out what she's been up to, with...

Squirrel Girl in a nutshell

Egg @imduderadtude
DOCTOR DOOM IS TAKNIG OVER NEW YORK CITY!!!!! PLEASE RT SO PPL KNO THAT DOC DOOM IS TAKNG OVER TEH CITY!!!!!!!

Squirrel Girl @unbeatablesg
@imduderadtude No it's not Doctor Doom, it's Melissa Morbeck! Also, me and my pals defeated her, so uh...we're good here

Egg @imduderadtude
DOCTOR DOOM IS GOING BY THE NAME "MELISSA MORBECK" NOW!!!!!! PLEASE RT!!!!!! #doctordoom

Squirrel Girl @unbeatablesg
@imduderadtude No, no, it was NEVER Doctor Doom, it was a NEW villain, Melissa Morbeck, who is COMPLETELY DIFFERENT from Doctor Doom!

Squirrel Girl @unbeatablesg
@imduderadtude Well, I mean, not COMPLETELY different. They both got that "take over the world" thing goin' on I guess

Squirrel Girl @unbeatablesg
@imduderadtude (also she briefly wore his clothes)

Squirrel Girl @unbeatablesg
@imduderadtude (or rather a bear under her control did)

Squirrel Girl @unbeatablesg
@imduderadtude (for reasons)

Squirrel Girl @unbeatablesg
@imduderadtude ANYWAY, point is, you don't need anyone to "please rt" anything, because the situation is under control!!

Egg @imduderadtude
@unbeatablesg wow it's almost like i said "please rt" and not "please @ me w fact checks"!!!!!

Egg @imduderadtude
@unbeatablesg OH WAIT I DID!!!!! blocked

Nancy W. @sewwiththeflo
@unbeatablesg whoooooo's up for a vacation?

Squirrel Girl @unbeatablesg
@sewwiththeflo Oh man! Negative Zone hangouts with Allene??

Tony Stark @starkmantony
@unbeatablesg @sewwiththeflo Should you really be posting that you're leaving NYC undefended while you hang out in an alternate dimension?

Squirrel Girl @unbeatablesg
@starkmantony @sewwiththeflo Oh pfft it's not undefended. It's got YOU.

Tony Stark @starkmantony
@unbeatablesg @sewwiththeflo I keep telling you, I'm a computer now. I put my consciousness into a computer. Because of course I did.

Squirrel Girl @unbeatablesg
@starkmantony @sewwiththeflo Tony I know you're trying to get me to make you another captcha pic but I'm busy packing for NEGAZONE TIMES

Squirrel Girl @unbeatablesg
@starkmantony @sewwiththeflo Besides, EVEN IF THAT WERE TRUE, Koi Boi, Chipmunk Hunk and Brain Drain are still gonna defend the city!!

Squirrel Girl @unbeatablesg
@starkmantony @sewwiththeflo I wonder what hilarious shenanigans THOSE crazy characters will get into! I, for one, would like to know!

Squirrel Girl @unbeatablesg
@starkmantony @sewwiththeflo And I WILL know, right after we return from visiting a friend in the Negative Zone SEE YOU LATER BYE

Tony Stark @starkmantony
@unbeatablesg @sewwiththeflo Wait, are you there? Squirrel Girl?

Tony Stark @starkmantony
@unbeatablesg @sewwiththeflo Squirrel Girl?

Tony Stark @starkmantony
@unbeatablesg @sewwiththeflo Hello?

Tony Stark @starkmantony
@unbeatablesg @sewwiththeflo ...

Tony Stark @starkmantony
@unbeatablesg @sewwiththeflo You've been gone five minutes and the news is

search!

- #braindrain
- #chipmunkhunk
- #koiboi
- #itsfabulous
- #diedandcamebackasfourguys
- #theoctopals

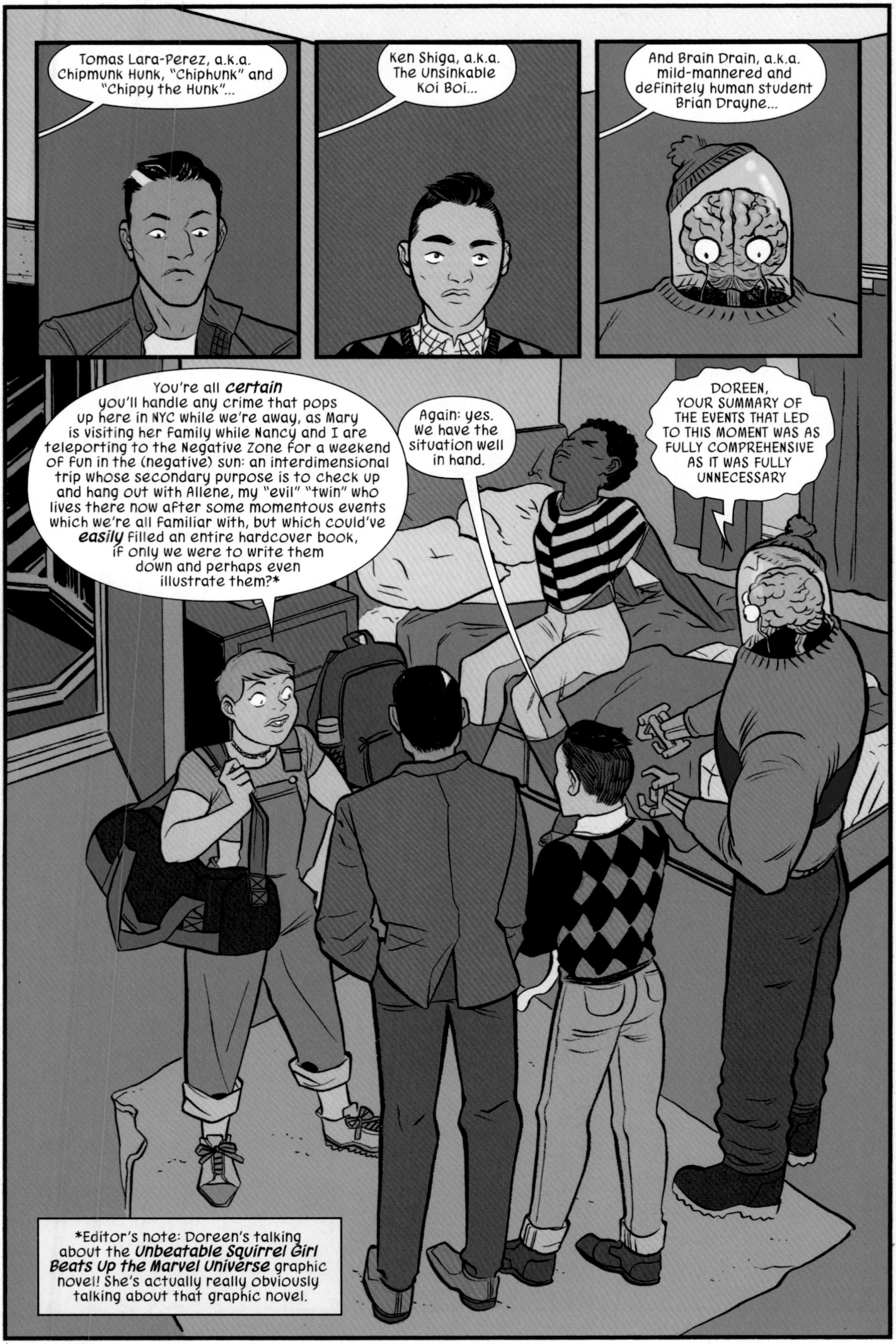
Tomas Lara-Perez, a.k.a. Chipmunk Hunk, "Chiphunk" and "Chippy the Hunk"...
Ken Shiga, a.k.a. The Unsinkable Koi Boi...
And Brain Drain, a.k.a. mild-mannered and definitely human student Brian Drayne...
You're all *certain* you'll handle any crime that pops up here in NYC while we're away, as Mary is visiting her family while Nancy and I are teleporting to the Negative Zone for a weekend of fun in the (negative) sun: an interdimensional trip whose secondary purpose is to check up and hang out with Allene, my "evil" "twin" who lives there now after some momentous events which we're all familiar with, but which could've *easily* filled an entire hardcover book, if only we were to write them down and perhaps even illustrate them?*
Again: yes. We have the situation well in hand.
DOREEN, YOUR SUMMARY OF THE EVENTS THAT LED TO THIS MOMENT WAS AS FULLY COMPREHENSIVE AS IT WAS FULLY UNNECESSARY
*Editor's note: Doreen's talking about the *Unbeatable Squirrel Girl Beats Up the Marvel Universe* graphic novel! She's actually really obviously talking about that graphic novel.

Doreen, if you are transforming the story of your life into some sort of "serialized illustrated picto-drama," then ***heed my warning well:*** it's actually really fun and I recommend it 100%!

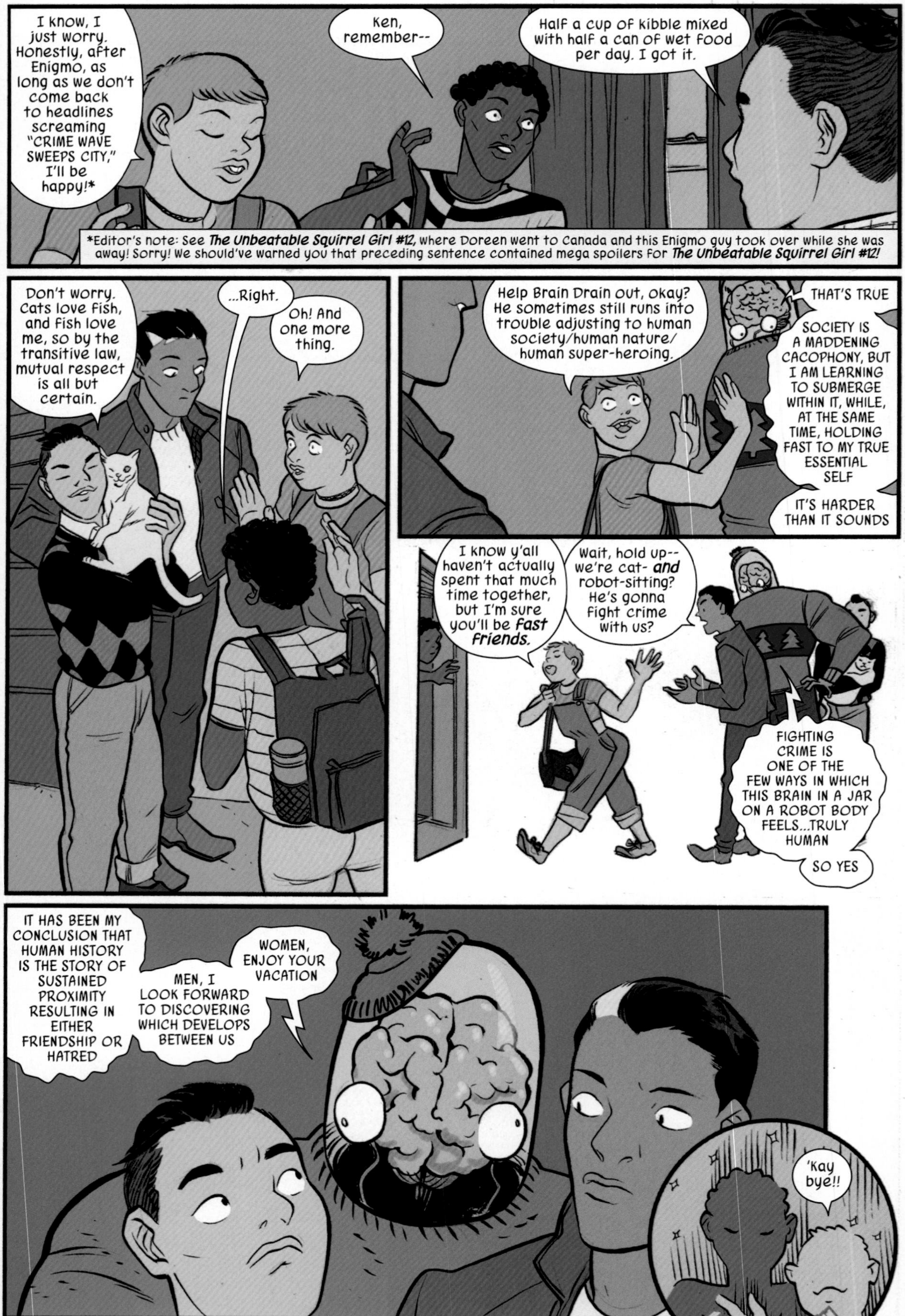
I know, I just worry. Honestly, after Enigmo, as long as we don't come back to headlines screaming "CRIME WAVE SWEEPS CITY," I'll be happy!*
Ken, remember--
Half a cup of kibble mixed with half a can of wet food per day. I got it.
*Editor's note: See The Unbeatable Squirrel Girl #12, where Doreen went to Canada and this Enigmo guy took over while she was away! Sorry! We should've warned you that preceding sentence contained mega spoilers for The Unbeatable Squirrel Girl #12!
Don't worry. Cats love fish, and fish love me, so by the transitive law, mutual respect is all but certain.
...Right.
Oh! And one more thing.
Help Brain Drain out, okay? He sometimes still runs into trouble adjusting to human society/human nature/ human super-heroing.
THAT'S TRUE
SOCIETY IS A MADDENING CACOPHONY, BUT I AM LEARNING TO SUBMERGE WITHIN IT, WHILE, AT THE SAME TIME, HOLDING FAST TO MY TRUE ESSENTIAL SELF
IT'S HARDER THAN IT SOUNDS
I know y'all haven't actually spent that much time together, but I'm sure you'll be fast friends.
Wait, hold up-- we're cat- and robot-sitting? He's gonna fight crime with us?
FIGHTING CRIME IS ONE OF THE FEW WAYS IN WHICH THIS BRAIN IN A JAR ON A ROBOT BODY FEELS...TRULY HUMAN
SO YES
IT HAS BEEN MY CONCLUSION THAT HUMAN HISTORY IS THE STORY OF SUSTAINED PROXIMITY RESULTING IN EITHER FRIENDSHIP OR HATRED
MEN, I LOOK FORWARD TO DISCOVERING WHICH DEVELOPS BETWEEN US
WOMEN, ENJOY YOUR VACATION
'Kay bye!!
VVZZHHNN

Cats love fish, and fish love me, and I love that feeling you get when you have a really inefficient SQL query but manage to optimize it by coming up with a gorgeously efficient way to reduce the number of joins required, so by the transitive law, every software development company should hire more cats. Q.E.D.

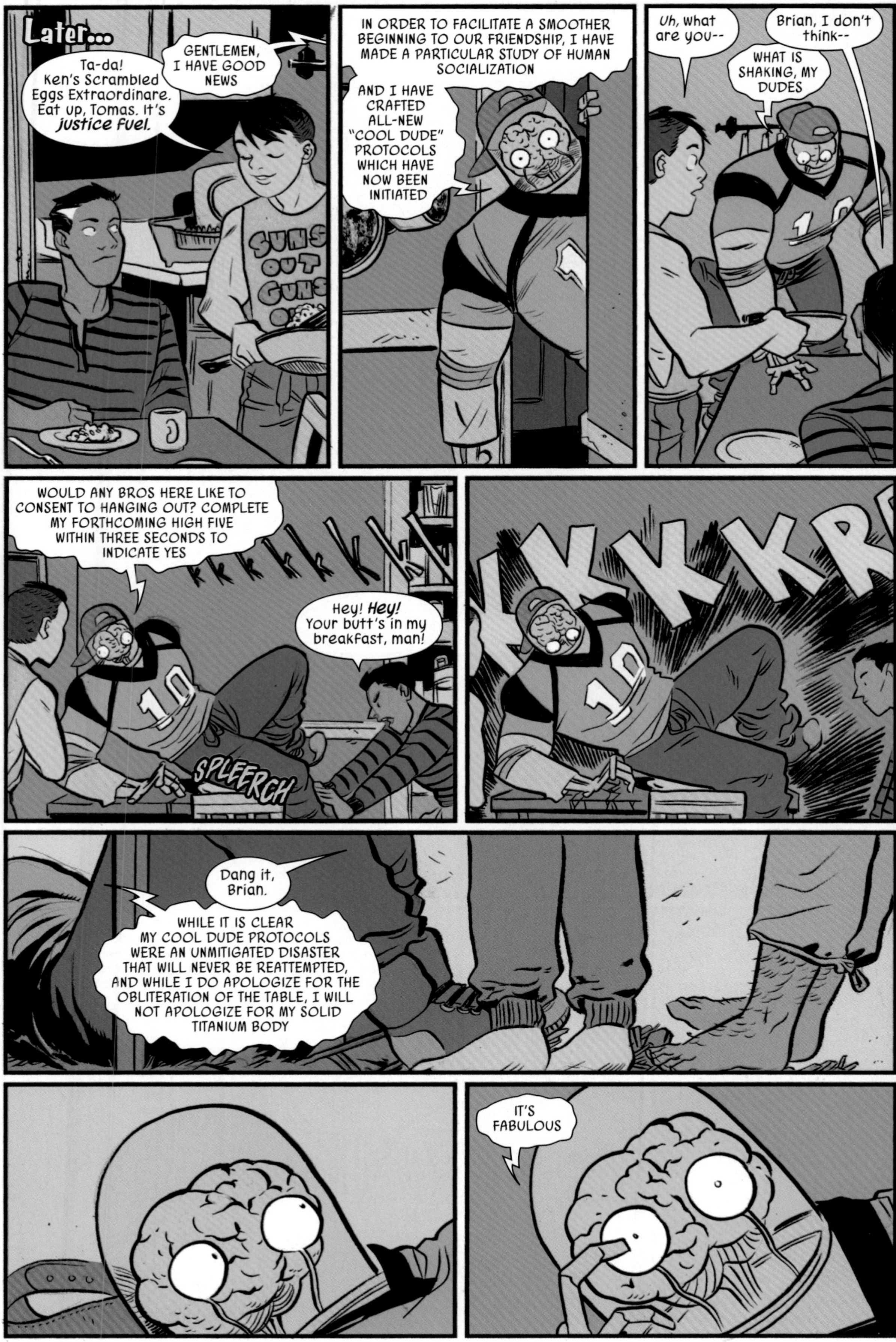
Later...
Ta-da! Ken's Scrambled Eggs Extraordinare. Eat up, Tomas. It's *justice fuel.*
GENTLEMEN, I HAVE GOOD NEWS
SUNS OUT GUNS
IN ORDER TO FACILITATE A SMOOTHER BEGINNING TO OUR FRIENDSHIP, I HAVE MADE A PARTICULAR STUDY OF HUMAN SOCIALIZATION
AND I HAVE CRAFTED ALL-NEW "COOL DUDE" PROTOCOLS WHICH HAVE NOW BEEN INITIATED
Uh, what are you--
Brian, I don't think--
WHAT IS SHAKING, MY DUDES
WOULD ANY BROS HERE LIKE TO CONSENT TO HANGING OUT? COMPLETE MY FORTHCOMING HIGH FIVE WITHIN THREE SECONDS TO INDICATE YES
KKKKKKKKK
Hey! **Hey!** Your butt's in my breakfast, man!
SPLEERCH
KKKKR
Dang it, Brian.
WHILE IT IS CLEAR MY COOL DUDE PROTOCOLS WERE AN UNMITIGATED DISASTER THAT WILL NEVER BE REATTEMPTED, AND WHILE I DO APOLOGIZE FOR THE OBLITERATION OF THE TABLE, I WILL NOT APOLOGIZE FOR MY SOLID TITANIUM BODY
IT'S FABULOUS

Do eggs truly make a "spleerch" sound when you sit on a plate of them? This answer is generously left as an exercise for the reader.

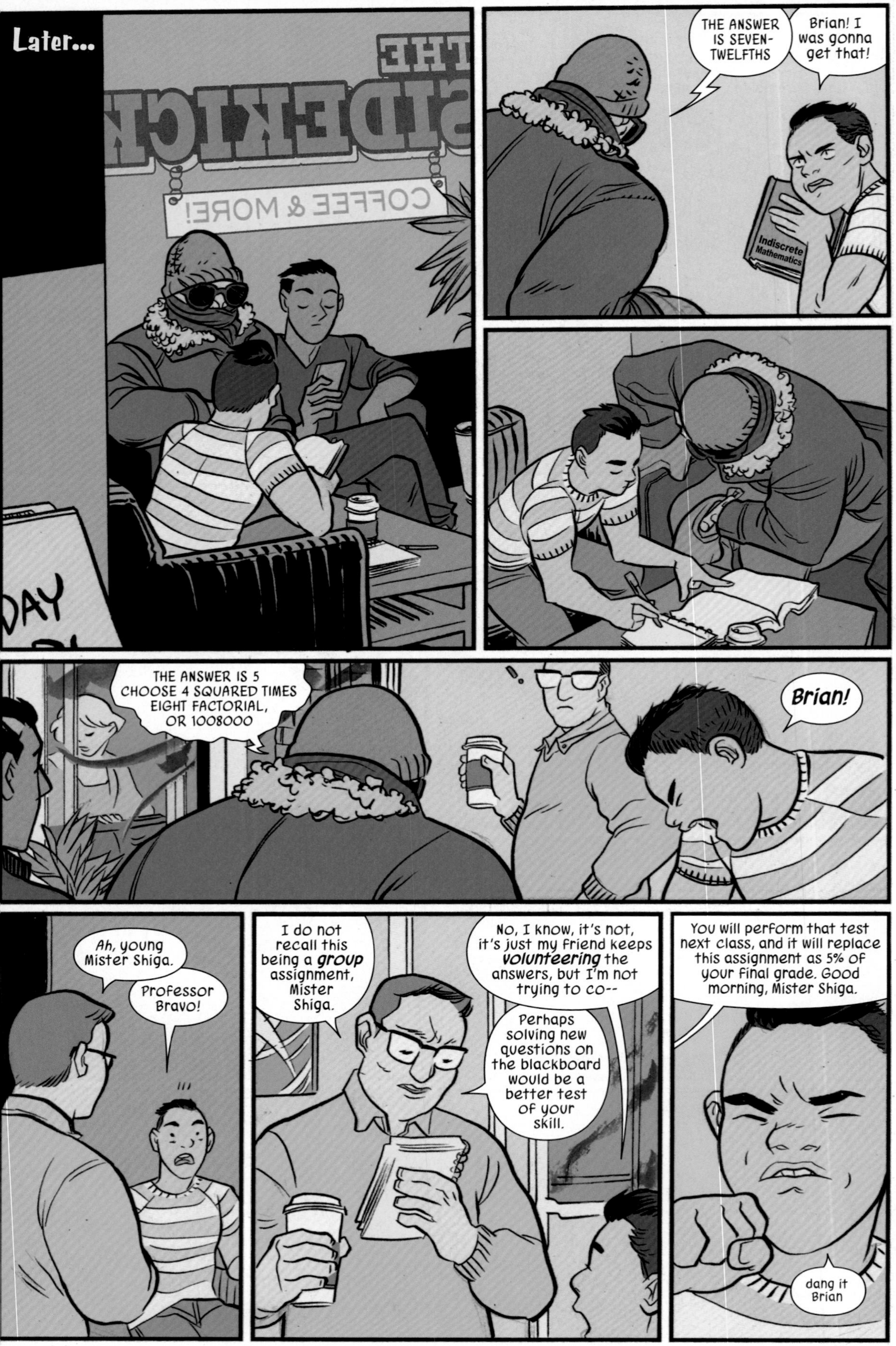
Later...
THE SIDEKICK
COFFEE & MORE!
THE ANSWER IS SEVEN-TWELFTHS
Brian! I was gonna get that!
Indiscrete Mathematics
THE ANSWER IS 5 CHOOSE 4 SQUARED TIMES EIGHT FACTORIAL, OR 1008000
Brian!
Ah, young Mister Shiga.
Professor Bravo!
I do not recall this being a *group* assignment, Mister Shiga.
No, I know, it's not, it's just my friend keeps *volunteering* the answers, but I'm not trying to co--
Perhaps solving new questions on the blackboard would be a better test of your skill.
You will perform that test next class, and it will replace this assignment as 5% of your final grade. Good morning, Mister Shiga.
dang it Brian

While "1008000" is the answer, what's the question? Well, let me say this: If one day you get on the bus and you don't have enough fare, and the bus driver says "I'll let you ride for free if you can tell me how many 8-digit numbers consist of exactly 4 distinct odd digits (i.e., 1, 3, 5, 7, 9) and 4 distinct even digits (i.e., 0, 2, 4, 6, 8)," you'll be laughing *all the way to your destination*.

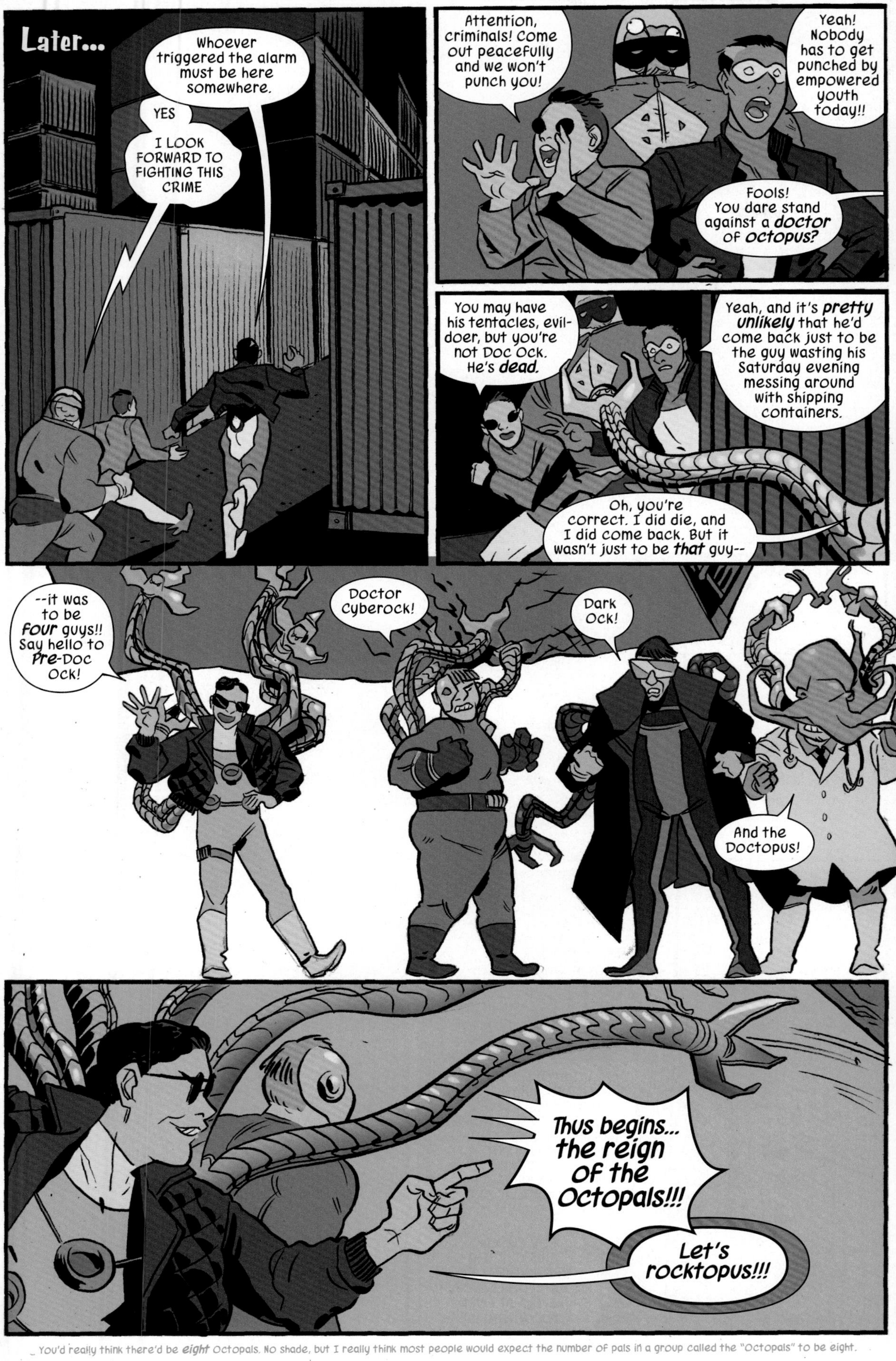
Later...
Whoever triggered the alarm must be here somewhere.
YES
I LOOK FORWARD TO FIGHTING THIS CRIME
Attention, criminals! Come out peacefully and we won't punch you!
Yeah! Nobody has to get punched by empowered youth today!!
Fools! You dare stand against a doctor of octopus?
You may have his tentacles, evil-doer, but you're not Doc Ock. He's dead.
Yeah, and it's pretty unlikely that he'd come back just to be the guy wasting his Saturday evening messing around with shipping containers.
Oh, you're correct. I did die, and I did come back. But it wasn't just to be that guy--
--it was to be four guys!! Say hello to Pre-Doc Ock!
Doctor Cyberock!
Dark Ock!
And the Doctopus!
Thus begins... the reign of the Octopals!!!
Let's rocktopus!!!

You'd really think there'd be *eight* Octopals. No shade, but I really think most people would expect the number of pals in a group called the "Octopals" to be eight.

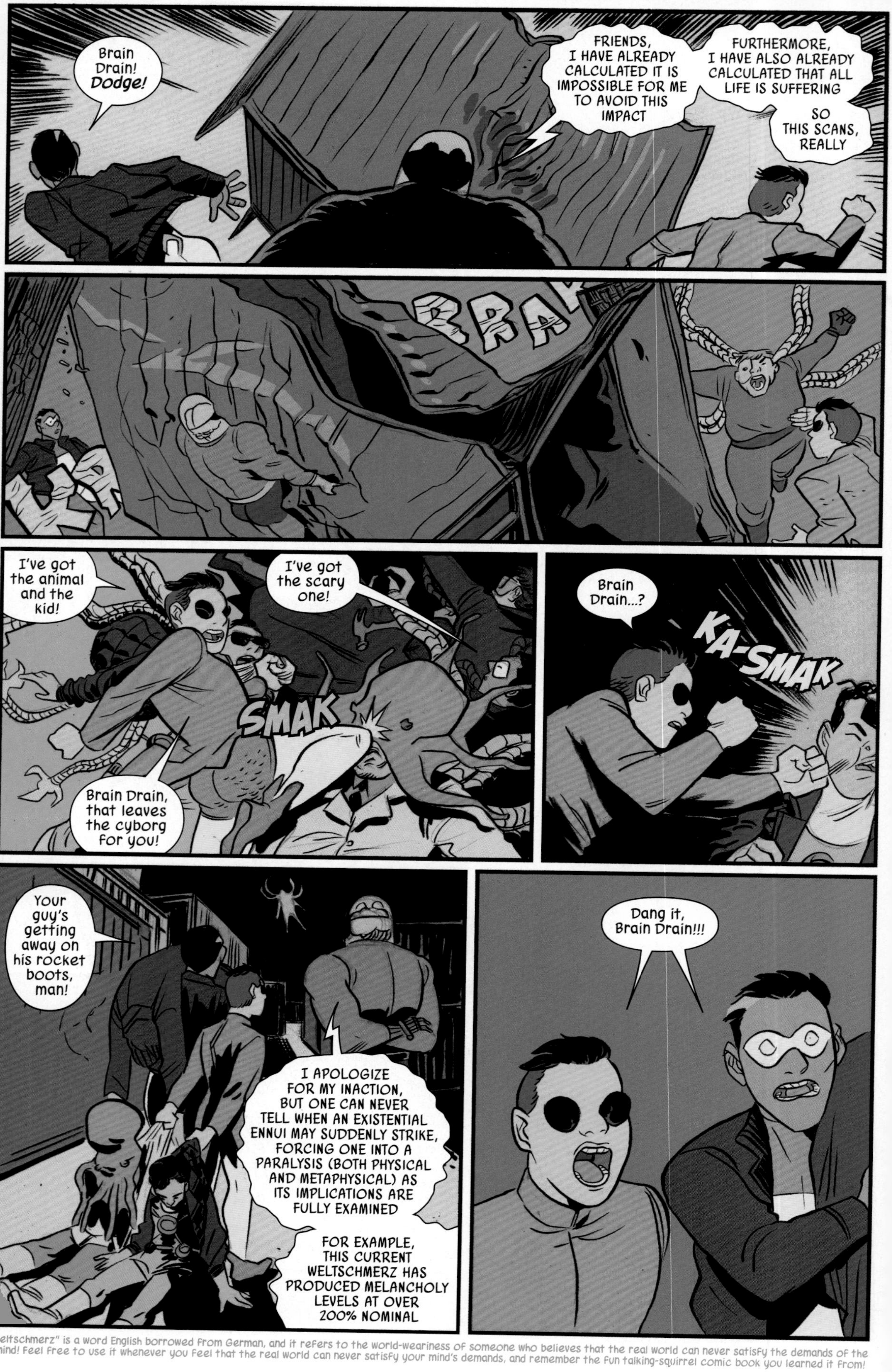

Brain Drain! *Dodge!*
FRIENDS, I HAVE ALREADY CALCULATED IT IS IMPOSSIBLE FOR ME TO AVOID THIS IMPACT
FURTHERMORE, I HAVE ALSO ALREADY CALCULATED THAT ALL LIFE IS SUFFERING
SO THIS SCANS, REALLY
BRAK
I've got the animal and the kid!
I've got the scary one!
SMAK
Brain Drain, that leaves the cyborg for you!
Brain Drain...?
KA-SMAK
Your guy's getting away on his rocket boots, man!
I APOLOGIZE FOR MY INACTION, BUT ONE CAN NEVER TELL WHEN AN EXISTENTIAL ENNUI MAY SUDDENLY STRIKE, FORCING ONE INTO A PARALYSIS (BOTH PHYSICAL AND METAPHYSICAL) AS ITS IMPLICATIONS ARE FULLY EXAMINED
FOR EXAMPLE, THIS CURRENT WELTSCHMERZ HAS PRODUCED MELANCHOLY LEVELS AT OVER 200% NOMINAL
Dang it, Brain Drain!!!

eltschmerz" is a word English borrowed from German, and it refers to the world-weariness of someone who believes that the real world can never satisfy the demands of the nind! Feel free to use it whenever you feel that the real world can never satisfy your mind's demands, and remember the fun talking-squirrel comic book you learned it from!

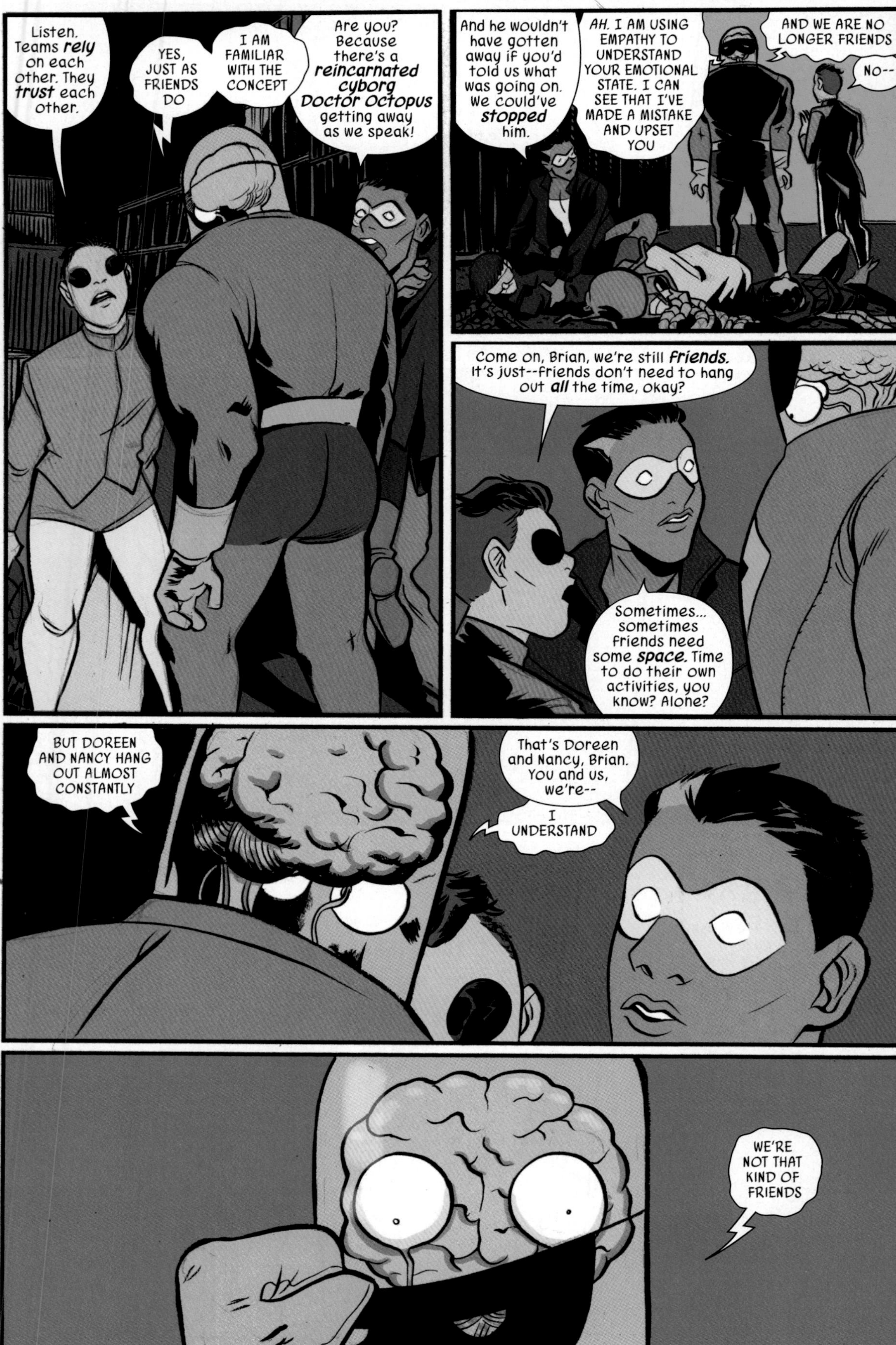
Listen. Teams *rely* on each other. They *trust* each other.
YES, JUST AS FRIENDS DO
I AM FAMILIAR WITH THE CONCEPT
Are you? Because there's a *reincarnated cyborg Doctor Octopus* getting away as we speak!
And he wouldn't have gotten away if you'd told us what was going on. We could've *stopped* him.
AH. I AM USING EMPATHY TO UNDERSTAND YOUR EMOTIONAL STATE. I CAN SEE THAT I'VE MADE A MISTAKE AND UPSET YOU
AND WE ARE NO LONGER FRIENDS
NO--
Come on, Brian, we're still *friends.* It's just--friends don't need to hang out *all* the time, okay?
Sometimes... sometimes friends need some *space.* Time to do their own activities, you know? Alone?
BUT DOREEN AND NANCY HANG OUT ALMOST CONSTANTLY
That's Doreen and Nancy, Brian. You and us, we're--
I UNDERSTAND
WE'RE NOT THAT KIND OF FRIENDS

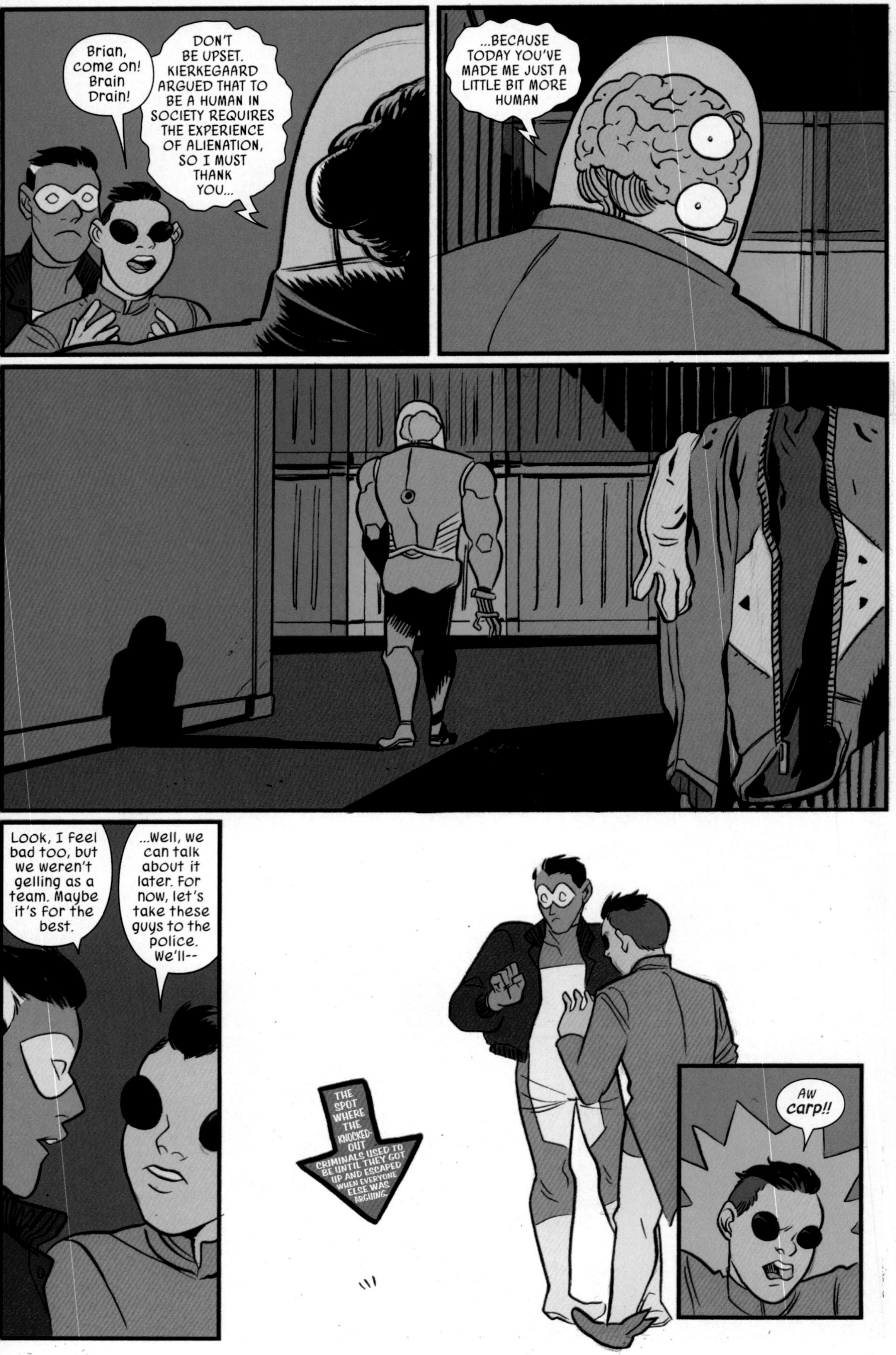
Brian, come on! Brain Drain!
DON'T BE UPSET. KIERKEGAARD ARGUED THAT TO BE A HUMAN IN SOCIETY REQUIRES THE EXPERIENCE OF ALIENATION, SO I MUST THANK YOU...
...BECAUSE TODAY YOU'VE MADE ME JUST A LITTLE BIT MORE HUMAN
Look, I feel bad too, but we weren't gelling as a team. Maybe it's for the best.
...Well, we can talk about it later. For now, let's take these guys to the police. We'll--
THE SPOT WHERE THE KNOCKED-OUT CRIMINALS USED TO BE UNTIL THEY GOT UP AND ESCAPED WHEN EVERYONE ELSE WAS ARGUING.
Aw carp!!

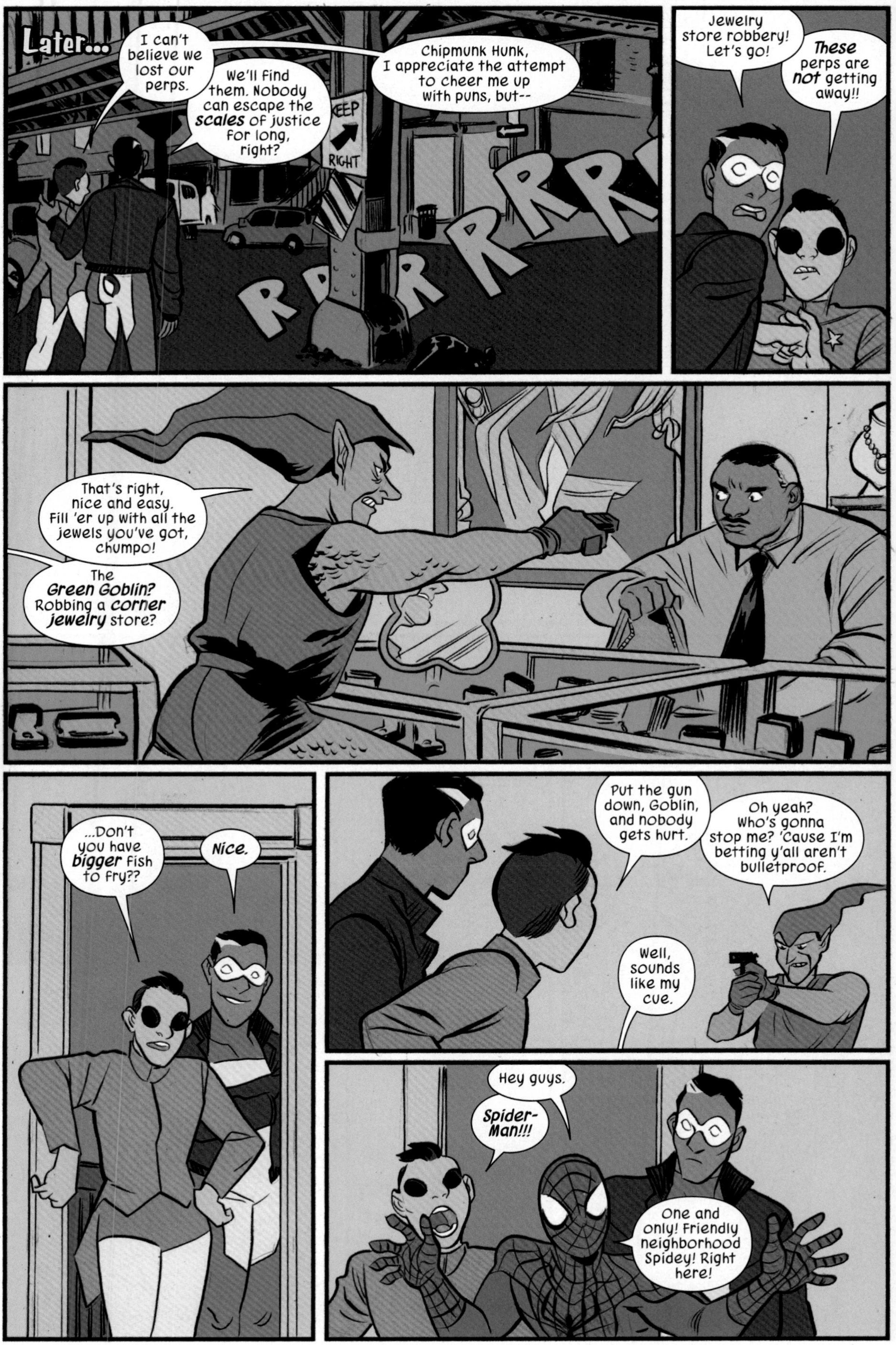
Later...
I can't believe we lost our perps.
We'll find them. Nobody can escape the scales of justice for long, right?
Chipmunk Hunk, I appreciate the attempt to cheer me up with puns, but--
KEEP RIGHT
RRRRRRR
Jewelry store robbery! Let's go!
These perps are not getting away!!
That's right, nice and easy. Fill 'er up with all the jewels you've got, chumpo!
The Green Goblin? Robbing a corner jewelry store?
...Don't you have bigger fish to fry??
Nice.
Put the gun down, Goblin, and nobody gets hurt.
Oh yeah? Who's gonna stop me? 'Cause I'm betting y'all aren't bulletproof.
Well, sounds like my cue.
Hey guys.
Spider-Man!!!
One and only! Friendly neighborhood Spidey! Right here!

You're seeing it here for the first time, but you just *know* Koi Boi is gonna use that line again approximately one million times.

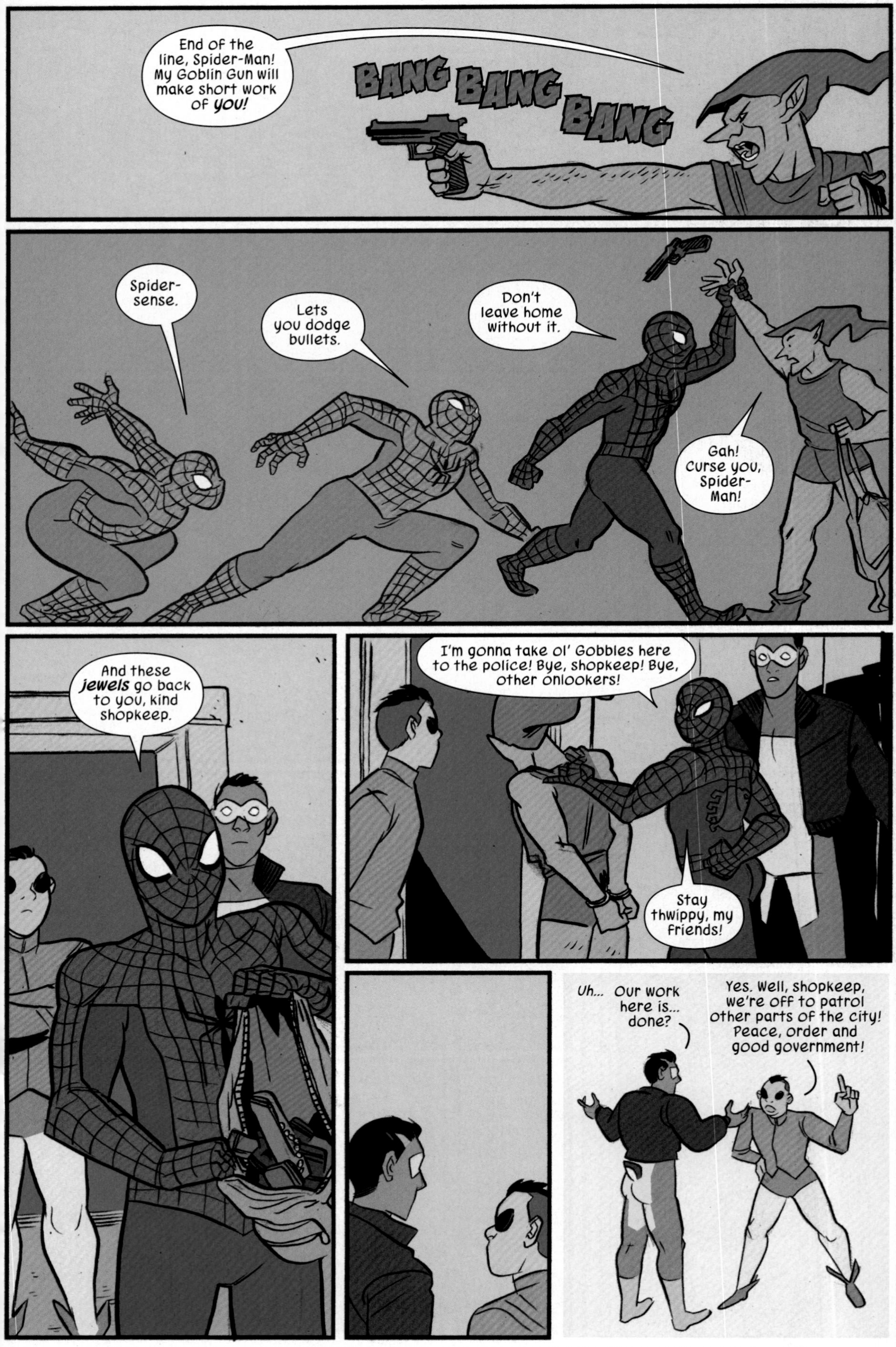
End of the line, Spider-Man! My Goblin Gun will make short work of *you!*
BANG BANG BANG
Spider-sense.
Lets you dodge bullets.
Don't leave home without it.
Gah! Curse you, Spider-Man!
And these *jewels* go back to you, kind shopkeep.
I'm gonna take ol' Gobbles here to the police! Bye, shopkeep! Bye, other onlookers!
Stay thwippy, my friends!
Uh... Our work here is... done?
Yes. Well, shopkeep, we're off to patrol other parts of the city! Peace, order and good government!

Spider-sense: Lets you dodge bullets, while also sensing if there are any cool spiders nearby. Honestly, I mostly only use the first part of it.

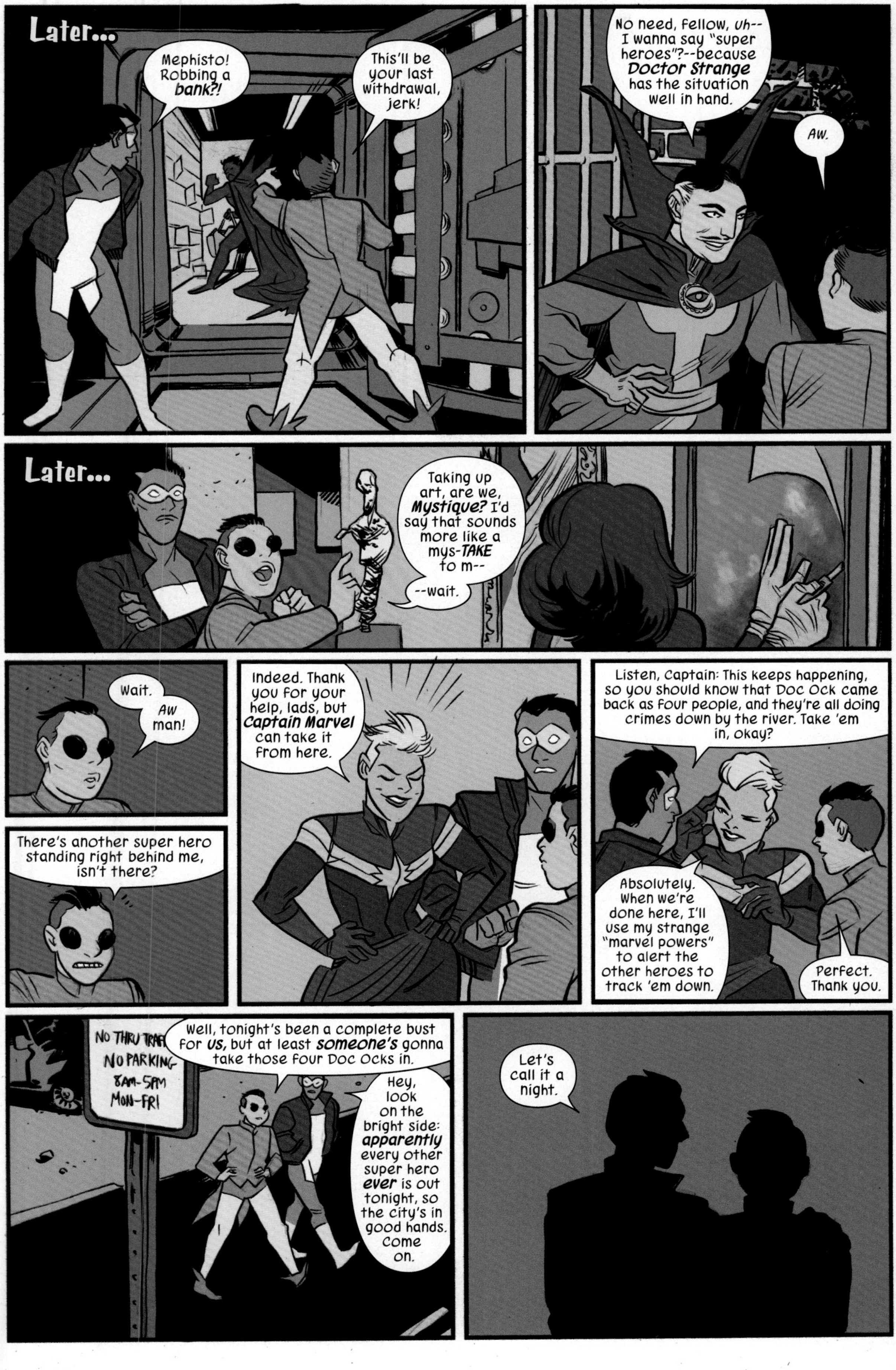

Later...
Mephisto! Robbing a bank?!
This'll be your last withdrawal, jerk!
No need, fellow, uh-- I wanna say "super heroes"?--because Doctor Strange has the situation well in hand.
AW.
Later...
Taking up art, are we, Mystique? I'd say that sounds more like a mys-TAKE to m--
--wait.
Wait.
AW man!
There's another super hero standing right behind me, isn't there?
Indeed. Thank you for your help, lads, but Captain Marvel can take it from here.
Listen, Captain: This keeps happening, so you should know that Doc Ock came back as four people, and they're all doing crimes down by the river. Take 'em in, okay?
Absolutely. When we're done here, I'll use my strange "marvel powers" to alert the other heroes to track 'em down.
Perfect. Thank you.
NO THRU TRAF
NO PARKING
8AM-5PM
MON-FRI
Well, tonight's been a complete bust for us, but at least someone's gonna take those four Doc Ocks in.
Hey, look on the bright side: apparently every other super hero ever is out tonight, so the city's in good hands. Come on.
Let's call it a night.

It must be fun to be a headline writer in the Marvel Universe. I bet it's never boring. You probably get to use a 72pt font any time you want and don't even have to wait for a moon landing to give you the excuse.

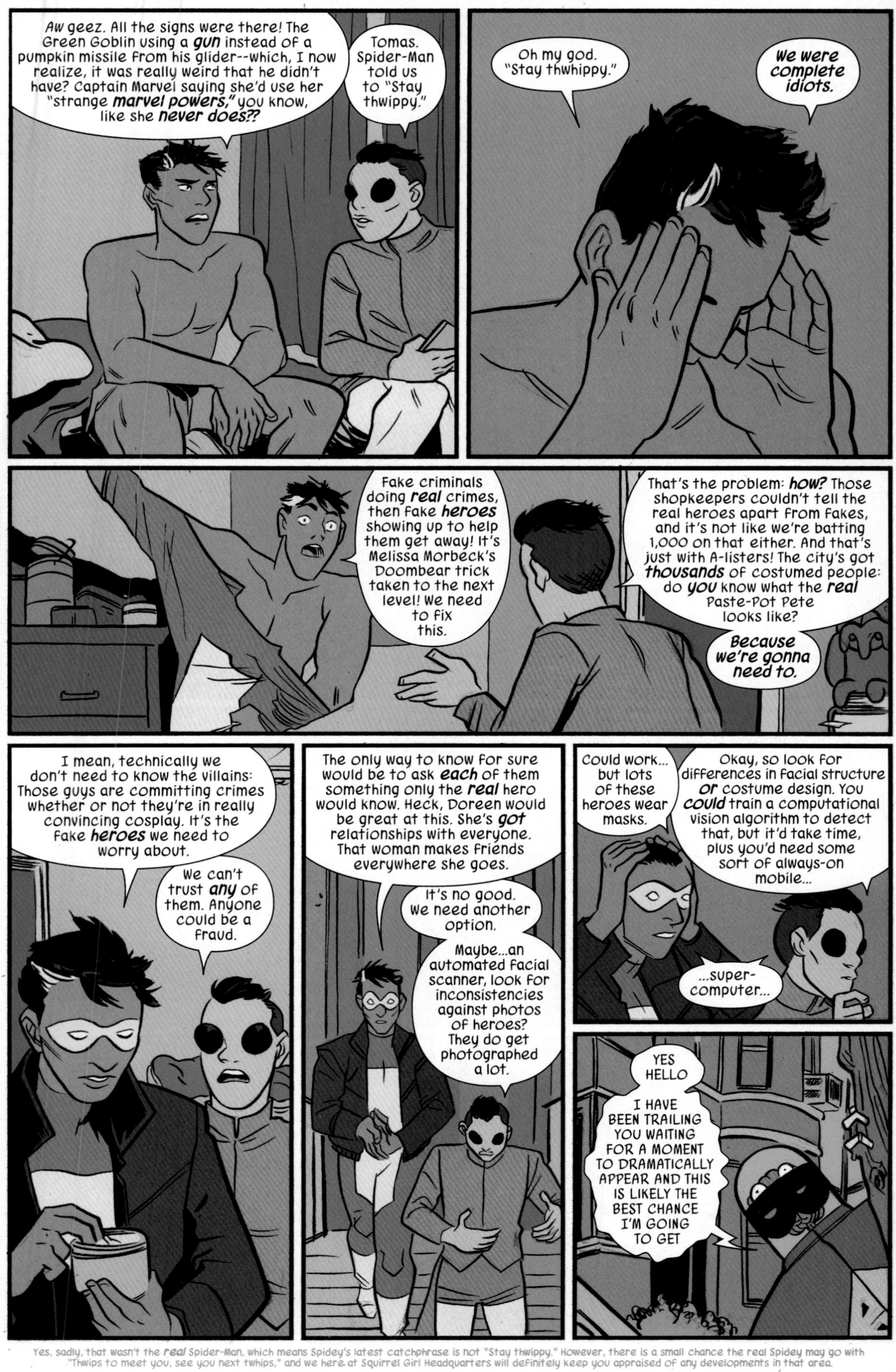
Aw geez. All the signs were there! The Green Goblin using a gun instead of a pumpkin missile from his glider--which, I now realize, it was really weird that he didn't have? Captain Marvel saying she'd use her "strange marvel powers," you know, like she never does??
Tomas. Spider-Man told us to "Stay thwippy."
Oh my god. "Stay thwhippy."
We were complete idiots.
Fake criminals doing real crimes, then fake heroes showing up to help them get away! It's Melissa Morbeck's Doombear trick taken to the next level! We need to fix this.
That's the problem: how? Those shopkeepers couldn't tell the real heroes apart from fakes, and it's not like we're batting 1,000 on that either. And that's just with A-listers! The city's got thousands of costumed people: do you know what the real Paste-Pot Pete looks like?
Because we're gonna need to.
I mean, technically we don't need to know the villains: Those guys are committing crimes whether or not they're in really convincing cosplay. It's the fake heroes we need to worry about.
We can't trust any of them. Anyone could be a fraud.
The only way to know for sure would be to ask each of them something only the real hero would know. Heck, Doreen would be great at this. She's got relationships with everyone. That woman makes friends everywhere she goes.
It's no good. We need another option.
Maybe...an automated facial scanner, look for inconsistencies against photos of heroes? They do get photographed a lot.
Could work... but lots of these heroes wear masks.
Okay, so look for differences in facial structure or costume design. You could train a computational vision algorithm to detect that, but it'd take time, plus you'd need some sort of always-on mobile...
...super-computer...
YES HELLO
I HAVE BEEN TRAILING YOU WAITING FOR A MOMENT TO DRAMATICALLY APPEAR AND THIS IS LIKELY THE BEST CHANCE I'M GOING TO GET

Yes, sadly, that wasn't the *real* Spider-Man, which means Spidey's latest catchphrase is not "Stay thwippy." However, there is a small chance the real Spidey may go with "Thwips to meet you, see you next twhips," and we here at Squirrel Girl Headquarters will definitely keep you appraised of any developments in that area.

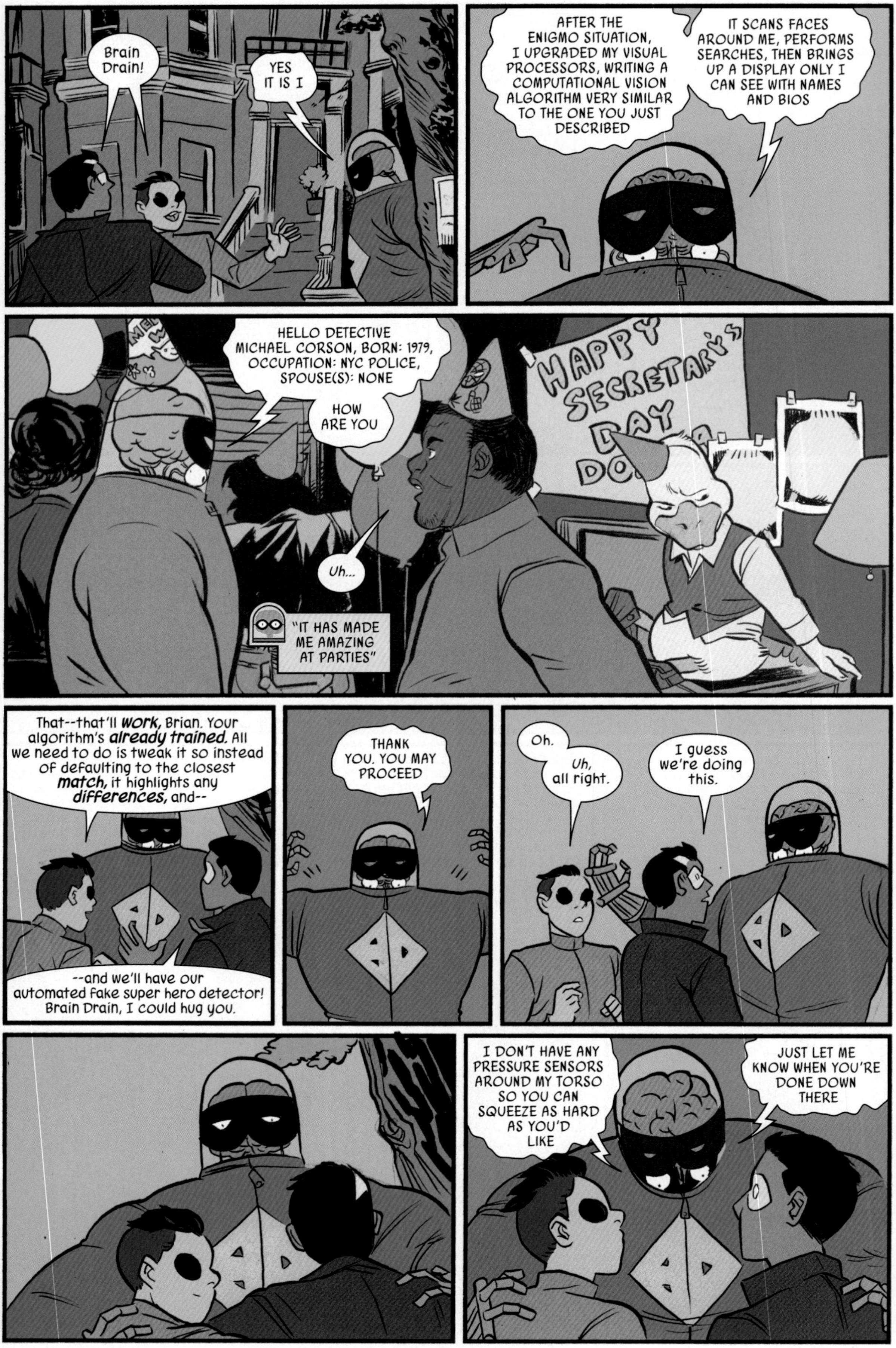
Brain Drain!
YES IT IS I
AFTER THE ENIGMO SITUATION, I UPGRADED MY VISUAL PROCESSORS, WRITING A COMPUTATIONAL VISION ALGORITHM VERY SIMILAR TO THE ONE YOU JUST DESCRIBED
IT SCANS FACES AROUND ME, PERFORMS SEARCHES, THEN BRINGS UP A DISPLAY ONLY I CAN SEE WITH NAMES AND BIOS
HAPPY SECRETARY'S DAY DO
HELLO DETECTIVE MICHAEL CORSON, BORN: 1979, OCCUPATION: NYC POLICE, SPOUSE(S): NONE
HOW ARE YOU
Uh...
"IT HAS MADE ME AMAZING AT PARTIES"
That--that'll ***work,*** Brian. Your algorithm's ***already trained.*** All we need to do is tweak it so instead of defaulting to the closest ***match,*** it highlights any ***differences,*** and--
--and we'll have our automated fake super hero detector! Brain Drain, I could hug you.
THANK YOU. YOU MAY PROCEED
Oh.
Uh, all right.
I guess we're doing this.
I DON'T HAVE ANY PRESSURE SENSORS AROUND MY TORSO SO YOU CAN SQUEEZE AS HARD AS YOU'D LIKE
JUST LET ME KNOW WHEN YOU'RE DONE DOWN THERE

DETECTIVE MICHAEL CORSON, HOW DID YOU ENJOY THAT STEAK YOU POSTED A PICTURE OF ON SOCIAL MEDIA THREE DAYS AGO? I NOTICE THE PHOTO EARNED A TOTAL OF TWO LIKES AND I HOPE IT WAS AS HASHTAG TASTYSTEAK AS YOU ANTICIPATED

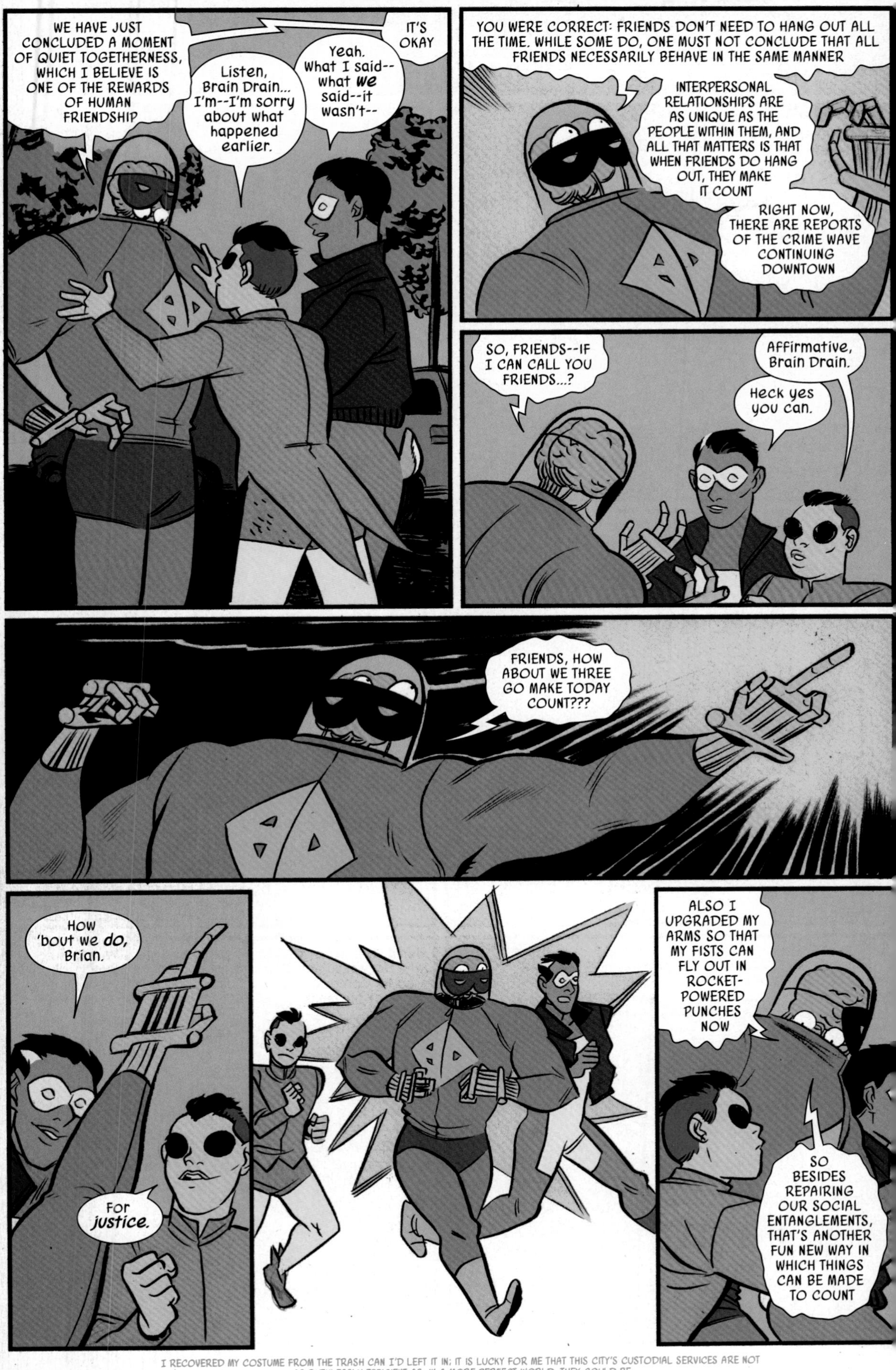
WE HAVE JUST CONCLUDED A MOMENT OF QUIET TOGETHERNESS, WHICH I BELIEVE IS ONE OF THE REWARDS OF HUMAN FRIENDSHIP
Listen, Brain Drain... I'm--I'm sorry about what happened earlier.
Yeah. What I said--what we said--it wasn't--
IT'S OKAY
YOU WERE CORRECT: FRIENDS DON'T NEED TO HANG OUT ALL THE TIME. WHILE SOME DO, ONE MUST NOT CONCLUDE THAT ALL FRIENDS NECESSARILY BEHAVE IN THE SAME MANNER
INTERPERSONAL RELATIONSHIPS ARE AS UNIQUE AS THE PEOPLE WITHIN THEM, AND ALL THAT MATTERS IS THAT WHEN FRIENDS DO HANG OUT, THEY MAKE IT COUNT
RIGHT NOW, THERE ARE REPORTS OF THE CRIME WAVE CONTINUING DOWNTOWN
SO, FRIENDS--IF I CAN CALL YOU FRIENDS...?
Affirmative, Brain Drain.
Heck yes you can.
FRIENDS, HOW ABOUT WE THREE GO MAKE TODAY COUNT???
How 'bout we do, Brian.
For justice.
ALSO I UPGRADED MY ARMS SO THAT MY FISTS CAN FLY OUT IN ROCKET-POWERED PUNCHES NOW
SO BESIDES REPAIRING OUR SOCIAL ENTANGLEMENTS, THAT'S ANOTHER FUN NEW WAY IN WHICH THINGS CAN BE MADE TO COUNT

I RECOVERED MY COSTUME FROM THE TRASH CAN I'D LEFT IT IN; IT IS LUCKY FOR ME THAT THIS CITY'S CUSTODIAL SERVICES ARE NOT AS RUTHLESSLY EFFICIENT AS, IN A MORE PERFECT WORLD, THEY COULD BE

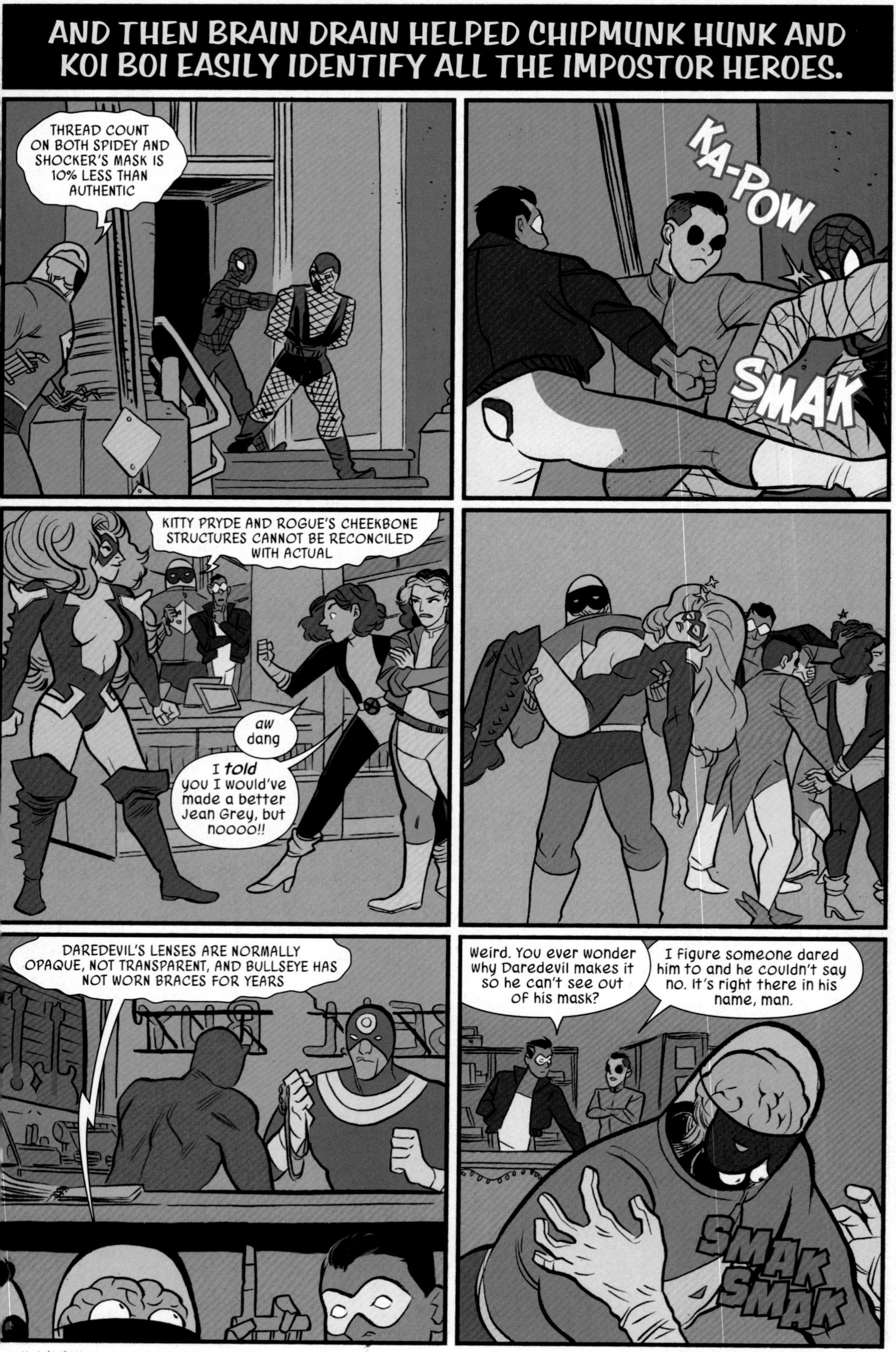
AND THEN BRAIN DRAIN HELPED CHIPMUNK HUNK AND KOI BOI EASILY IDENTIFY ALL THE IMPOSTOR HEROES.
THREAD COUNT ON BOTH SPIDEY AND SHOCKER'S MASK IS 10% LESS THAN AUTHENTIC
KA-POW
SMAK
KITTY PRYDE AND ROGUE'S CHEEKBONE STRUCTURES CANNOT BE RECONCILED WITH ACTUAL
aw dang
I told you I would've made a better Jean Grey, but noooo!!
DAREDEVIL'S LENSES ARE NORMALLY OPAQUE, NOT TRANSPARENT, AND BULLSEYE HAS NOT WORN BRACES FOR YEARS
Weird. You ever wonder why Daredevil makes it so he can't see out of his mask?
I figure someone dared him to and he couldn't say no. It's right there in his name, man.
SMAK
SMAK

Is that *truly* the reason he's named "Daredevil"? Or is it more likely his *real* name is actually "Da Red Evil," but Daredevil has such horrible handwriting that all the words run together, and that, combined with crippling shyness about correcting anyone, means we never found out the truth...*until this very moment???*

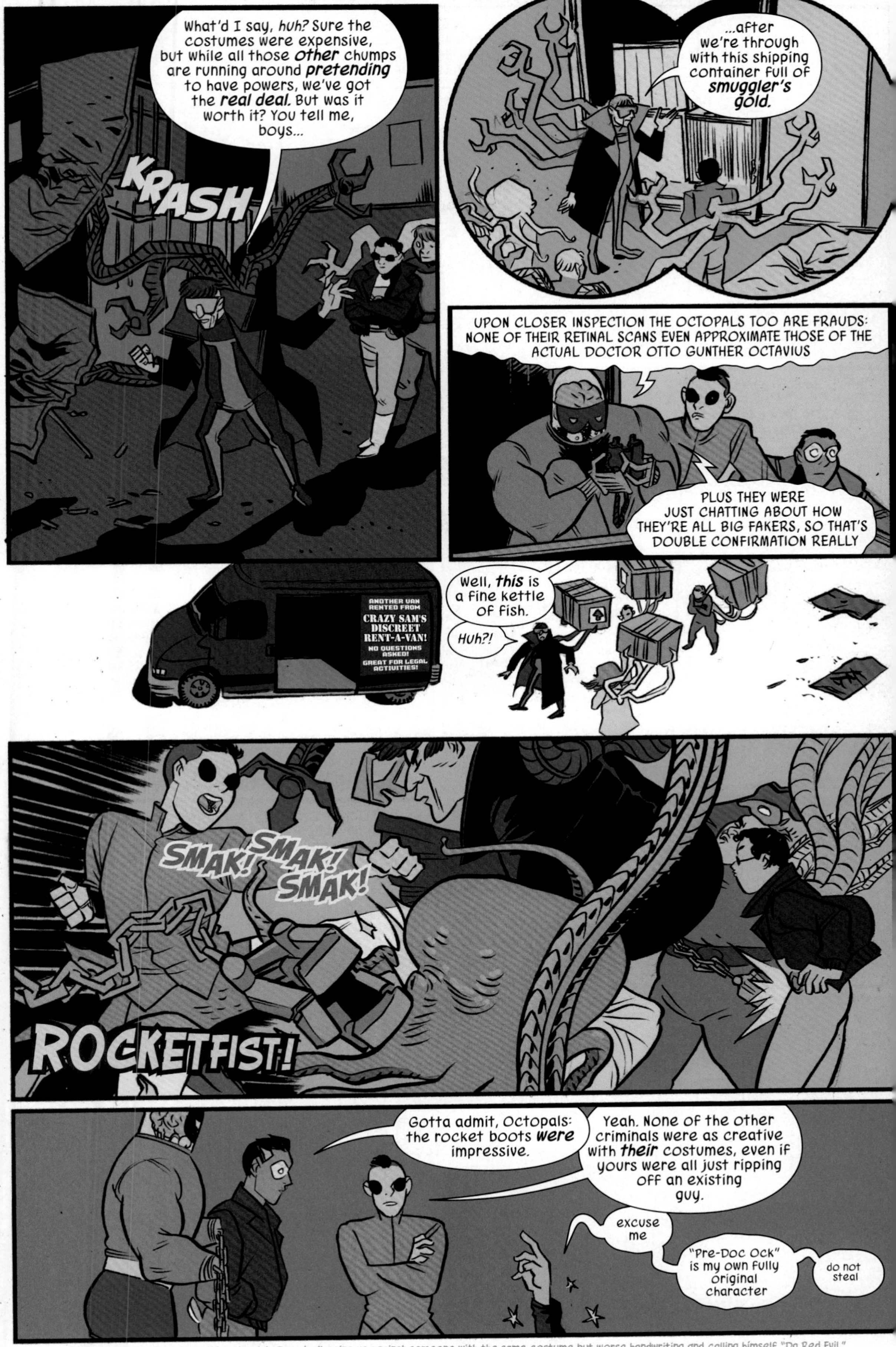
What'd I say, *huh?* Sure the costumes were expensive, but while all those *other* chumps are running around *pretending* to have powers, we've got the *real deal.* But was it worth it? You tell me, boys...
KRASH
...after we're through with this shipping container full of *smuggler's gold.*
UPON CLOSER INSPECTION THE OCTOPALS TOO ARE FRAUDS: NONE OF THEIR RETINAL SCANS EVEN APPROXIMATE THOSE OF THE ACTUAL DOCTOR OTTO GUNTHER OCTAVIUS
PLUS THEY WERE JUST CHATTING ABOUT HOW THEY'RE ALL BIG FAKERS, SO THAT'S DOUBLE CONFIRMATION REALLY
ANOTHER VAN RENTED FROM CRAZY SAM'S DISCREET RENT-A-VAN! NO QUESTIONS ASKED! GREAT FOR LEGAL ACTIVITIES!
Well, *this* is a fine kettle of fish.
Huh?!
SMAK! SMAK! SMAK!
ROCKETFIST!
Gotta admit, Octopals: the rocket boots *were* impressive.
Yeah. None of the other criminals were as creative with *their* costumes, even if yours were all just ripping off an existing guy.
excuse me
"Pre-Doc Ock" is my own fully original character
do not steal

I'm sorry, but now all I can think about is Daredevil going up against someone with the same costume but worse handwriting and calling himself "Da Red Evil."
Attention, creators of the Daredevil TV series: I believe history may judge your next season harshly if you don't incorporate this extremely excellent idea??

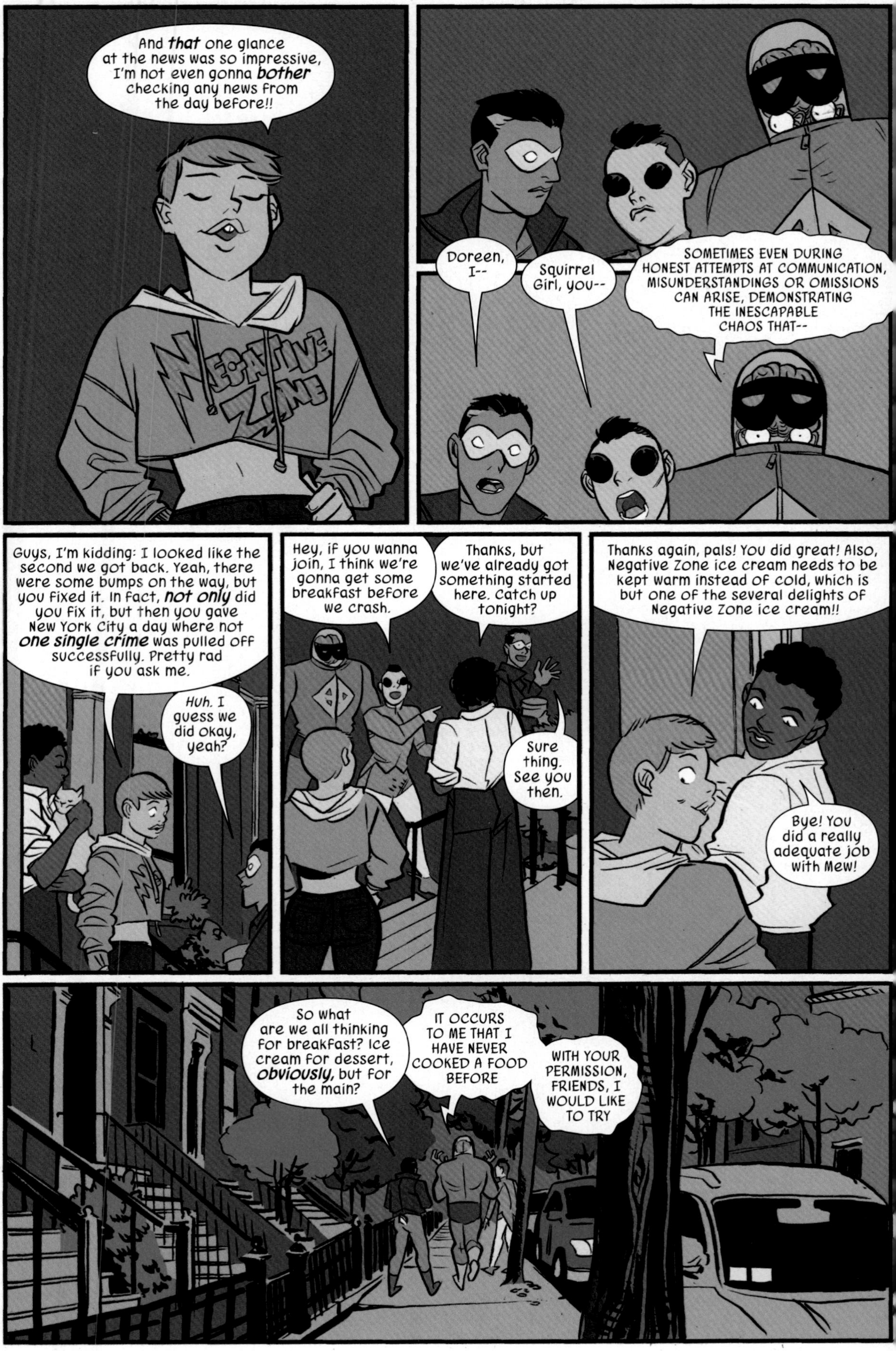

And *that* one glance at the news was so impressive, I'm not even gonna *bother* checking any news from the day before!!
Doreen, I--
Squirrel Girl, you--
SOMETIMES EVEN DURING HONEST ATTEMPTS AT COMMUNICATION, MISUNDERSTANDINGS OR OMISSIONS CAN ARISE, DEMONSTRATING THE INESCAPABLE CHAOS THAT--
Guys, I'm kidding: I looked like the second we got back. Yeah, there were some bumps on the way, but you fixed it. In fact, *not only* did you fix it, but then you gave New York City a day where not *one single crime* was pulled off successfully. Pretty rad if you ask me.
Huh. I guess we did okay, yeah?
Hey, if you wanna join, I think we're gonna get some breakfast before we crash.
Thanks, but we've already got something started here. Catch up tonight?
Sure thing. See you then.
Thanks again, pals! You did great! Also, Negative Zone ice cream needs to be kept warm instead of cold, which is but one of the several delights of Negative Zone ice cream!!
Bye! You did a really adequate job with Mew!
So what are we all thinking for breakfast? Ice cream for dessert, *obviously*, but for the main?
IT OCCURS TO ME THAT I HAVE NEVER COOKED A FOOD BEFORE
WITH YOUR PERMISSION, FRIENDS, I WOULD LIKE TO TRY

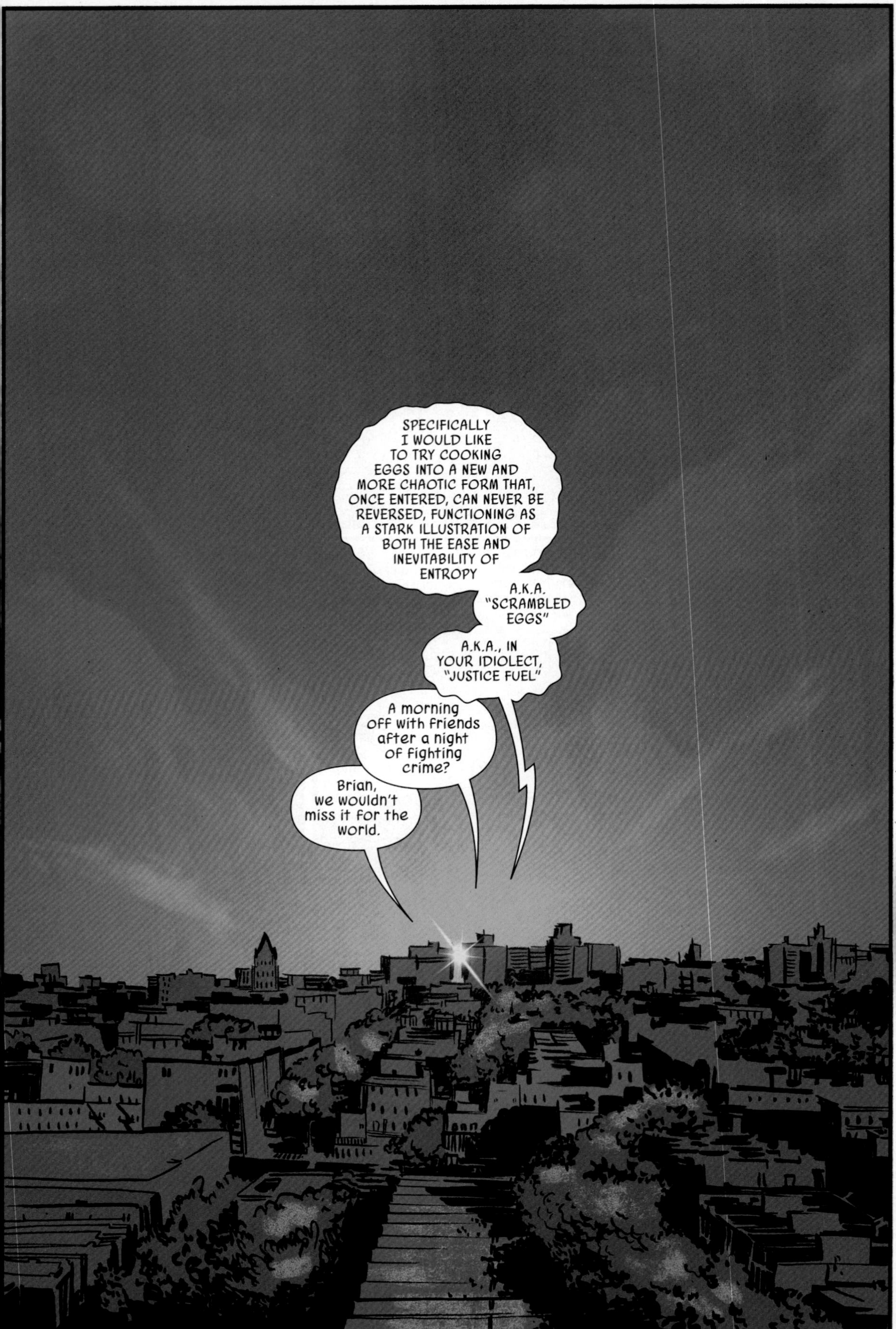
SPECIFICALLY I WOULD LIKE TO TRY COOKING EGGS INTO A NEW AND MORE CHAOTIC FORM THAT, ONCE ENTERED, CAN NEVER BE REVERSED, FUNCTIONING AS A STARK ILLUSTRATION OF BOTH THE EASE AND INEVITABILITY OF ENTROPY
A.K.A. "SCRAMBLED EGGS"
A.K.A., IN YOUR IDIOLECT, "JUSTICE FUEL"
A morning off with friends after a night of fighting crime?
Brian, we wouldn't miss it for the world.

THE END.

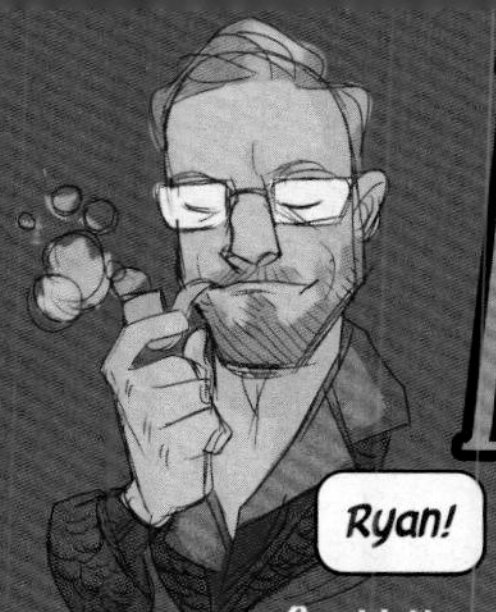
Ryan!

Letters From Nuts

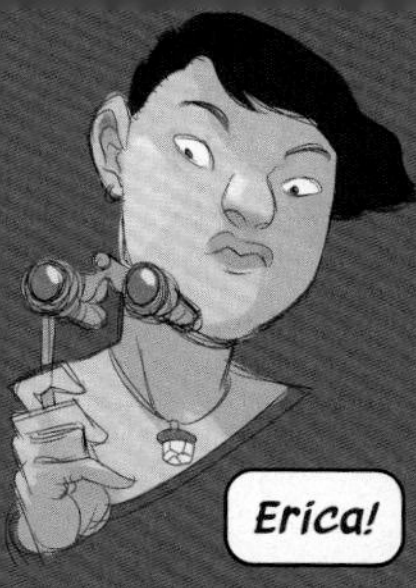
Erica!

Send letters to mheroes@marvel.com or 135 W 50th St, 7th Floor, New York, NY 10020 (Please mark "OKAY TO PRINT")

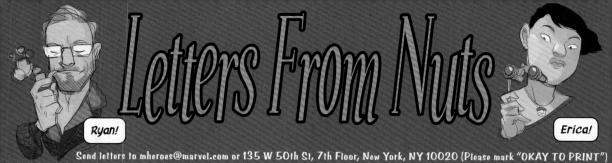

How great is Brain Drain, y'all? (The correct answer is: MEGA great.)

So hey, the nominations for the 2017 Eisner Awards (which are like the Academy Awards, but for comics!) were recently announced, and THE UNBEATABLE SQUIRREL GIRL is up for Best Publication for Teens (ages 13-17)! Plus, the *JUGHEAD* series that Erica and Ryan both worked on is also up for Best Publication for Teens (ages 13-17) and for Best Humor Publication! That's right, Erica and Ryan have to prepare *three separate acceptance speeches!!!* (And by the way, if you're a fan of USG and you haven't read that *JUGHEAD* series, what are you waiting for?? It's crazy good!)

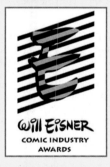

Will Eisner
COMIC INDUSTRY AWARDS

Also: We were thrilled to have Squirrel Girl co-creator Will Murray write a story in USG #16, the issue where we celebrated the 25th anniversary of Doreen's first appearance! Will did a signing at New England Comics back when issue #16 went on sale, and the real-life inspiration for Doreen--Doreen Greeley--was in attendance! How cool is that?? Here's a photo of Will and the IRL Doreen at the signing:

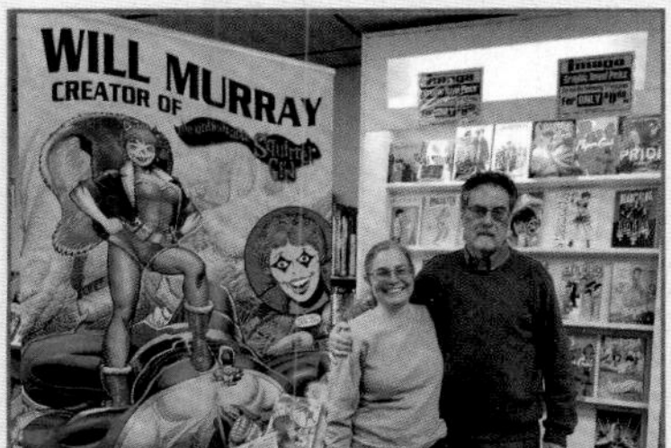
WILL MURRAY
CREATOR OF

And to show you just how far Squirrel Girl's fan base now reaches, here's a photo of a Squirrel Girl that USG Executive Editor/Godfather Tom Brevoort took when he was a guest at the opening of "The Marvel Age of Heroes Exhibition" in Tokyo back in April:

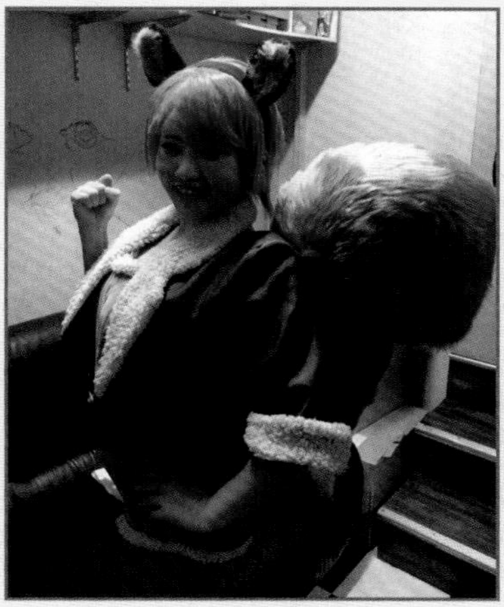

That tail is A+! Okay, now on to your letters, and Erica and Ryan's responses!!!

Dear Team Squirrel Girl,

The last time I sent a letter to Marvel was in the mid-'80s when I wanted to find out how I could find back issues of *ELFQUEST.* So it's been a while.

Happily, I've reached an age where I now understand how to find back issues of excellent comics, so I can focus this letter on what's really important: that y'all are awesome. I started picking up Squirrel Girl for my wife's cousin; I give her a stack of comics every year for Christmas, which is what my grandma used to do for me (back when JC Penney sold the 30-pack of Marvel comics out of their Christmas catalog, y'all need to find a way to bring that back). And the nice thing about giving the gift of comics is that you can read them before you wrap them up. No surprise, I was immediately hooked. You've heard it all before, but this book is so clever and intelligent and positive and lol funny.

But what prompted me to plunk down in front of my computer and send you an electronic message (did you hear that, '80s? We can send our mail electronically now!) was Alfredo the Chicken. When Ms. Morehead told Chef Bear to go cook Alfredo after Doreen left, I was caught off guard. It was a dark moment that was out of step for the book. I shouldn't have been worried, though. I was relieved and delighted to see that not only was Alfredo alive and well, but that he wasn't going down without a hilarious fight.

The Alfredo and Chef Bear subplot sums up how amazing this book is. In just a few pages, you got me to really care about a sentient chicken. I will allow you to use that blurb for any subsequent Squirrel Girl collections.

Keep up the amazing work.
Jason

RYAN: Thank you! The Alfredo backups in the Melissa arc ended up being one of my favorite parts, and they began life entirely for the reason you saw: I didn't want Alfredo to get eaten, and then the relationship with Chef Bear began to develop, and it was lots and lots of fun. I got a message from someone on Twitter once who was upset that Alfredo died and I got to say "keep reading!"--they had messaged before they'd even finished the book, assuming he was definitely 100% dead! BUT THAT NEVER HAPPENS IN COMICS, especially OUR talking-squirrel comics. And I'm glad Alfredo broke your 30-year drought of not writing in letters to comic books!

ERICA: I feel like given how much we've fallen for Alfredo, this isn't the last we've seen of him. P.S. ELFQUEST! That brings me back.

Heyo, Erica and Ryan!

So, first: I love love love this comic book! Sometimes my friends say, "Isn't a Squirrel Girl a joke character? And I say, "Have you ever been surrounded by a mob of angry squirrels? They can bite you, in places." So, let it be said: Squirrel Girl is the coolest, fiercest super hero with a tail ever!!

Second: I have a proposition. I just saw Squirrel Girl make a cameo in HOWARD THE DUCK (2016) #6, as well as PATSY WALKER, A.K.A. HELLCAT. So I was thinking, "Hey, I've seen a lot of Marvel cameos recently: Ms. Marvel cameos in MOON GIRL AND DEVIL DINOSAUR, Howard the Duck cameos in PATSY WALKER, A.K.A. HELLCAT, Squirrel Girl cameos in HOWARD THE DUCK, etc." So, what if we had a super ultimate amazing (you catch my drift) crossover? Specifically, between:

Squirrel Girl (and Chipmunk Hunk, Koi Boy, Nancy and Tippy-Toe), Moon Girl and Devil Dinosaur, America Chávez, Hellcat (and Telekinian, Attaché, Jubilee, and She-Hulk), Howard the Duck and Ms. Marvel (Kamala Khan).

Would that be great or what? (Rhetorical question. Of course it would). Maybe Loki

could even join in on the fun. What would we call such an event? Something cool I hope. What would these guys do together? Maybe fight Black Cat, Casiolena, The Inventor, The Skrull, the Collector and Doctor Doom all at once! That would be interesting...

Peace out and tune in,
Claudine Gale
Tigard, Oregon

RYAN: Claudine, I see no problems with your ideas and would like to see this ultimate team-up happen. Now that Chip Zdarsky is writing PETER PARKER: THE SPECTACULAR SPIDER-MAN [First issue is on sale next week! – Chip] instead of HOWARD THE DUCK, we should probably throw Spidey in the mix too, so Chip doesn't feel left out. It's hard when you have to write a story about a man with gross spider-powers instead of a cool-talking duck, so we should all send our sympathies to him. [PP:TSS #2 on sale July 19! – Chip]

ERICA: How many of these people are in one place at a time?

Hi Ryan and Erica,

I'm a big fan of THE UNBEATABLE SQUIRREL GIRL and I'm enjoying the latest adventure, including the backup feature introducing us to the breakout creations of 2017: Alfredo the Chicken and Chef Bear. I had to let you know that there is a real (fake) Chef Bear here in San Diego! You can sign up for a special dinner at a secret location where an anonymous chef in a bear costume in a chef costume will serve you and your friends a five-course meal with wine pairings. I won't include it here, because I'm sure Marvel doesn't want plugs for other businesses in their letter columns, but I'm sure you can find the website, including video of Chef Bear, with your considerable computer finesse. Thanks for the great comics!

Chris Martin
San Diego, CA

RYAN: WHAT. WHAT EVEN IS THIS. Marvel, please send me and Erica to San Diego ON THE DOUBLE, because I didn't even know I wanted to be served dinner by an anonymous chef in a bear costume in a chef costume until this moment, and now it's the only thing I've ever wanted. CHEF BEAR IS REAL!!

ERICA: Ryan, I guess we have our night-before-SDCC plans set. There's no turning back on your destiny, Ryan. Ryan. We're doing this.

I've never written a letter to a comic before... But as I was reading the latest issue of SQUIRREL GIRL (#19), I noticed that Melissa called the geese "Canadian" geese. Funny enough, on the morning news today, they were watching a video of a goose attacking a man (which in retrospect is not too dissimilar to the videos of animals attacking people reference in the book as well) and one anchor said Canadian geese and the other corrected her with an off-camera affirmation that "Hey, they are called Canada geese, not 'Canadian.'" And on most occasions, after learning this, for someone to misname them wouldn't be a big deal, but for Melissa Morbeck to misname them seems out of place. She seems like someone who knows a lot about animals and wouldn't make this mistake. Just saying.

Funny thing is, if I read this yesterday, I wouldn't have thought twice about it.

Always reading,
Asher Humm

RYAN: I have lived in Canada my entire life and never distinguished between the two! But that may just be me not paying attention. Perhaps Melissa meant to say they were merely Canadian Canada geese and she just dropped out the "Canada" because it was redundant in that construction? Does that solve all the problems? Let's say it does, and I'll say "Canada goose" moving forward!

ERICA: I can say with full confidence that Melissa doesn't really care all that much about animals.

Hey hey Team Squirrel Girl!

I love this comic book so much, words fail me. Between Erica's anime-esque illustrations and Ryan's hilarious writing, you two combine to make an amazing series (it's almost like you're a Dynamic Duo, huh?). There is one little suggestion I have that would make this comic even more amazing: A Madcap adventure! You know, the purple-and-yellow harlequin who can't be hurt and likes to mind-control people for laughs? He's one of my favorite villains, and seeing Squirrel Girl and Co. take him on would be the best!

Stay squirrelly,
Lucy James
Wilsonville, Oregon

RYAN: Well, with Ratatoskr showing up in the last issue--who already has mind-control powers of her own--Doreen may have her hands full! That is, once she realizes Ratatoskr has returned, which she hasn't yet, because clearly that Norse Squirrel God is gathering her powers and hasn't tipped her hand, but something is going on there!

Erica, Ryan, Rico and the rest of the team:

Thanks for putting out what is consistently one of the funniest, most emotionally-compelling comics on the market. My daughter Thessaly and I anxiously await SQUIRREL GIRL every month, and it's always one of the first books we read together. I'm so incredibly thankful for this book and for the positive representation it provides for her and for other girls—Doreen is effortlessly awesome in two fields too-long dominated by men, she's not afraid to stand up for herself, and she always looks for (and helps people find) the best in others. Keep up the fantastic work, and may you be able to continue to make SQUIRREL GIRL until you've completely run out of nut-themed puns.

Charles Paul Hoffman (and Thessaly)
Indianapolis, Indiana

Oh, here's a picture Thessaly drew of Squirrel Girl. Thessaly met Erica at C2E2, which she said was her favorite part of the convention.

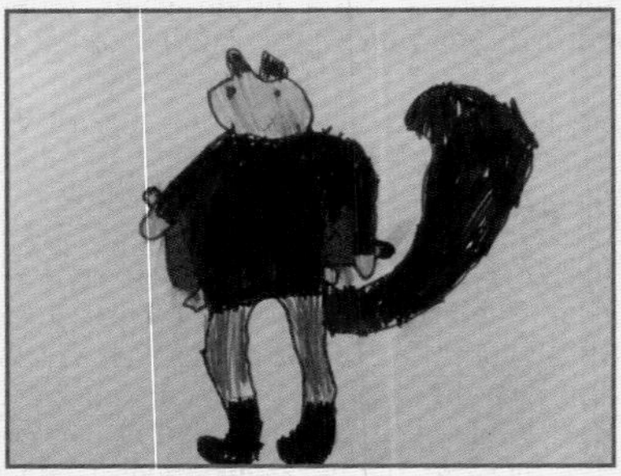

RYAN: LOVE IT. Thessaly's drawing is now officially my favorite part of this letters page too! Also: The idea of running out of nut-themed puns is terrifying. THEY'RE ALL I HAVE, AND I NEED MORE. Please send more.

ERICA: SHE'S THE FIRST (and only, but C2E2 wasn't that long ago) SQUIRREL GIRL COSPLAYER I'VE SEEN WITH THE NEW COSTUME WITH WINGS! It was amazing y'all. It's on my Twitter if you want to dig back several months (not recommended, I tweet A LOT). Anyway, letters like all of these--bringing families together and getting people back into the lost art of letter writing--makes it all worth it.

Next Issue:

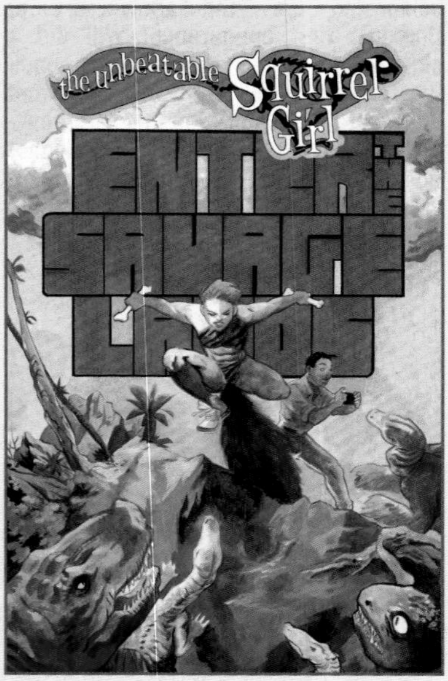
the unbeatable Squirrel Girl

Attention, Squirrel Scouts! Make sure to check out our production blog, **unbeatablesquirrelgirl.tumblr.com**, where we post behind-the-scenes stuff on how the book gets made, along with all sorts of cool things *you* make: fanart, cosplay, whatever!

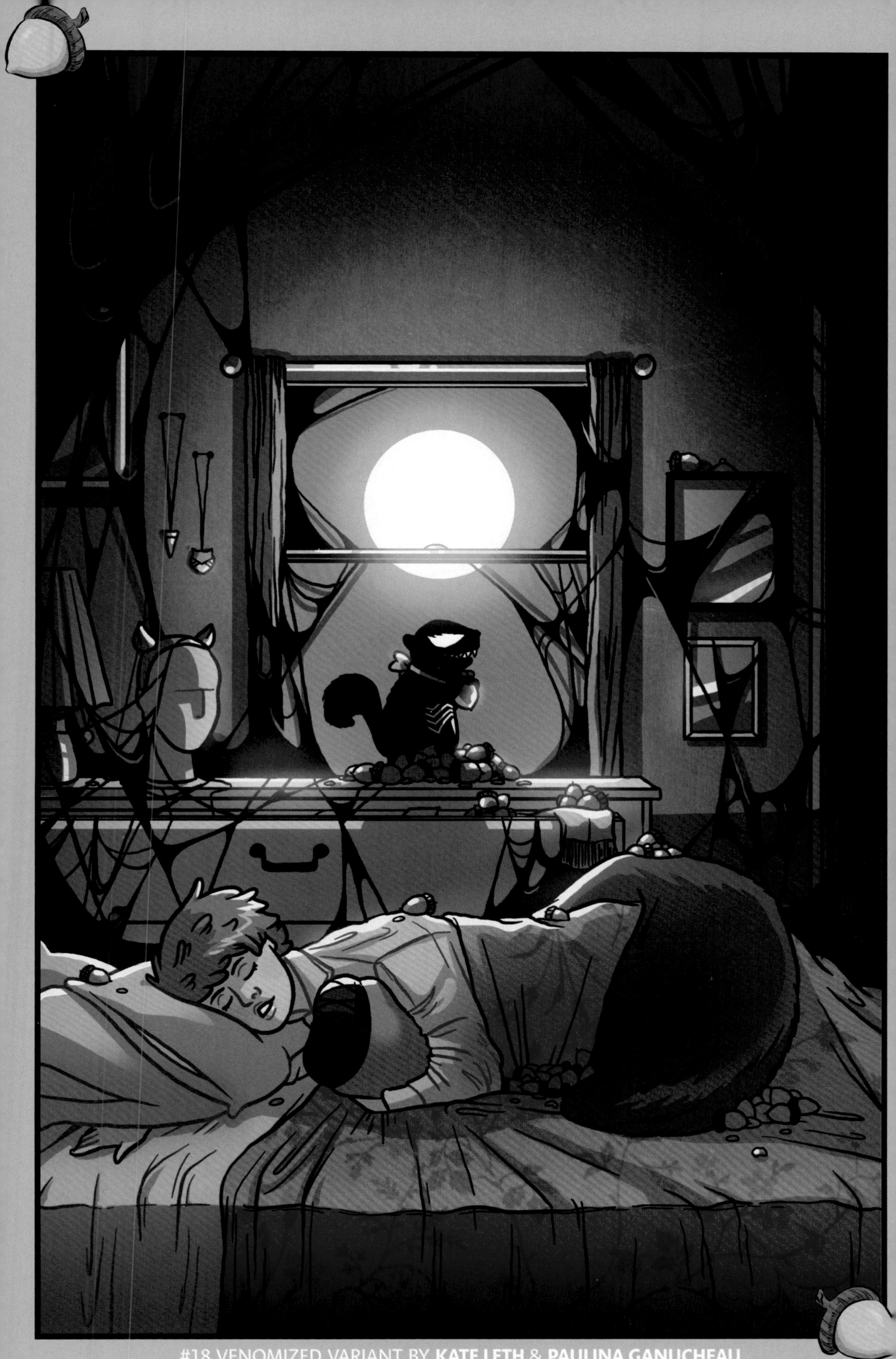

#18 VENOMIZED VARIANT BY **KATE LETH** & **PAULINA GANUCHEAU**

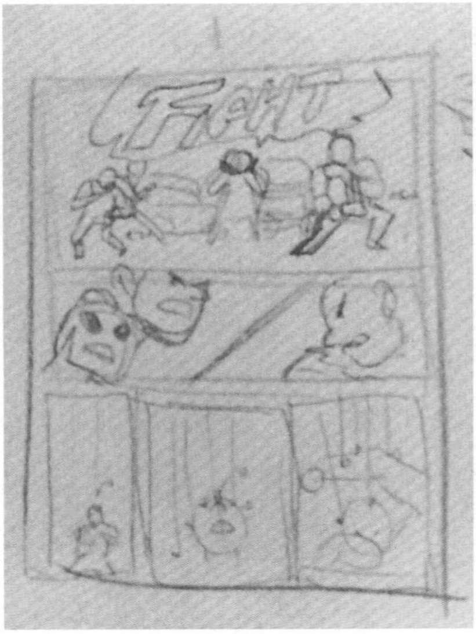

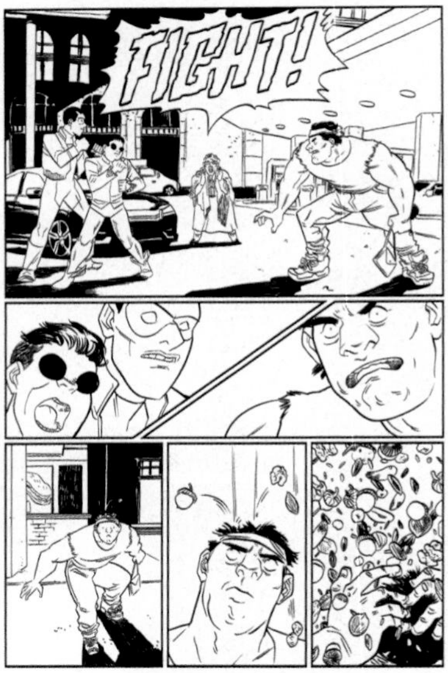
FIGHT!

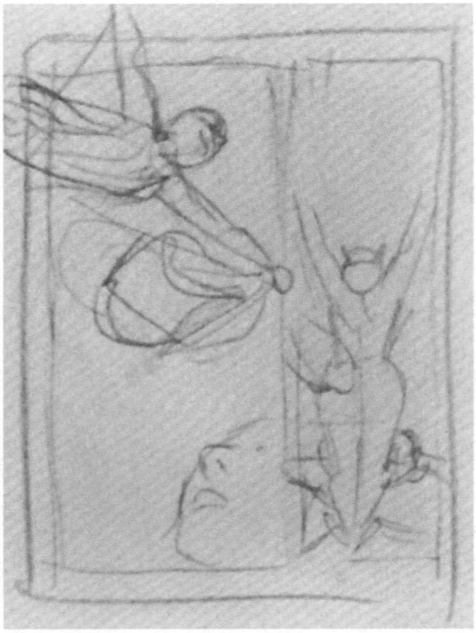

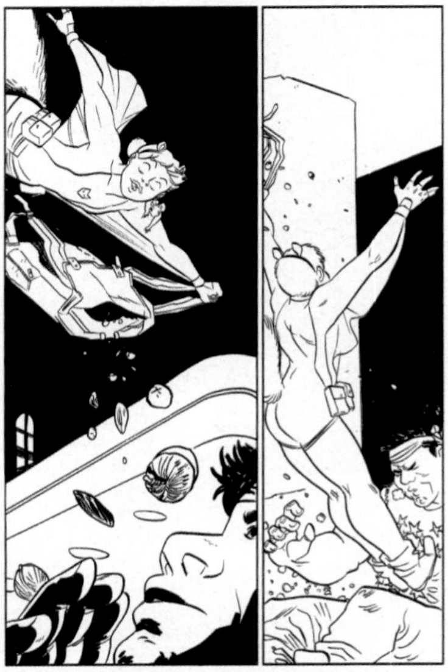

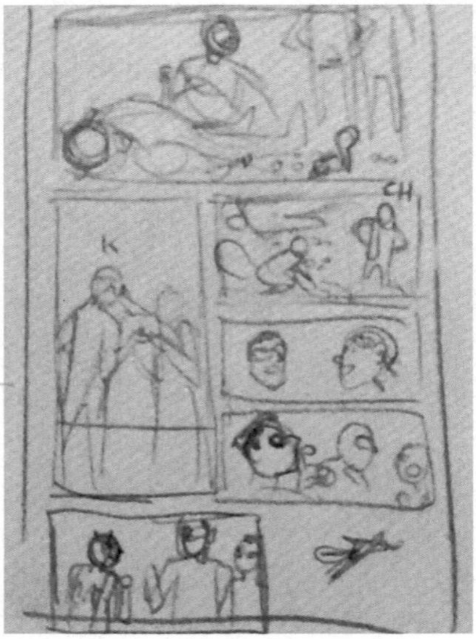

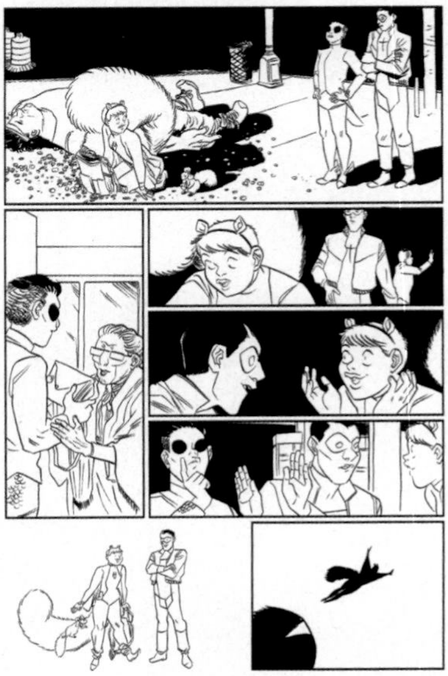

#18 PAGES 1-3 LAYOUTS AND INKS BY **ERICA HENDERSON**